FLASH 3D CHEATS
MOST WANTED

Aral Balkan
Josh Dura
Anthony Eden
Brian Monnone
James Dean Palmer
Jared Tarbell
Todd Yard

friendsof

DESIGNER TO DESIGNER™

an Apress® company

BRIEF CONTENTS

ABOUT THE AUTHORS

Aral Balkan: An interstellar marauder since age 12... Oh, wait, I wasn't supposed to mention that! What I meant to say is: Born in Turkey a little over a quarter of a century ago, Aral spent most of his childhood and early teens in a tropical paradise called Malaysia and currently lives in the murky wetlands of London (oh yes, the weather is that bad, thank you very much!). Coding and design both grew out of hobbies that started at age 7, when his Dad brought home an IBM XT instead of a Commodore 64, leaving him to either write his own games or go without (thanks, Dad!). His true passions in life are acting and singing, both of which he wants to pursue professionally.

In between globetrotting, Aral got the chance to produce a musical in North Cyprus (*Jesus Christ Superstar*) and grab a master's degree in film and video (with an emphasis on multimedia design) from American University in Washington, DC. Nowadays, he runs his own company in London called Bits And Pixels, specializing in Flash for web and mobile applications.

Aral would like to thank his amazing parents, Mehlika and Haluk, for making everything possible and for supporting him no matter what: I loves and appreciate you more than you'll ever know. And of course, to the angel whom I am honored to be able to call my wife, Emilie, for sticking with me through late nights spent absorbing the glow of my monitors.

Aral's photo by Emilie Balkan

Josh Dura: Josh Dura started his career as most web developers do, designing simple HTML pages with little graphics here and there, etc. About 3 years ago, Josh started coding Cold Fusion, learning basic OOP skills through that language, which brought him to learning ActionScript. Josh currently works for ReadyHosting.com out of Richardson, Texas, doing most of the web and graphic/print design work for them. On the side, he updates his personal website, www.joshdura.com, a basic weblog/photography/open source Flash project. Josh also currently owns and runs Dura Media, LLC (www.duramedia.com) with his brother Daniel. Josh would like to dedicate this book to his brother, as he was really the one who introduced and walked Josh through the computer/technical world. Josh would also like to personally thank many people: Shauna Dudley; Keran McKenzie; Brian Monnone; Samuel Granato; everyone from Flashkit, Actionscripts.org, and Were-Here; everyone who posts on his weblog; and last but certainly not least, Mom and Dad. Without you, this would have never been possible.

Anthony Eden: From an early age, Anthony developed a love of interaction with mathematics and computational languages, gaining along the way an appreciation of any given natural environment and the ability to transform his environment into a digital construct. Inspiration for his latest project, www.arseiam.com (essentially an ActionScript anthology of his Flash work), is testament to this philosophy.

The last decade has included commercial roles with Microsoft, Disney, Toyota, and Adobe, providing a sound framework from which to explore and diversify his project development life cycle skills.

Spare time? If he's not thinking about it, he's doing it.

Brian Monnone: Brian is the senior multimedia producer/developer for Tocquigny Advertising in Austin, Texas. Tocquigny Advertising received the *Austin Business Journal*'s Top 25 Web Developers #1 position for 2002–2003 in web design and development in Austin. Brian has been computing for over 17 years and has found himself doing what he loves to do: "making really cool stuff." Brian works on projects with AMD, Dell, HP, USAA, GlobalScape, and a host of other companies creating Flash demos, websites, video, and other types of multimedia. Brian has won awards for his works and many accolades for his personal site. Living in a home nestled in the hills, he finds inspiration for his work and plenty to do with his wife and children. He enjoys creating interactive content and hopes in the future to become a filmmaker. According to Brian, "The fact is this: I work with lots of people on a daily basis, listening to ideas and reviewing storyboards, but it boils down to one simple concept for me—'I'm just a guy...who wants to make really cool stuff.'"

James Dean Palmer: James graduated in 1998 from the Texas A&M Computer Engineering program. In 2000 he completed his master's degree in computer visualization. Deeply technical and profoundly visual, James has been working professionally both in print and the web since 1994. James founded Caramba Designs in 2001 to develop web-based applications and end-to-end solutions for unique problems.

James would like to extend his thanks to his beautiful wife, Yaya, whom he is madly in love with; his free-thinking parents; his little sister and her husband; and the entire Tiger Marmalade clan for being the great friends that they are.

Jared Tarbell: Jared is originally from the high deserts of Albuquerque, New Mexico. He is most interested in the interactive visualization of large data sets and the emergent, life-like properties of complex computational systems. Jared sits on the board of the Austin Museum of Digital Arts, www.amoda.org, where he actively assists in the growth and development of the digital arts kingdom. He holds a degree in computer science from New Mexico State University.

Todd Yard: After studying theatre in London, then working for several years as an actor in the United States, Todd was introduced to Flash in 2000 and was quickly taken by how it allowed for both stunning creativity and programmatic logic application—a truly left-brain/right-brain approach to production—and he has not looked back. He now works as creative director for Daedalus Media in New York City, a company that specializes in the creation of Flash-based corporate presentations primarily for clients in the investment banking industry. His more frivolous work and experimentation can be found at his personal website, www.27Bobs.com.

As his new line of employment makes it incredibly unlikely that Todd will ever accept a best acting Oscar, he'd like to take this opportunity to thank his parents for their support through the years and to thank Lydian for her continued understanding as he sits hunched over a keyboard through many a night.

Introduction to Flash 3D

A couple of years ago we started trying to include three-dimensional (3D) effects in our Flash designs. Back then there were very few resources available to help us out, so the design process was all about applying a diverse range of techniques and tricks to produce believable 3D. These days, the story is similar—but now there are even more designers who are specifically using Flash to generate amazing pseudo-3D graphics.

That's where *Flash 3D Cheats Most Wanted* comes in. For this book, we've done extensive research, scouring the Flash and 3D communities to find out exactly what it is that people are craving to build with Flash 3D. We've taken these topics and crafted chapters designed to give you what you want. From the most basic tips and tricks relating to shading, scaling, and perspective, through isometric design and parallax scrolling effects, as far as using advanced scripted 3D engines—this book will show you how to fake it in the best possible way!

What is 3D?

3D is actually pretty simple: basically, there are three **axes**, or **planes**. The diagram below illustrates this.

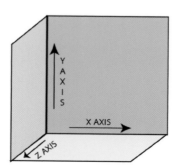

Typically, the x-axis is the horizontal plane, the y-axis is the vertical plane, and the z-axis is the depth plane. If you want to move something up and down, or scale an object so that it's taller, you use the y-axis. If you want to move something left or right, or make something wider, this relates to the x-axis. Moving something forward or back, or giving it more depth is associated with the z-axis. That's a little of the general explanation of 3D out the way—now let's turn our attention to Flash 3D.

3D with Flash MX

While Flash wasn't originally intended for generating 3D creations, there are actually numerous ways, basic and advanced, in which you can manipulate graphics to give the impression of 3D—so many that we wrote a whole book on them! The important thing to remember is that using Flash to create faux-3D graphics is all done using various *cheats* and *tricks*. Flash obviously isn't a 3D graphics package like 3D Studio Max, Maya, Swift 3D, and so on, but you can use certain standard techniques, along with a little ActionScript, bitmap tracing, importing from external programs, and so on to produce some great 3D designs.

Starting with the fundamentals, in this chapter we'll study some simple and effective methods of hinting at that elusive third dimension in Flash. The examples we show here deal with using perspective, shading, and gradients to create that 3D look.

3D drawing techniques

When I was in third grade, I remember coming in to class one day, and the teacher had drawn three examples of simple 3D drawings on the board. From the second I saw them, I knew it was going to be a fun day! Those three basic examples were a cube, a cylinder, and a pyramid:

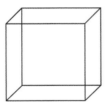 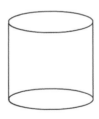 

Back then it was just pencil and paper, which in some respects is easier than Flash, but not as precise and clean. There are some areas where pencil and paper just don't make the grade. For example, it's not so easy to flood fill like you would with the Paint Bucket Tool in Flash, and it's also a lot harder to use gradients well with a pencil. So Flash it is!

These 3D shapes are very simple to draw, but a tip before you start working through these examples is to have the Snap to Objects option selected (make sure View > Snap to Objects is checked).

Cube

1. Select the Rectangle Tool (R) with a black stroke color and whatever fill color you prefer. Now hold down the SHIFT key and draw a perfect square about 100x100 pixels in size—we will refer

to this as square A. Don't worry if it's not exactly the right size; you can easily adjust these dimensions through the Property Inspector after drawing the square:

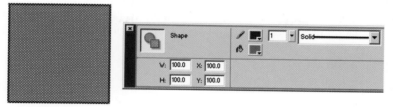

2. Select square A and its stroke by double-clicking its fill. Copy it (CTRL/CMD+C), unselect it, and then paste it in place (CTRL/CMD+SHIFT+V). We will call this square B.

3. With square B still selected, hold down your SHIFT key and press the DOWN arrow twice, and then the left arrow twice. If you are in 100% view, this should move square B 20 pixels down and 20 pixels left.

4. Now, using the Line Tool (N), connect the top-left corner of square B with the top-left corner of square A—this should be pretty easy if you've got Snap to Objects selected. Do the same thing with the top-right corner of both squares. Next, delete the extra lines that will not be seen (selected in the image below):

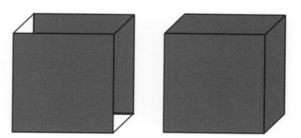

5. Fill the blank areas left by the deleted lines with the same color as used in the square's fill. For this, you can use the Eyedropper Tool (I) to sample the appropriate color and then the Paint Bucket Tool (K) to fill. You now have a complete cube.

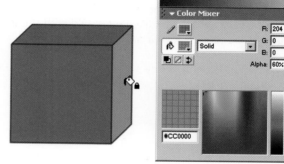

6. You will now fill the right and top sides of your cube with a different shade to create a better lighting effect. Select the right side of the cube and, using the Color Mixer panel (Window > Color Mixer or SHIFT+F9), set the Alpha of this fill to 60%.

7. Next, select the top fill of the cube, and set the alpha to 40%. Now, this does look OK, but because of the way that alpha works (**alpha** refers to the opacity of an object), if you ever put anything behind it on a lower layer (like a shadow you will put in later), you'll see straight through to it, and it will make this effect pointless.

    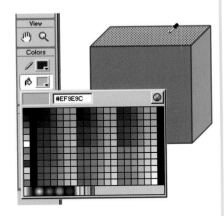

    So, to get the actual color values of these alpha-valued fills, you need to click on the Fill Color option on the toolbar. When you mouse over any fills in the Flash MX authoring environment, it will tell you the exact color values (in hexadecimal form), which you can suck up with the Eyedropper and plug back in to your fills with the Paint Bucket Tool.

8. Finally, delete all the lines and you're left with a beautiful cube.

    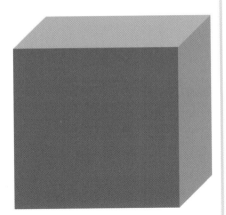

Cylinder

1. Select the Oval Tool (O), and draw an oval like the one shown at right. We'll call this oval A.

    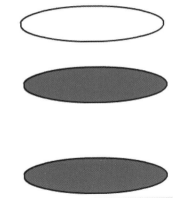

2. Use the Paint Bucket Tool (K) to fill oval A with a color of your choice, select it (double-click on the fill or press CTRL/CMD+A to select the whole object), and then copy it (CTRL/CMD+C) and paste it in place (CTRL/CMD+SHIFT+V). We'll call this new one oval B. Again, while you hold the SHIFT key down, press the UP arrow about ten times (in 100% view mode this will move oval B up 100 pixels).

3. Next, take the Line Tool (N) and draw a line from the leftmost edge of oval A to the leftmost edge of oval B. Do the same for the rightmost edge of the two ovals.

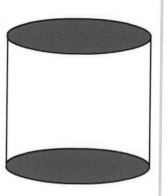

4. Now fill the middle portion with the same color as the fills on ovals A and B. Change the fill of oval A to match the top portion of your cube from the previous section. As before, you can use the Eyedropper Tool (I) to sample this color and the Paint Bucket Tool (K) to fill.

5. Now delete the top half of the stroke on oval B (shown selected in the image at right) to produce a solid cylinder with borders.

6. To take it that one step further, you can delete all the lines to leave a perfect cylinder.

Pyramid

1. Select the Line Tool (N), and draw a line about 100 pixels long, at about a 30 degree angle. If you want to be precise, you can draw a vertical line of any size and set its height (H) to 100 pixels through the Property Inspector and then rotate it by 30 degrees using the Transform panel (Window > Transform or CTRL/CMD+T):

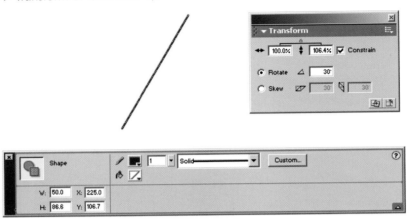

2. Select your line. Then copy (CTRL/CMD+C) and paste it in place (CTRL/CMD+SHIFT+V) in the usual way.

3. While you hold down the SHIFT key, press the RIGHT arrow key a couple times to move it off of the previous line. Then select Modify > Transform > Flip Horizontal. With this line still selected, grab the top edge of the line and snap it to the top edge of the other line.

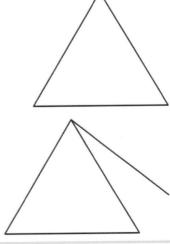

4. Select the Line Tool again and draw a line from the bottom of the first line to the bottom of the second line, thus completing a triangle.

5. Next, draw a line from the top of the triangle with the Line Tool to about 25 pixels above and 25 pixels to the right of the bottom right of the triangle.

6. Then, draw another line connecting the end of that line to the bottom right of the triangle. You're probably starting to realize the benefits of having View > Snap to Objects selected right now.

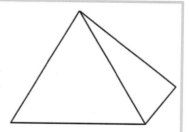

7. Fill the front of the pyramid with the main red color you've been using (for the record, it's #CE0000), and fill the right side of the pyramid with the secondary red that you used in the cube example. Finally, delete all the lines and you have a neat little pyramid.

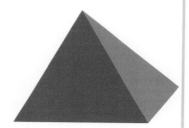

Shadowing

Shadowing is a very simple effect that can add a lot of depth and realism to any object. There are a variety of shadowing effects that can be used, and we cover a couple of the main techniques here. There are many things to consider when you put a shadow of any sort on a 3D object. You must remember that since that object has a shadow, it must have an imaginary light shining on it creating that shadow. For example, consider the simple 3D objects that you created in the previous sections—your cube, for instance, would look a little odd if all the sides were exactly the same color *and* there was a shadow behind it. In reality, a shadow behind the cube implies that light is hitting it from the front, therefore you'd naturally expect the front face of the cube to be a little brighter than the other faces. It's pretty simple when you think about it like that!

The two types of shadows we'll look at here are **drop shadows** and **inner shadows**. For more details on shadows and all sorts of tips relating to shading and highlighting, be sure to check out the next chapter on light and shadow in Flash 3D.

Drop shadows

1. Select the Text Tool (T) and click anywhere on the stage to create some text. For this example, we will use the text JoshDura.com.

2. With the text selected, refer to the Property Inspector and change the font to Arial Black and the font size to 36. Change the text fill color to a light gray.

3. Copy the text (CTRL/CMD+C), paste it in place (CTRL/CMD+SHIFT+V), and then move the object 2 pixels down and 2 pixels to the left with the cursor keys. Now change the font color to black and you've got a very simple drop shadow effect:

4. Note that if you are working on a darker background color when trying to use a drop shadow, you might want to try using a lighter text color on the top text and a darker text color on the bottom text (but not as dark as the background):

Inner shadows

Inner shadows are really just a variation of a drop shadow, but rather than seeming to appear *below* the object, they appear *inside* the object.

1. Choose the Rectangle Tool (R) with a black fill color selected (and no stroke color), and draw a rectangle on your stage about 250 pixels wide by 150 pixels tall.

2. Select the rectangle, copy it (CTRL/CMD+C), and paste it in place (CTRL/CMD+SHIFT+V). Then move it 2 pixels up and 2 pixels to the left. Change the fill in this rectangle to a dark red color (we've used #CC0000).

3. Next, using the Rectangle Tool again, draw a square about 100x100 pixels with a white fill color and a black stroke color.

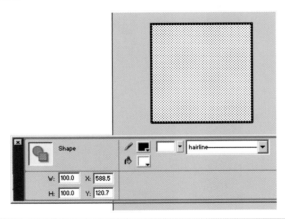

4. Select the top and left stroke lines of this square and move them 2 pixels down and 2 pixels to the right. Now, select the fill that is left—this should be a small 2-pixel-tall inverted L-shaped section like the picture shown at right.

5. Copy this selection and then paste it in place. Group this object (CTRL/CMD+G), and then double-click the object and edit the color to be black.

6. Now, go back to your main edit window and delete all strokes/lines from the square. If you followed these instructions correctly, you should now have a very simple inner shadow on the square. Take this square and center it on the red rectangle you created earlier for a neat inner shadowing effect.

In the sample files that accompany this book, available for download from www.friendsofed.com, you'll find the file basic3Dshapes.fla in this chapter's folder. Open this up and you'll see that we've included some slightly more complex inner shadow examples that you can study. They have all been created using these same fundamental techniques.

Bevels

Bevels are one of the most effective ways to show simple 3D in any interface object. There are only a few ways to bevel an object, which makes it pretty easy to learn how to achieve this effect.

Outer bevel

The **outer bevel** is the most simple of all, as it includes just two line colors. This is the bevel style that you see in most web designs today.

1. First, draw a square with a black (#000000) stroke color and a light gray (#EEEEEE) fill color.

2. Select the left and top lines, and set the stroke color to #CCCCCC.

3. Select the right and bottom lines, and set the stroke color to #666666. This is your very simple outer bevel effect—it looks like it is dented outward. It's also worth noting that if you increase the size of the stroke (from the Property Inspector) to 2 or 3 points, then the bevel effect becomes even more prominent:

Inner bevel

To create an **inner bevel**, just rotate this same square 180 degrees (it will look like it is indented).

Pillow emboss

A **pillow emboss** is just an outer bevel with an inner bevel edge, which creates a bordered emboss.

1. To create this effect, repeat the outer bevel that you created earlier. Group the beveled square (CTRL/CMD+G) and then duplicate it (CTRL/CMD+D). Now simply scale this second square down by about 75% and rotate it 180 degrees (you can use the Transform panel—CTRL/CMD+T).

2. Change the fill color of the smaller square to white, and then place in the center of your original outer bevel rectangle. An easy way to do this is to select both this new rectangle and the outer bevel rectangle, and using the Align panel (CTRL/CMD+K), click the Horizontal Center and Vertical Center buttons (make sure the To Stage button isn't selected).

3. There you have it—a simple pillow emboss:

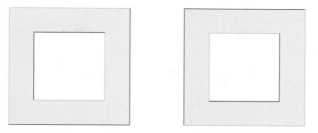

Gradients

Gradients are a key aspect of 3D in Flash. They provide a kind of realistic shine to your objects that most other techniques can't achieve. As you will see in the following example, gradients provide a much more believable 3D feel to an object than simple bevels and embossing do.

1. Select the Oval Tool with a dark red fill color and no stroke color. Holding down the SHIFT key, create a circle approximately 150x150 pixels.

2. Next, select the circle, and in the Color Mixer panel (SHIFT+F9), pull down the fill menu and select a Radial gradient. This will most likely come up with the default black–white gradient. Select the black arrow portion of the gradient and change its color to #CC0000. Then select the white arrow portion of the gradient and change its color to #990000. Slide the #CC0000 arrow about 75% of the way down the gradient bar (toward the right), so the majority of the gradient consists of the #CC0000 color. Your circle should reflect these color changes:

3. Now click on the circle again and group the object (CTRL/CMD+G). Copy the circle (CTRL/CMD+C) and then paste it in place (CTRL/CMD+SHIFT+V). Scale the object down by something like 93%.

4. Double-click the object to edit the group, and select the circle. Go back to the Color Mixer. Select the first arrow (#CC0000), change its color to white (#FFFFFF), and set the alpha on it to 0%. Select the second arrow (the one 100% down), change its color to white, and set the alpha

on it to 50%. Now, using the Arrow Tool (V), grab the center-bottom of the unselected white/white alpha circle and drag it to the middle of the circle:

5.   Go back to the main window, and your circle is complete. It doesn't look exactly right yet as you still have to put something in the middle. For instance, check out the sample FLA from the source files download. At right, we've used the inner shadow technique to create the Flash MX stylized F in the middle of the 3D circle.

As you can see, gradients may not be the most difficult effect to apply in Flash, but they can be tricky to use *effectively*. Using the right kind of gradient in the appropriate situation can be a real art form, so the more practice you get, the better you'll become.

How to use this book

This book offers a comprehensive look into the many cheats you can use in Flash MX to achieve believable pseudo-3D effects in your designs. Each chapter guides you through the most wanted 3D cheats using a series of stepped tutorials, giving you tips and tricks along the way.

Layout conventions

We want this book to be as clear and easy to use as possible, so we've introduced a number of layout styles that we've used throughout—you've probably already noticed a few of them in this chapter:

- Instructions in exercises appear as numbered steps.
- Different styles emphasize things that appear on the screen.
- Hyperlinks appear in the following format: www.friendsofed.com.
- Code appears in this style, and any new code or code that we want to emphasize appears like **this**. You'll also see input information and element names in the same style.
- Keyboard shortcuts appear as follows: CTRL/CMD+S indicates that PC users should press the CTRL (Control) key and the S key at the same time, while Mac users the ⌘ (Command) key and S key. We've attempted to cater to both PC and Mac users throughout.
- New, **important terms** appear in bold.
- If a page isn't wide enough to display a long line of code, we have employed a code continuation symbol (➡). Where you see this, it means the code should all be on the same line.
- Menu selections are indicated as follows: Text > Style > Bold (see the following screen shot).

Download files

Throughout each of the chapters, you'll see references to download files. These are the completed files for everything you will build throughout the book and extra files to help you along the way. In fact, you can get an entire bonus chapter, "Interactive Scaling." These files can be downloaded from the link on the friends of ED homepage (www.friendsofed.com).

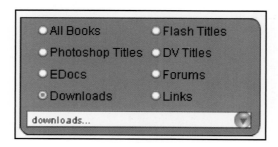

Support—we're here to help

All books from friends of ED should be easy to follow and error-free. However, if you do run into problems, don't hesitate to get in touch—our support is fast, friendly, and free.

You can reach us at www.friendsofed.com. We'd love to hear from you, even if it's just to request future books, ask about friends of ED, or tell us how much you loved *Flash 3D Cheats Most Wanted*. If your inquiry concerns an issue not directly related to book content, then the best place for these types of questions is our message boards at www.friendsofed.com. Here, you'll find a variety of designers talking about what they do, who should be able to provide some ideas and solutions.

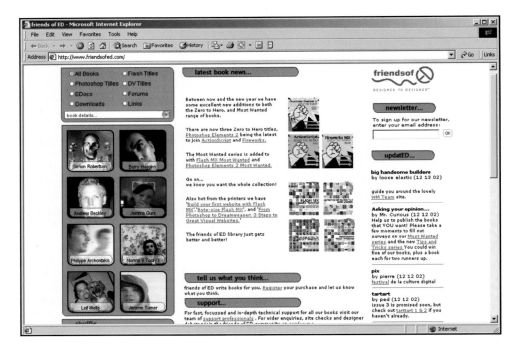

Light and Shadow

What is it we like so much about creating designs with three-dimensional elements? It seems that we can't get enough of 3D work, but why is it so eye-catching? After all, we see in real 3D every day of our lives! Some find creating 3D objects fun or neat, whereas others feel it is a way to express thoughts or ideas we may be familiar with in everyday lives. We like the idea of creating something that we've never seen in real life, such as a dinosaur or a spaceship. Seeing such a thing in 3D tricks your brain, even if for only a split second, that it might be real.

3D is fun because when we see this type of object, whether it be some kind of elaborate sci-fi spacecraft, a fantastic gel button on a website, or an animated 3D cartoon, we attempt to visualize what it would be like to actually have the thing in our hands or actually be in the same make-believe 3D environment. You can almost imagine what a gel button, for instance, would feel like. Is it smooth, squishy, or solid?

Of course, you realize that we are not quite talking about creating ultra-realistic spaceships straight out of *Starship Troopers* in this book (although stay tuned for Chapter 5, in which a flying saucer plays a central character). With the 3D cheats we concentrate on in this book, we're talking about generating really cool 3D effects with a program that is not specifically intended for 3D creation.

Flash is traditionally known as a 2D vector animation tool, but it has grown up over the years and is now being used to produce some of the coolest websites and movies around. With some creativity and a little know-how, Flash can used to create really cool pseudo-3D graphics as well.

Seeing the light

Before we dive right into the vector 3D world, let's take a moment to examine the key signatures of 3D objects. 3D essentially boils down to a few concepts: perspective, distance, speed, motion, and light and shadow. Without light and shadow, all we see are flat 2D objects, so that's what we focus on in this chapter. Consider the circle at right.

It's just that: a circle. Or could it be a ball? It doesn't look like the kind of ball that we are familiar with. It's just a flat, lifeless, blue circle. Looking at this "ball" we have no sense of placement, depth, or texture, or even the fact that it is indeed a ball at all.

Now let's take a look at that same circle with some texture, light and shadow (see the image at right).

It's obvious that this is the number 4 ball for a pool table. What made the simple blue circle into a shiny blue pool table ball is light and shadow and, of course, the telltale number 4 in a white circle. But more important, the light and shadow really define the ball. The light is coming from the top-right section of the ball, highlighting it. This light produces both the highlight and the shadow at the same time. The area of the ball not getting as much light is obviously darker, and the 3D solid form of our sphere casts a shadow. Looking at the circle, we get a natural sense that it is three-dimensionally spherical. This is because the top half of the circle is lighter than the bottom, but more important because the areas where the darker and lighter parts of the circle meet curve a little.

Now look at the pool ball again, this time with some hints (see the image at right).

You can see that the shadow does indeed have a slight curve to it, giving us the illusion that it is truly round. This curve in the shadow suggests that the circle has dimension or depth and is a real ball. The additional lines that you see here serve to accentuate the curve of the shadow so you can really see it.

Most objects that we see in the real world have some sort of highlight and lowlight. The highlights are caused by a light source such as the sun illuminating or reflecting off an object. The shadows are caused by places where light cannot reach. This concept seems rather elementary and obvious, but unless you are thinking in terms of 3D you may not have actually thought how important light and shadow are. Let's look at another example before we begin. Look at this beautiful ocean picture taken in Hawaii:

There's hardly anything there! This represents the scene with very little light source.

Here is the same picture again, except with much better light this time:

This is a simple but effective explanation of how light is important in creating 3D effects. It's clear this is a picture of a rocky cove with the ocean splashing against it. We know this is the ocean because of the lights and darks of the rippling in the waves. It's obvious that the rocks in this cove are really rough and jagged. We get this visual clue because of where the light shines on the rocks and where it does not. In fact, there are many different visual clues—the white water splashing against the rocks, for example, and the color of the rocks give the viewer more hints about the perspective and motion of the image. More fundamentally speaking, we wouldn't be able to see any color at all without light.

Elements of light and shadow

In order to better understand the use of light and shadows to produce realistic graphics, let's take a closer look at the number 4 pool ball:

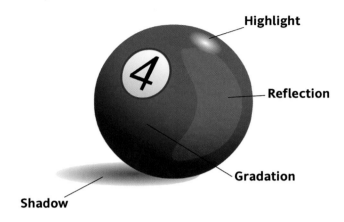

Highlight

Reflection

Gradation

Shadow

Highlight

The highlight in this case lets us know that the ball has a smooth, shiny surface. It also tells us the direction of the light source and how far away it may be, which we will need to know later for creating the shadow.

Reflection

This confirms that the ball is in fact shiny—this shiny surface reflects objects in the scene. Even though we do not have any actual objects in this scene other than the ball itself, it is implied that the ball is perhaps part of a larger picture. Maybe the ball is sitting on a pool table and we are seeing the reflection of a doorway. Look at the ball a little closer and you'll see!

This leads us to another important point: the *subtlety* of certain elements that make up an image can work to our advantage. There are lots of things we take for granted on a daily basis when we look at real objects. For example, lighting, color variations, gradients, reflections, and the relation to other objects are all taken for granted and must be included in some combination, be it explicit or implicit, when trying to create believable 3D effects.

The reflection in this ball may not be entirely necessary, but it does add to the believability that this is supposed to be a number 4 pool ball.

Gradation

This is where the light begins to lose its luminosity and fades to a darker color, creating the shadow. This not only leads to the shadow but also allows us to create some sort of dimension to the object. In this case, the gradient has a bent shape, giving the object the appearance of a sphere or of roundness.

Where the gradation begins on the object is important because it strengthens the idea that the object has a third dimension (also referred to mathematically as a z-axis). It tells us what direction the light source is coming from and maybe how far away it is. With this particular image, however, it is difficult to tell how big the light source actually is—the light could be very large and very far away or very small and very close to the ball. That's where other objects in the scene can help out.

Shadow

The shadow lets the viewer know where the light source is coming from and from about what angle. If the light were directly above the ball, the shadow would naturally be directly under the ball. If the light were hitting the ball at a 90-degree angle, then the shadow would be very long against the surface the ball is sitting on.

3D shading techniques

Before you begin to use some of the theory that we've just covered, it's worth clarifying that creating realistic 3D and producing believable 3D are two different things. In Flash MX, a 2D vector graphics application, we're simply concerned with creating believable 3D effects. On the other hand, realistic 3D is something that might be used in a motion picture, or something that could be created in a specific 3D software package (3D Studio Max, for example). In such cases, the designers need the audience to believe that the 3D is in fact real. In contrast, in this chapter we're not trying to emulate any kind of super-realism—we'll just create objects and scenes that the viewer can believe are meant to be 3D, such as our humble pool ball.

Throughout the following tutorials, keep in mind that there are always many different ways to create effects in Flash. You may eventually find that you like creating these visuals differently, but the fundamental ideas behind each example are what you should remember. That may simply mean that the highlight gets drawn before the reflection or vice versa. Our point is that we explain how to re-create these objects linearly from the bottom up. You may find that when you do them from scratch you'll create them differently, and that's just fine. Also, because color is so important in creating believable 3D, we focus on gradients and colors a bit as well.

These demonstrations will hopefully serve to inspire and motivate you, and from here you should just go with your feeling and create the best looking Flash 3D possible.

Pool ball

Let's start out re-creating that blue pool ball you've heard so much about. Open Flash MX and let's get cracking:

1. Open a new Flash movie (CTRL/CMD+N). The size of the stage and the frame rate are not important, so the default values will work fine: 550x400 for the stage size and 12 fps for the frame rate.

2. Create six layers and name them as shown opposite.

    Naming layers makes referencing them later much easier. And, of course, it makes explaining procedures much easier in this book!

3. Let's start with the circle layer. Click the Oval Tool (O) and make sure the stroke color around the circle is turned off. I've chosen a shade of blue (#3265C9) for the fill color.

4. Create a circle using the Oval Tool, holding down the shift key to constrain it to a perfect circle. With the circle selected, you can set its diameter to 150 by changing its W and H dimensions in the Property Inspector.

    For good measure, center the circle in the middle of the stage. You can use the Align panel (CTRL/CMD+K) to center it.

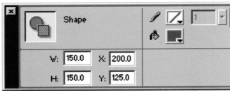

5. Let's go ahead and add the gradient. Select your blue filled circle and refer to the Color Mixer panel (Window > Color Mixer or SHIFT+F9). After you choose a Radial gradient, add a couple of gradient markers (the little house-shaped icons) and make sure your gradient matches the palette (see the image at right).

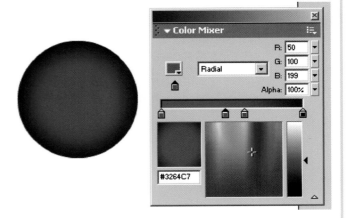

The gradient color changes, from left to right, are as follows: #3366CC, #3264C7, #2F5FB8, and #132D46. It's important to know that this gradient color was not thought up out of thin air—there was a great deal of tweaking to get the right color pattern. You should expect to have to experiment and tweak the colors of your gradient when creating it from scratch.

6. Now you need to move the gradient in the right position on the circle. Choose the Fill Transform Tool (F). With this tool you can position the shadow such that it has a curve. Again, the curve is important because it denotes that the circle might have a z-axis, or third dimension:

 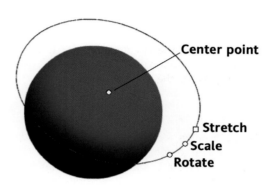

A good point of reference is to place the white center dot of the Fill Transform Tool over the spot where the highlight will approximately be, as shown above. You can use the four edit handles to move, stretch, scale, and rotate the gradient. It's worth spending a moment playing around with these powerful controls, if you're not already familiar with them.

7. While we are talking about where the highlight will be, let's go ahead and add it. Choose the Oval Tool (O) again and drag out an oval with no stroke anywhere on the stage in the highlight layer of your Flash movie. As before, be sure to select Radial for the gradient type.

The important thing about the color for the highlight is that the blue must match the blue that the highlight is going to be sitting on. In this case, #3265C9 is the hex code for the blue on the outer edge. The other color in the middle is simply white.

8. Next you need to set the size of the highlight so you can set the gradient correctly. Make the oval 32x23 pixels. Using the rotate and scale modifiers of the Free Transform Tool (Q) (or the Transform panel—CTRL/CMD+T) and the Arrow Tool (V), set the highlight to match the position and angle of the ball as shown on right (the rotation on the highlight should be about 30 degrees, where the long side of the shadow is parallel to the side of the ball).

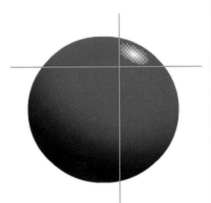

9. You'll add the reflection next. This is basically a distorted circle that has been tweaked to form the shape shown at right. With the Oval Tool (O), create a white oval on the reflection layer. Again, you'll need to distort the oval to get it about the shape shown at right. To distort the shape, simply use the Arrow Tool and place the cursor near the edge of the unselected oval. Once the arrow turns into an arrow with a curve, you can start to distort the oval (alternatively, you can use the Free Transform Tool again, but this time with distort and envelope modifiers).

10. After you get your reflection just right, turn the distorted shape into a movie clip (select it and choose Insert > Convert to Symbol..., or press F8). With the reflection now in the form of a movie clip, you can easily adjust the alpha channel so it is just a subtle reflection against the blue ball. With the movie clip selected, examine the Property Inspector and adjust the alpha to 10%.

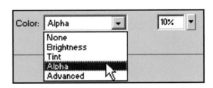

11. OK, let's move on and create the surface shadow. With the Oval Tool selected, on the shadow layer create a black oval shape approximately the same size as the one shown below. You may find that you need to distort your shadow, as you did with the reflection, to make it just right. To see the surface shadow easily, select the Show Layer As Outline icon in the timeline:

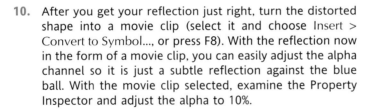

12. With the shadow selected, create the gradient shown at right.

13. Now with the Fill Transform Tool (Q), make the gradient centered on the shadow and shaped like the oval of the shadow.

14. At this point, you should have a rather convincing shiny blue ball.

Let's go ahead and add the finishing touch: the small circle with the number 4. This 4 is important because it further illustrates that the ball is indeed supposed to be 3D. This is because the 4 is distorted and off to the side of the ball, giving the illusion of depth.

With the Oval Tool, create a light gray circle with a black stroke in the 4-circle layer. Again, slight tweaking of the circle will be in order here to achieve better 3D-looking results. With the circle finished, select the Text Tool (T) and type in a number 4 using a simple font in the layer named 4.

Now you need to break apart your 4 so you can distort it. Select Modify > Break Apart (or just press CTRL/CMD+B) to break the text apart into a simple vector graphic. Now you can select the 4 and then choose Modify > Transform > Distort from the menu (similarly, you could use the Free Transform Tool (Q) with the distort modifier). Tilt the top part of the 4 slightly to the right. Now rotate the 4 slightly and center it inside the gray circle.

Once again, you'll probably need to make slight adjustments here and there to get the 4 and circle looking just right. When everything is done, you should have a very convincing number 4 pool ball.

Open up `ball.fla` in Flash to see the finished design. This file is available for download from www.friendsofed.com, along with all the other sample files featured in this book.

Now that you're familiar with using some of the basic concepts of light and shadow to produce 3D effects in Flash, let's look at a slightly more complex example.

Gel button

The gel button is probably one of the most popular and duplicated button styles ever made. There's a lot to think about when creating this gem, so we briefly explain the unofficial design requirements. The button typically resembles a pill and it is supposed to be transparent and shiny. Also, any text on the button should reflect to the bottom of the pill. Let's get started:

1. Open a new Flash movie. Again, the default values on stage size and frame rate will work fine. Next, create eight layers and name them as shown below:

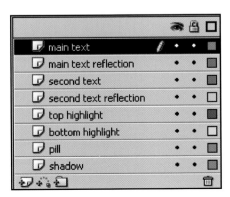

2.   Select the Rectangle Tool (R), click on the Round Rectangle Radius button, and give the rectangle a radius of `100`. While you're working with the Tools panel, make sure that the stroke color (line) is turned off.

With these options selected, drag out a rectangle on the pill layer (which will look like a rounded-edge rectangle) to around 430x98 (it doesn't have to be exact—that's just what we used). The fill color is not important at this point.

3.   With the rectangle drawn, make sure to fill it with the appropriate fill gradient. Select the rounded rectangle on the stage and adjust the color mixer for a Linear gradient with these colors (refer to the previous tutorial for further instructions):

The colors from left to right are as follows: `#5ABAF3`, `#64BEF4`, `#2A73A6`, `#0B578C`, and `#0A4E76`. Likely the gradient will be from left to right. You need to reposition this gradient for top to bottom.

4.   Now choose the Fill Transform Tool (F) and click on the rectangle. You'll see the edit handles appear on the pill for the gradient. Click and hold down the rotation handle and rotate the gradient such that the dark color is on top and the gradient is as tight on the pill as possible. It may help to get the gradient perfectly straight on the pill if you make sure that View > Snap to Objects is on.

5.   Next, you add the lower highlight. In the bottom highlight layer you are going to create an object that looks something like this:

It really doesn't matter how you make this shape as long as it looks something like the one shown and has the color #9CD2F8. We made ours by creating another rectangle with the same properties as the main part of the pill. We then used the Arrow Tool to select the area that we wanted to trim and deleted it—simple enough!

Convert this shape into a movie clip (press F8) and call it bottom_highlight. You now need to add the fade on the outside of the shape. Double-click into this new movie clip and select the shape. In the menu, select Modify > Shape > Soften Fill Edges.... Set Distance to 40, Number of Steps to 10, and Direction to Expand. The shape should look something like this now:

6. Click back to Scene 1 (the root timeline) and select the bottom highlight movie clip. In the Property Inspector at the bottom of the screen in the Color setting, choose Advanced and then Settings.... Make sure that your settings match those shown at right.

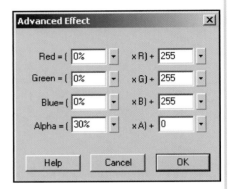

7. Position the highlight so that your pill now looks like this:

8. Now let's create the upper highlight. In the top highlight layer you will need to create another shape. This one should resemble the following shape:

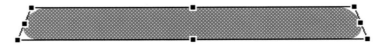

9. Again, there are probably quite a few ways that you could create this shape. We used the Rectangle Tool with the same settings as above and drew out a long, thin rectangle slightly smaller in width than the main pill. Then, with the distortion tool (Modify > Transform > Distort), we grabbed the two top edges and pulled them in slightly to give the shape a bend that roughly matched the shape of the main pill:

10. You now need to add the gradient fill. Make sure the new highlight shape is selected and adjust your gradient fill to match those shown at right.

   The colors from left to right are as follows: #E8F4FC, #B5DCF6, and #62B4EC.

11. Once again you will need to adjust the direction of the gradient by selecting the Fill Transform Tool and rotating the gradient where the lightest color is at the top and moving the top highlight to match this one:

12. Now you will create the shadow. You may want to hide the other layers for now so you can see the shadow layer. Again, choose the Rectangle Tool with a round radius, using the same parameters as before. In the shadow layer, draw a rectangle that is about 10% smaller than your original pill. Use a solid fill and the color #3C8BBE.

   With the shape selected, make it a movie clip (F8) and call it pill_shadow. Now double-click the new movie clip to edit it. Make sure the shape is selected and select Modify > Shape > Soften Fill Edges... from the top menu. In the Soften Fill Edges dialog box, adjust the settings as shown below:

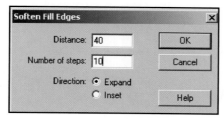

13. Now back in the main timeline (Scene 1), select the pill_shadow movie clip and adjust its width to 106%, its height to 90%, and its alpha to 40%.

   Again, the reason we are re-adjusting the shadow movie clip to these settings here rather than making them like that to begin with is to illustrate that there is usually a lot of tweaking to be done before you are satisfied with your results. In this case, we made the shadow and then decided that it had to be adjusted to 106% x 90% to look right.

So at this point you have a really convincing gel button. But let's take it one more step by adding some text.

14. To complete the button you'll add the text friendsofED in the main text and main text reflection layers of your movie. You will use a common font, Arial Black, a point size of 45, Auto Kern selected, and the color #3C8BBE.

    With that text selected, make it a movie clip and call it `foe_shadow`. Position your text in the middle. Now copy that movie clip and paste a copy of it in the main text layer in the same position (you can use Edit > Paste in Place). You need to break apart the pasted movie clip down to a simple graphic. With that newly pasted movie clip selected, press CTRL/CMD+B twice to get the text down to its raw vector graphics. You will know that it is a vector graphic because it will look like it has little dots over the graphic when selected. Lock all the layers except the main text layer.

    With the Arrow Tool, select the top half of the text. Your selection should include only the part of the text graphics that overlaps the upper highlight.

15. Change the color of this selected area to #454545. Now choose the other half and make it black. This has the effect of making the text look as if it's part of the button, picking up some of the highlight.

16. Finally, unlock the shadow layer, set its alpha to 25%, and move it slightly down and to the left. This produces the reflection in the pill of the friendsofED text. You can repeat this procedure for whatever other text you'd like to feature on your button, and voila—the 3D pill-shaped gel button is complete! Take a look at the file `gel_button.fla` to see the final version of this design:

You should have a clear idea by now of how light and shadow plays an important role in creating the impression of 3D. Other concepts play a role in 3D as well. In the case of the pool ball and gel button examples that you've just studied, you used reflection to indicate that the surface of your objects is smooth. In the gel button, you used the lower highlight to give the button a sense of transparency and depth—it actually looks as if the light is shining through the button as well as reflecting off its smooth surface.

As a bonus, we've provided another variation of this button that includes previous techniques. It's called `foe_button.fla`, and it's essentially a flat version of this technique with a few extras:

Navigation bar

Let's look at how 3D can be useful in Flash navigation. You'll create a simple navigation bar where the buttons look as though they can be physically pushed down. You'll take a look at how the shadow really convinces you that the button is indeed *down* as opposed to *up*. Although this is a simple navigation bar, explaining how to create it can get tricky. Read closely and dig in:

1. Open a new Flash document. The stage size is not really important for this demonstration, but you will need to adjust your frame rate to 31 fps—this is a workaround to ensure that both PCs and Macs will play back at the intended frame rate (in previous versions of Flash, if the frame rate was set to 30, then it would play back at 21 to 24 fps on a Mac).

2. Create seven layers and name them as shown at right.

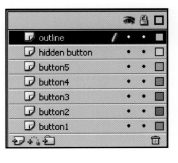

3. In the outline layer, create a frame for your navigation bar with the Rectangle Tool. Hide the fill, make the stroke black, and make sure the weight of the stroke is set to 2. Drag out a rectangular outline of 464x21 pixels, and then center it on the stage:

4. Next, build one of the buttons. Create a new movie clip (Insert > New Symbol... or CTRL/CMD+F8) and call it button1. Make four layers inside this clip labeled as shown below:

5. In the background layer, create a black rectangle that is 93x21 pixels. Make sure that it is centered within the movie clip:

6. The main button needs to be created next. Create a new movie clip (CTRL/CMD+F8) and call it `button_graphic`. Make two layers in this movie clip and call the bottom layer bottom and the top layer (yep—you guessed it) top. With the top layer selected, drag out a rectangle that is 89x17 pixels. Fill the rectangle with a gradient pattern as shown at right.

The colors from left to right are as follows: `#D5D5D5`, `#C7C7C7`, and `#626262`.

7. Now select the Fill Transform Tool and rotate the gradient to match the following:

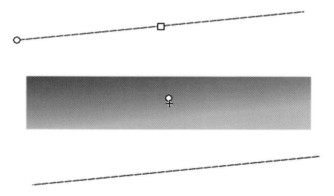

8. For the beveled edge, create a rectangle 93x21 pixels in size in the bottom layer, centered on the stage. You will need to select different parts of this rectangle and colorize them like this (light: `#E6E6E6`, dark: `#333333`):

We've found that using the Line Tool to cut the rectangle so we can select the different sections is easiest. Be sure to set the line weight to Hairline. With the line drawn out, you can select the different sections and color them accordingly. After you are finished, be sure to select and delete the lines.

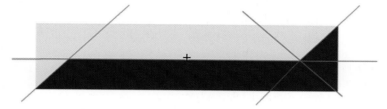

9. Now that you have the main part of the button complete, edit the `button1` movie clip located in the Library. Drag the `main_button` movie clip into the `main button` layer in the `button` movie clip. Make sure the `button_graphic` is centered on the `button1` stage.

10. You will now create the down movement of the button. Still editing `button1`, on the `main button` layer create a keyframe on frames 4 and 8. Select `button_graphic` in the fourth frame, resize it to 98% x 86%, and move it approximately to the x position `-44` and y position `-8`. It should look something like the image at right:

11. Finally, for this down state you need to add a darker tint to the button to indicate that it is being pushed down, creating a sort of shadow. So with the button in the fourth keyframe selected, choose Tint from the Property Inspector and give it the color `#ACA899`:

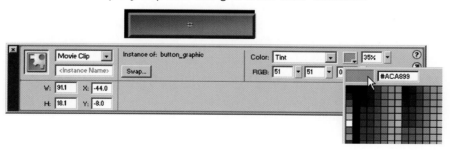

As usual, we like to tweak things until we feel comfortable with them. This being the case, we wanted to change the color of the button's up state. Select the button in frame 1 and tint it with the color `#ECE9D8`. Do the same for the button in frame 8—this keyframe should be a duplicate of the first so no change is needed. Now create a motion tween (Insert > Create Motion Tween) between each keyframe in the `main button` layer.

12. Next you will create the label. In the layer named `label` in the first frame, select the Text Tool (T). We chose Arial Black with a point size of 11 and the color black (of course, you can choose any font you like). Type Button One , or whatever you want, and make sure that the text is centered. Next, make the text a movie clip (F8) and call it `button1_text`. Again, create keyframes in frames 4 and 8.

13. Back in frame 1, with your new `button1_text` movie clip selected, apply a tint to the movie clip with the color `#666666` (dark gray). Do the same in the frame 8, but leave frame 4 as it is—no tint, just black. In frame 4, resize `button1_text` to 98% and move it to where it is centered with the main button but more toward the bottom of the button, as shown at right.

14. Now tween all the frames in the labels.layer. In the actions layer put stop commands (`stop();`) in frames 1, 2, and 4. You should now have the button ready to go. If you scrub the timeline back and forth, you should see the button basically looks like it's moving up and down.

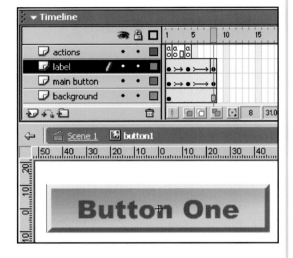

15. Next, you need to create five more of these buttons, all with different names and different labels. The best way to do this is to open the Library and duplicate `button1`, calling it `button2`, and so on until you have five different button movie clips. You will need to do the same for the label movie clips, `button1_text`, `button2_text`, and so on. For reference, at right are the contents of our Library (F11) at this point. Edit each button and each text label accordingly.

16. Back on the root timeline (Scene 1), add each of the buttons from the Library into its respective layer, `button2`, `button3`, and so on, to the stage. Place each button side by side, 1 through 5:

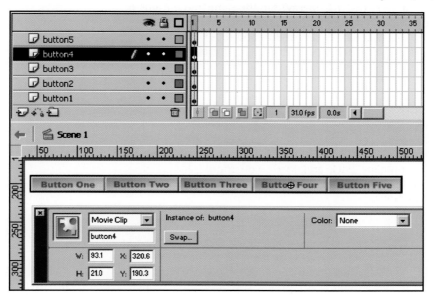

At this point, you can label each button so that you will be able to control each button separately with some simple ActionScript. Select the first button and in the Property Inspector give it an instance name of `button1`. Now select all of the other buttons and name them accordingly (as shown above): `button2`, `button3`, `button4`, and `button5`.

17. You're nearly finished now—you just need to add a hidden button that will control the timeline of each navigation button so you can manage the push down effect you've created. In the `hidden_button` layer drag out a rectangle 93x21 pixels. With the rectangle selected, make it a button (F8) and name it (you guessed it) `hidden_button`. Edit this button and move the rectangle from frame 1 to frame 4 (the Hit state frame). Navigate back to the root timeline, Scene 1.

18. You should notice that your button is now a greenish-blue. That indicates that it is a *hot spot* and you can now add actions to the button. Copy and paste `hidden_button` four times on the layer hidden button and move them directly over the other buttons below it.

On the hidden buttons, you need to add the ActionScript that controls the movement of each button. Select the first hidden button and place the following code in the Actions panel (F9):

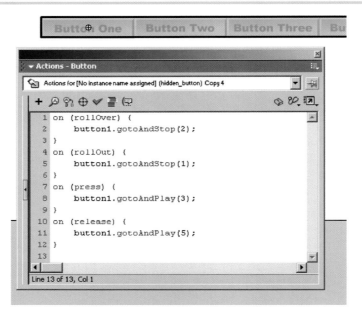

In the code, button1 is the reference to your movie clip button (remember, you gave it this instance name in Step 16). For the other four hidden buttons, copy this code and place it on the button. For each button, you will need to replace the `button1` reference with the name of the button the code is to control. For example, when you copy this code on the second hidden button, the hidden button that controls `button2`, the code will look like this:

```
on (rollOver) {
  button2.gotoAndStop(2);
}
on (rollOut) {
  button2.gotoAndStop(1);
}
on (press) {
  button2.gotoAndPlay(3);
}
on (release){
  button2.gotoAndPlay(5);
}
```

Continue with the rest of the buttons, modifying the code as needed.

The finished effect, `nav_bar.fla`, can be found with this chapter's sample files. On testing your navigation bar movie (CTRL/CMD+ENTER), you should have a set of buttons that appear darker when they are pushed down:

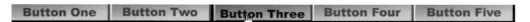

Several concepts about light and shadow are in use here. The highlight around the button in its up state tells you where the light is coming from (the top left). When the button is pressed, it gets darker, denoting that it is below the area that light can reach, which further emphasizes the idea that it is being depressed. The black around the button, once the button is pushed down, also tells you that this is an area that light cannot reach, and the overall effect is of a believable 3D navigation bar.

Animated shadows

The last concept of light and shadow we discuss is actually pretty straightforward. In this example, we discuss the direct correlation between light and shadow, and how you might use this to enhance your 3D animations. Instead of creating this next piece in the standard step-by-step tutorial style, you'll examine some sample Flash movies.

First of all, open `sun.swf`. Here you have a scene showing a building with the sun in the background. The sun is initially high, causing the building to cast a shadow. If you click the Move button, the sun starts to move across the sky, and you see the shadow from the building move to the opposite direction and get a little longer:

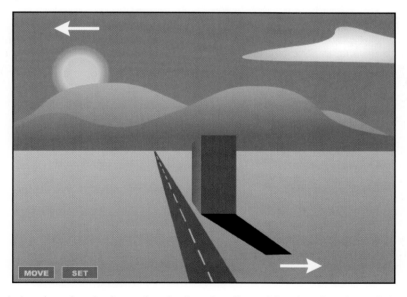

The direction and size that the shadow takes is directly affected by the direction of the light source. This is important to consider when you create believable 3D and, although logical enough, it's often overlooked. As the sun moves further down into the horizon, the building shadow gets even longer. Now click the Set button, and you'll see that as the sun starts to go below the mountains and the horizon, the scene begins to get dark—it's night time. Take a look at `sun.fla` to see how these simple ideas were put together.

Returning to the shadow animation, the shadow gets longer because the amount of direct light that actually hits the building's side is greater when the sun is lower in the horizon versus when it's higher in the sky. In this case, the object is a building and the source is the sun.

Let's take a quick look at this relationship using parts of the ball you made earlier in the chapter. We've re-created the ball and its associated shadow in `ball_shadow.swf` (you can also open up `ball_shadow.fla` to see how this example was constructed). Open `ball_shadow.swf` and pay particular attention to both the shadow and highlight of the ball when it is in the air and on the ground.

In this movie we have another simple demonstration of a light source affecting an object. It's clear that the highlight is large when it's closer to the source, but the shadow, on the other hand, is small and faint. This is because the object is far away from the surface where the shadow is being cast. A faint shadow also tells the viewer that the object is much smaller than the light source. The reason for this is the light source is actually shining around the ball onto the surface.

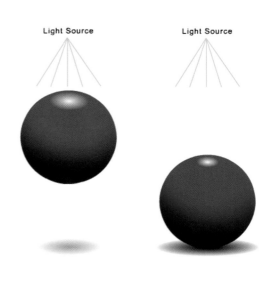

When the ball falls closer to the ground, the shadow will get bigger and darker because the light cannot reach the area under the ball as easily. The changing shadow in this case tells the viewer that the light affects the ball and that it is in motion. It also tells the viewer that the ball is getting closer to the landing surface. Also notice that the highlight is smaller when the light source is further away—this is a subtle yet effective indication of the relative positioning of the light source and the object.

The reason we take the time to include shadows and highlights is to add to the believability that the object is supposed to be 3D, moving up then down, casting shadows, and creating highlights. Experiment with `ball_shadow.fla` to see what other kind of light and shadow effects you can create.

Summary

Light and shadow define just about everything we look at, whether it's a photo of Hawaii or an image of a pool ball. They defines space perception and depth, and allow us to perceive colors. Take a look at the cube at right and its associated light source.

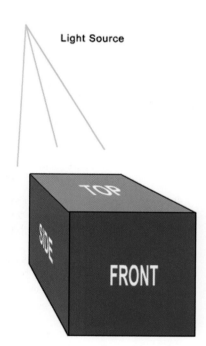

Light Source

The box is light blue—we know this by looking at the top. The light source from above is clearly illuminating the top of the box, showing its true color. The side of the box is receiving less light, making its color look darker. The front of the box is getting even less light, making its color even darker. We know the box is light blue, but the direction of the source light has made it appear three different colors—this gives it depth. More fundamentally, this lighting effect helps us to recognize that the object it actually a box.

The effects of light and shadow are played out everywhere we look: on cars, on buildings, on people, on mountains, indoors, and so on. Because of these simple effects, we can gain a sense of the object placed in a three-dimensional space. This applies to *everything* we see. The challenge is re-creating that third dimension in the 2D format of digital art to make our viewers believe it is 3D. The nice thing about creating 3D in Flash is that Flash is very forgiving; if you make a mistake, you can just undo and try again. We've already established that Flash MX is not a true 3D program (perhaps that's the reason you're reading this book on 3D cheats), but with a little know-how and imagination we can produce some really nice pseudo-3D. There are many more techniques involved in creating 3D effects with Flash MX, so keep reading!

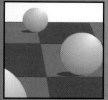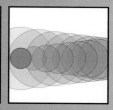

Scaling for 3D

In case the first two chapters of this book have not drilled this into you so completely that you now have nightmares about it every night, we're going to repeat it once again. All of the cheats in this book are about one thing: fooling the user into seeing 3D on a 2D screen. There are many different methods for achieving this. At the very high end, we have complicated 3D engines that allow the creation and traversing of 3D worlds, complete with photo-realistic lighting and textures. On the other end of the scale, there's the kind of faux-3D that we're talking about in this book. Since Flash doesn't have a built-in 3D engine or the computational firepower for creating such an engine in ActionScript, we need to resort to trickery. This chapter is about using one of the most important clues that our brain processes when judging depth and perspective: the relative sizes of various objects. In other words, **scale**.

We take for granted that when we look down a long corridor or across a wide plain to a person in the distance, that person appears smaller to our eyes than if she were standing right in front of us. Although the person appears smaller in our view, our brain knows that this is because she is standing far away and not because she's pulling an "Alice in Wonderland" on us. In other words, our brain understands that people don't shrink, so it interprets impossibly small people as standing far away. In fact, this is not an automatic reaction but one that is socially learned. We can manipulate the fact that our brains have learned to correlate size with distance to create the effect of the third dimension on our flat 2D monitors.

Lights... cameras... Flash!

Creating the illusion of 3D is a bit more complicated than simply scattering a couple of objects of different sizes on the stage. The realism of your scenes will depend on factors such as lighting, camera angle, and depth of field. If this is beginning to sound like an introductory film course, there's a reason for that: what we're doing is very similar to shooting a film. Whereas with film we have a camera that we can manipulate to affect depth of field, exposure, and focus, we have to create these effects manually in Flash. Similarly, when filming we use carefully placed lights (or the sun and reflectors) to control shadows. When creating our 3D scenes, we have to visualize imaginary light sources and shade our objects accordingly. In creating the upcoming effects, we're going to look at the stage in a new way: as the viewfinder of our camera, looking out into a 3D world that we will sculpt using all manner of trickery to create lighting, depth of field, and perspective. To do this, we'll start out using the 2D drawing tools in Flash and, later on, a little bit of ActionScript.

Basic 3D scaling

Knowing that smaller objects appear farther away, we can immediately put this knowledge to use and trick our eyes into seeing depth where there actually is none. Before we can think of setting up our scene (or *mise-en-scène*), we need to create some objects to place in it. For the sake of simplicity, we're going to create one of the simplest fake 3D objects you can create in Flash: a sphere, complete with lighting and shadow effects.

1. Start a new Flash movie (File > New or CTRL/CMD+N), set the stage dimensions to 400x300 using the Document Properties dialog box (Modify > Document... or CTRL/CMD+J, or simply click the Size button in the Property Inspector), and set the frame rate to 24 fps. Whenever you set the stage size, the main stage gets displaced with the new settings. A quick way to get back to the full stage view is to double-click on the Hand Tool.

2. Our sphere is going to start a life as a reddish-orange circle without an outline (stroke). Disable the stroke by clicking on the stroke color and then selecting the disable button (no color). Next, select a web-safe orange using the Fill Color selector and draw a circle using the Oval Tool (O). Make sure to hold down the SHIFT key while you're drawing to constrain your oval to a perfect circle. At this point you're probably thinking, "Now that doesn't look very three-dimensional!" Of course you'd be right, so let's jazz it up a bit, keeping in mind some of the tricks you learned in the previous chapter.

3. You're going to be adding depth to your otherwise two-dimensional circle using a method called **chiaroscuro**, a technique first developed in painting during the Italian Renaissance. You may know it more simply as "using a gradient fill." In fact, the chiaroscuro technique is a little more involved, but not by much. So let's set sail: select the default black-to-white radial gradient for the fill color in the lower-left corner of the color palette, as shown in the figure opposite.

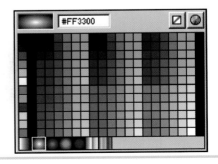

4. If the Color Mixer panel isn't showing, make it visible (Window > Color Mixer or SHIFT+F9). You should be able to see the black-to-white radial gradient that you selected in the Color Mixer panel. Click on the small black color swatch at the rightmost end of the rectangular gradient strip to select it. The larger color swatch next to the Fill Style drop-down menu should turn black. Click on this swatch and select the web-safe orange with the hexadecimal color value of FF6600. When you're done, the gradient in the Color Mixer panel should look like the one in the figure opposite.

5. If you like, you can save this custom gradient by selecting Add Swatch from the Color Mixer panel menu (the small drop-down menu on the title bar of this panel). This will add your custom gradient to the Color Swatches panel so you can use it again in the future without having to re-create it.

6. Now it's time to add the radial gradient you just created to your circle to give it the appearance of volume and thus transform it into a sphere. With your radial gradient selected, use the Paint Bucket Tool (K) and click toward the upper-right of the circle that you drew a moment ago. There's a lot you can do with gradients to simulate lighting and give objects the appearance of volume. Thanks to the gradient, your sphere looks like it is being lit from the top and slightly to the side, just as it would be if it were a real sphere being lit by the sun at around 2pm.

    If you haven't done so already, it's worth looking at Chapter 2 for more neat tricks with gradients.

7. Things are looking a bit more three-dimensional now, but we can do better. On earth, objects that are illuminated tend to cast shadows. To make things look more lifelike, you're going to add a shadow to your sphere. Before you get too carried away, however, you'll convert your sphere to a movie clip so you can manipulate it easily later on. Click on the sphere to select it and choose Insert > Convert to Symbol... (F8) to transform it into a symbol. Make the symbol a movie clip and call it `mySphere`. This will create a movie clip symbol in your Library called `mySphere` and replace the sphere that was on the stage with an instance of this mySphere symbol.

8. Double-click on your new `mySphere` movie clip instance to open up the symbol for editing. Here, create a new layer (Insert > Layer, or click the little icon in the bottom-left corner of the timeline). Give these layers some meaningful names: rename Layer 1 as sphere and Layer 2 as shadow by double-clicking on their layer names and typing over the default names. Now drag the shadow layer underneath the sphere layer.

9. To draw the shadow, choose a dark shade of gray as your fill color, disable the stroke color, and create an oval similar to the one in the figure opposite. Position the shadow toward the bottom and to the left of the sphere. Note how you're positioning it opposite the highlight on the sphere. That's the direction the light is coming from, so the shadow has to be cast in the opposite direction. Pay attention to the light sources in your scenes. Just because they're imaginary doesn't mean that they're any less important!

10. Now that you have your faux-3D sphere symbol, you need to add a few more instances of it to the stage before you can manipulate them to trick your eyes into seeing perspective. Double-click on an empty part of your work area to exit out of editing the mySphere symbol. With the instance of your sphere symbol selected, press CTRL/CMD+D twice to create two duplicates of it.

11. Here comes the important bit: you're going to scale the duplicated clips to give the illusion of depth. With one of the spheres selected, activate the Free Transform Tool (Q) and begin to resize the sphere using the transformation handle in the lower-left corner of the movie clip. Hold down the SHIFT key while you're doing this to ensure that you maintain the aspect ratio of the sphere. Drag outward to make the sphere larger and inward to make it smaller, using the final layout to the right as a guide. Repeat with the other spheres, positioning them as necessary to create a scene something like that shown opposite.

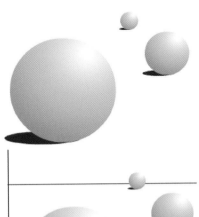

12. Although all you have are three differently-sized objects on a flat screen, your eyes start to try and read some perspective into the picture. You can heighten the effect greatly by adding a single horizontal line, the horizon, to give your scene a ground plane and vanishing point. By adding a horizon, using the Line Tool (N), and playing with the placement of the spheres slightly, you arrive at the final effect. The horizon line is central to any illustration that aims to depict depth, as you'll see in the next effect, where you'll tackle creating a perspective grid.

You can also take a look at `sphere_layout.fla` from this chapter's sample files to see this finished effect. To recap, for the preceding effect you first created a sphere using the chiaroscuro method and you then used a combination of **blocking** (placing objects within the scene) and **framing** (choosing your view of the scene) to set up your scene. If you were shooting a film, you would block a scene in exactly the way you've done here (by placing your objects, or props, within your scene). In Flash, the placement of objects also constitutes the only means of framing a scene. Unlike 3D programs, such as 3D Studio Max or Maya, you don't have a camera that you can move around to frame—or select your view of—the scene. So as not to waste time on the creation of new objects (you can use the chiaroscuro method for any object, not just spheres), you're going to use the sphere you created here in some of the other effects in this chapter, so it's a good idea to save your work so far. (Of course, you can always use the sphere from `sphere_layout.fla`, available with this book's examples download.)

Perspective grids

In the previous effect, you saw that your sense of depth is primarily affected by the size and placement of objects within the scene. To create the effect, you eyeballed the scaling of the objects and used trial and error until you arrived at a scene that was aesthetically pleasing and believable. For a simple scene, this isn't too much of a problem, but what if you want to create an illustration of a busy downtown street with people, cars, buildings, and streets? How can you make sure that everything fits into the perspective of the scene? Fortunately, painters started pondering the same question thousands of years before the first line of code that was eventually to become the program we now know and love as Flash was ever written. The solution they came up with, sometime around the 1500s, was to use **perspective grids**. There are three types of perspective grids that you can create to help you lay out your faux-3D scenes: one-point, two-point, and three-point. The points refer to the number of vanishing points in each grid.

For example, here's a hand-drawn one-point perspective grid with the spheres from the previous example. It is a one-point grid since, if you were to extend the vertical lines up past the horizon, you would see that they eventually meet at a single vanishing point.

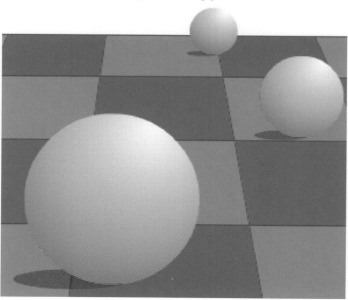

To save you the trouble of having to create these grids by hand, we've created a perspective grid tool that lets you play around with one- and two-point perspective grids. Take a look at `two_point_grid.swf` in this chapter's downloaded code folder. Play around with different two-point perspective grids by moving the vanishing points.

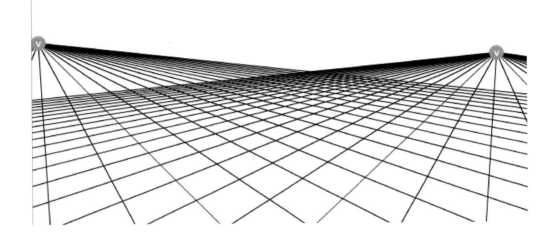

Macromedia FreeHand: The mother of all perspective grids

The perspective grids that we've discussed are essential to creating 3D scenes with accurate perspective; however, they do not go beyond being helpful static guides (or cool background images for our scenes). Wouldn't it be nice if we could somehow draw an object and have it fit into our perspective grid automatically? Although the Flash authoring environment doesn't currently have this as a built-in feature, it is entirely possible that someone will eventually come up with a layout manager component that does just this, using Live Preview from within the authoring environment. A program that does have this ability as a standard feature is FreeHand, Macromedia's vector illustration tool.

We are actually die-hard Adobe Illustrator fans, but starting with FreeHand 9, Macromedia introduced a perspective grid in FreeHand that blows Illustrator away. Basically, it allows you to create an object (say a square), turn on a perspective grid, and have the object snap onto it. Once you've snapped your object onto the perspective grid, you can move it around and it will stay in correct perspective. Macromedia FreeHand 10 has one-point, two-point, and three-point (shown over the page) perspective grids that you can snap objects to.

If you don't have FreeHand, download the trial version (www.macromedia.com/downloads/) and take it for a spin. Then send an email to wishlist@macromedia.com asking them nicely if they wouldn't mind including this killer feature in the next version of Flash to make all our lives easier!

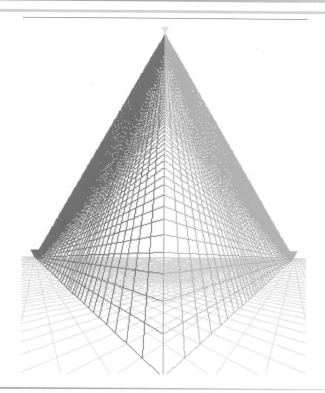

3D scaling text with atmospheric perspective

Although the crux of this chapter concerns manipulating scale to create 3D effects, there are other important aspects besides the size of objects that will affect the realism of your 3D scenes. These are factors that have been observed on Earth, where the atmosphere interferes with and degrades our vision. Specifically, atmospheric interference causes our eyes to see objects that are far away with less contrast, detail, and focus than those that are close by. Leonardo da Vinci called this "the perspective of disappearance." You may have seen this effect used many times under the guise of the popular 3D scaling text effect. Due to the computational and bandwidth costs of blurring objects in Flash, you are going to simulate loss of contrast, detail, and focus in a different way: by manipulating the opacity, or alpha property, of the text along with its scale.

1. Create a new movie (CTRL/CMD+N), and then click the Size button in the Property Inspector to bring up the Document Properties box. Now set the stage size to 600x300px and the frame rate to 24 fps, as shown at right.

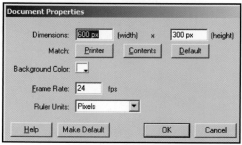

2. Using the Text Tool (T), enter whatever text you'd like to feature in your 3D effect. Type the text at the final size that you want it to scale to (in other words, large rather than small), and position it as you want it to appear in the final frame of the animation. We used 96pt Arial, Bold.

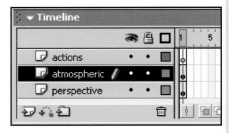

3. Make sure that you put each word, phrase, or sentence that you want to scale separately in its own layer. As you can see, for this example we're scaling two words— Atmospheric and Perspective!—so we've placed them in layers named likewise. Don't be afraid to be blatantly obvious when setting up your Flash movies—it's much better than being cryptic! We've also added an actions layer, since we'll need to stop() the animation once it reaches the end (we'll cover this shortly).

4. Before you start to animate the text, you need to change each word into a movie clip. In addition to being good practice, this will help when it comes time to scale the text since, in Flash, text is scaled from the lower-left corner and you want your text to scale from the center out. Converting the text to movie clips will automatically allow us to do this since the registration point of movie clips is set to the center of the clip by default.

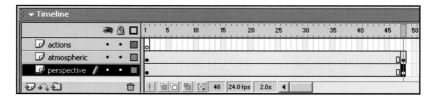

To convert the word Atmospheric to a movie clip, click on frame 1 of the atmospheric layer to select all objects on that frame—in this case, the solitary word—and press F8. Call the movie clip atmospheric, and repeat this for the Perspective! text, calling the movie clip perspective.

5. Let's start animating now. Click on frame 48 of the atmospheric layer and insert a keyframe (Insert > Keyframe or F6). Repeat this for the perspective layer. Since your frame rate is 24 fps, the animation will take 2 seconds:

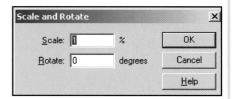

6. Now click back to frame 1 of the atmospheric layer to select the atmospheric movie clip. Initially, you want the text to start out tiny and zoom in, so resize the clip using Modify > Transform > Scale And Rotate (CTRL/CMD+ALT/OPT+S) and setting the Scale to 1%.

7.   Click on the `atmospheric` movie clip in frame 1, and click on its instance in the canvas (now very small) to bring up its details in the Property Inspector. Choose Alpha in the Color drop-down menu and set it to 0%. This is going to create the atmospheric perspective effect by making the text appear to fade in as it gets closer.

8.   To actually make the text scale up and fade in, make sure that one of the frames between 1 and 48 are selected in the timeline and use Insert > Create Motion Tween. (You can also create a motion tween from the Property Inspector by choosing Motion from the Tween drop-down.)

9.   Repeat Steps 6 to 8 for the `perspective` layer. You can test the movie at this point to see the effect. The two words should scale up in a perfectly synchronized animation that loops.

10. To make the motion more interesting (and appear to arc slightly as the text scales), select the `atmospheric` movie clip in frame 1 and move it down slightly. Do the opposite with the `perspective` movie clip (nudge it up) so that they start out from approximately the same place. For our purposes, this will be the horizon.

11. Let's also separate the two animations a little. Click on the keyframe on the perspective layer (frame 1) to select it. Click (again) and drag it to frame 25.

12. Finally, let's stop the animation after it has played through once by adding a stop action to frame 48 of the actions layer. Click on frame 48 of this layer and insert a blank keyframe (F7). Click on the newly created keyframe and type `stop();` in the Actions panel (Window > Actions or F9 if it's not already open). Once you're done, your timeline should resemble the one below:

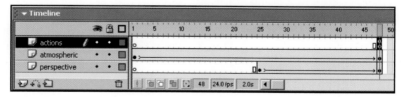

Test the movie and you should see the text scale up and fade in from a single vanishing point:

Atmospheric
Perspective!

There are times when making objects transparent will not work within the context of your movies. A variant on this effect would be to animate the color of the movie clip from a washed-out bluish-gray to its actual color as it gets closer to our view. Objects that are further away also have denser textures and appear out of focus. Re-creating these effects in Flash, however, usually requires the use of multiple prerendered bitmaps and can be both CPU- and bandwidth-intensive. Be sure to check out Chapter 7 for some more neat tricks along the lines of manipulating text in pseudo-3D space.

Basic 3D rotation using scaling

A lot of fake 3D rotation effects involve scaling. Here's the simplest way to achieve this effect using tweening:

1. Start a new movie (CTRL/CMD+N) and set the stage size to 400x300px and the frame rate to 24 fps, as you did in the previous example.

2. Select a stroke and fill color of your liking—we've chosen black for the stroke and orange (#FF6600) for the fill. Now draw a circle using the Oval Tool (O), remembering to hold down the SHIFT key to constrain it to a circle.

3. Using the Arrow Tool (V), double-click on the fill of your circle to select both the fill and the stroke and, using the Property Inspector, set both the width (W) and height (H) of your shape to 90:

4. With both the fill and stroke of your circle still selected, convert it to a movie clip symbol by pressing F8, and call it myCircle.

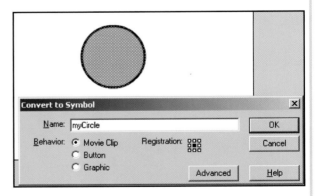

5. With your newly created instance of the myCircle symbol selected on stage, open up the Align panel if it isn't already showing (Window > Align or CTRL/CMD+K). Click the To Stage button to align your movie clip in relation to the stage and click the Align horizontal center and Align vertical center buttons to center your circle on the stage.

6. In the timeline, rename the default layer 1 to myCircle and then, in turn, click on frames 8, 16, 24, and 32 in the timeline and press F6 (or Insert > Keyframe) for each one to create five keyframes in total. Your animation will last 32 frames and, at 24 fps, it will take a little over 1 second.

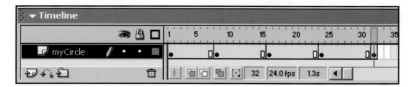

7. Now click on the frame 8 to select the myCircle movie clip and, holding down the SHIFT key to ensure that the movie clip moves in increments of 10 pixels instead of 1, press the right arrow key 12 times to move the circle toward the right edge of the stage.

8. Click on frame 24 and repeat the instructions in step 7, but this time in the opposite direction to bring the circle near the left edge of the stage. If you drag the playhead all the way through your animation at this point, you should see the circle start in the center, jump to the right, jump back to the center, jump to the left and, finally, jump back to the center again.

9. To smooth out the motion, you need to create motion tweens between the keyframes. To do this, right-click (CTRL+click on a Mac) on each of the keyframes and select Create Motion Tween from the context-sensitive menu:

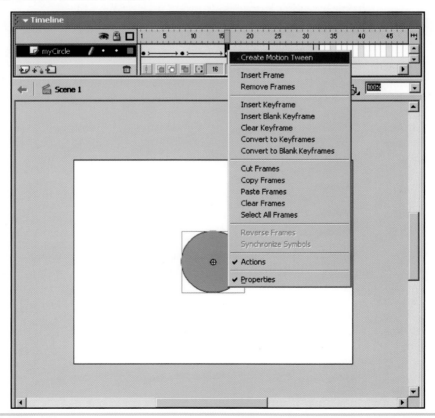

10. If you test the movie at this point, you should see the circle animate from one side of the stage to the other and return to rest in the middle. Let's now add some 3D magic! As always, this is going to involve some scaling. Click on frame 8 and select Modify > Transform > Scale And Rotate... (CTRL/CMD+ALT/OPT+S). Leaving the Rotation setting at zero, enter 66 for the Scale setting and click OK.

11. Next click on frame 16 and repeat the instructions in step 10. This time, however, set the Scale setting to 33%. Finally, click on frame 24 and, once again, set the scale to 66%.

12. Now test the movie (Control > Test Movie or CTRL/CMD+ENTER) and you should see the circle appear to rotate around the y-axis. There are two problems with the animation at this point. First, it appears to stop slightly when it reaches the end of the animation, before looping around. Second, the transitions from one quadrant of the animation to the next are too abrupt. You'll fix these next.

13. The first issue arises because the last leg of the animation contains an extra frame: the last keyframe loops back to the first keyframe and the circle is in exactly the same position in both, leading to it appearing to halt momentarily as the animation loops. The way to fix this is to select the frame immediately before the last keyframe (frame 31 here) and make it into a keyframe. So click on frame 31 and press F6:

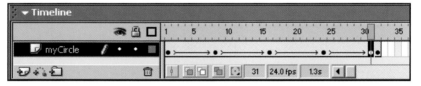

14. Now all you need to do is remove the keyframe on frame 32. To do this, click on frame 32 and select Insert > Remove Frames (SHIFT+F5). Why anyone would put an option that begins with Remove under a menu called Insert is beyond us! Perhaps this is why we use keyboard shortcuts almost exclusively in Flash and why we've taken care to include them in these examples—they will save you a lot of time and mousing around in the long run. Additionally, you can access many options in Flash by using the right-click/CTRL-click context-sensitive menus.

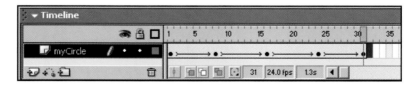

15. If you test the movie at this point, you should see that steps 13 and 14 have fixed the first issue and that the animation loops perfectly. Now let's tackle the second issue: the abrupt change of directions. These happen because you aren't easing your tweens.

    Yes, ladies and gentlemen, you need to **ease your tweens**. Easing refers to the acceleration of motion in our animations. When you ease in from a keyframe, the motion in your animation gradually speeds up as it gets further away from the keyframe. Conversely, when you ease out from a keyframe, the motion in your animation gradually slows down as it approaches the next keyframe. Easing is central to both traditional animation and animation with Flash. Using a combination of easing in and out, you can create all sorts of effects.

For this example's purposes, you're going to alternately Ease In and Ease Out of your keyframes. This will create a sort of gravity at these points, smoothing out the motion and lending some added authenticity to your effect. To start off, click on frame 1 and set the Ease value for the keyframe to 50 using the Property Inspector.

16. Repeat by setting the Ease value at −24 for frame 8, 50 for frame 16, and −50 for frame 24. Leave the Ease value for frame 31 at 0.

17. Test the movie (CTRL/CMD+ENTER) and you should notice that the motion appears smoother. This finished example can be found in the sample files as `basic_tweened_rotate.fla`. Experiment with some other ease settings to see how they affect the motion, trying to get the change of directions as smooth as possible.

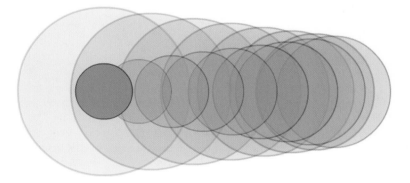

3D rotation around another object

In the previous effect, you animated a circle to make it appear to rotate in 3D space. Although rotating objects are fine by themselves, the effect of depth is heightened when you make one object appear to orbit another. This is an effect that you'll have no doubt seen various times with text. Here you're going to make your circle from the previous effect orbit a larger circle. To achieve this you need to manipulate the **z-order** of movie clips on the stage.

Z-ordering in Flash

Z-order determines which movie clips appear on top of others when two or more movie clips overlap. Clips with higher z-order (or depth) appear on top of (and if opaque, obstruct) clips with lower depths. Flash has the following rules that determine the z-order of movie clips.

For dynamically created movie clips:

- *Movie clips that are dynamically created using ActionScript (using the* `duplicateMovie()`, `attachMovie()`, *and* `createEmptyMovieClip()` *methods) are created on a separate z-order stack, the depth of which is higher than the z-order stack for movie clips that you create on the stage. This means that dynamically created movie clips will always appear on top of movie clips that are created on the stage.*

- *The depths of dynamically created clips must be explicitly set when the clips are created.*

For movie clips placed on the stage during authoring:

- *Clips on higher layers will have higher depths and appear in front of clips on lower layers.*

- *For clips on the same layer, the latest clips to be added to the layer appear in front of clips added earlier (for example, if you have a movie clip partially obstructing another one on the same layer, you can select the partially obstructed clip, cut it and then paste it in place and it will appear in front of the clip that was previously obstructing it).*

Knowing the z-order rules noted above will come in handy when following a great number of the effects in this book from this point on, since achieving 3D realism in Flash relies heavily on juggling z-orders.

1. Follow along with the steps in the previous effect (3D rotation using scaling) to create a rotating sphere (or you can use `basic_tweened_rotate.fla` as a starting point for this example).

2. Insert a new layer (Insert > Layer), label it background, and move it under the `myCircle` layer.

3. In frame 1 of the background layer, choose a fill color that's different from the color you chose for your circle and draw a larger circle using the Oval Tool (O) (holding down the SHIFT key to constrain it, as usual). For our new circle we've chosen a dark gray color with a black stroke.

4. Select your new background circle and center it behind the smaller one. If you'd rather not eyeball it, you can use the Align horizontal center and Align vertical center buttons on the Align panel (CTRL/CMD+K), with the To Stage button toggled. Your stage should now have an object that looks somewhat like a wheel smack in the middle of it.

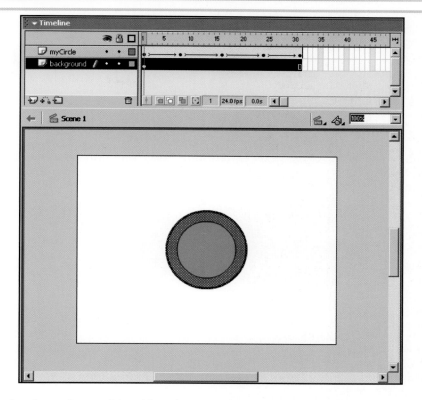

5. Go ahead and test the movie at this point. You will see that the smaller circle rotates in front of the larger one. You want it to rotate around it. For this you need to manipulate the z-order of the two circles at key points within the animation. In this case, manipulating the z-order is as simple as placing the larger circle in a higher layer for certain parts of the animation. You can also achieve this effect by masking the myCircle layer with a rectangular fill that covers the whole stage and has a hole the size of the larger circle in the middle of it. The effect is achieved by placing this mask over the myCircle layer during those frames that it should appear behind the larger sphere—see `tween_around_mask.fla` for a working example.

6. Returning to the present example, to start you need a new layer *above* the myCircle layer, so create a new layer (Insert > Layer) and call it foreground:

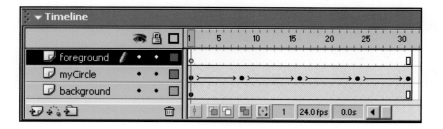

7. If the playhead isn't on frame 1, rewind the movie using Control > Rewind (CTRL/CMD+ALT/OPT+R) and then step through the animation one frame at a time using Control > Step Forward (.) until you reach the frame where the smaller circle first overlaps the larger one on its way back from the right edge of the stage. In our movie, this occurs at frame 11.

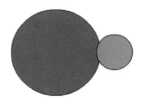

8. Click on the foreground layer to activate it and make sure that the playhead is in the frame you identified in the previous step. Insert a blank keyframe (F7) in the foreground layer to mark this position.

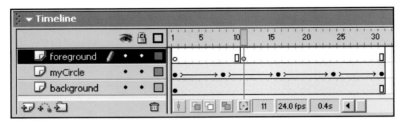

9. Continue scrubbing the timeline using Control > Step Forward (.) until you reach the frame where the small circle overlaps the larger one on its way back from the left edge of the stage. Create another blank keyframe at this frame on the foreground layer (F7). In our movie this occurs at frame 27.

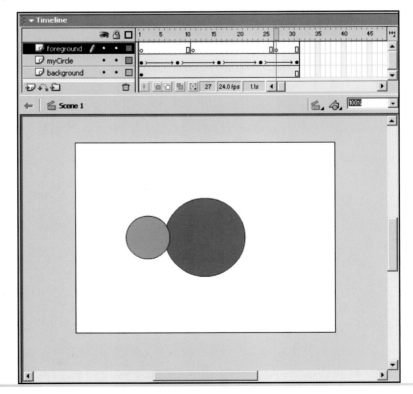

10. On the same frame that you put the *second* blank keyframe on the foreground layer, select Insert > Keyframe (F6) for the background layer (click on the background layer to activate it if it isn't active).

11. On the same frame that you put the first blank keyframe on the foreground layer, insert a blank keyframe (F7) for the background layer, making sure that the background layer is still selected. Once you're done, your timeline should resemble the one shown below:

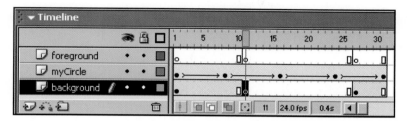

12. The only thing left to do is to copy the larger circle to the first blank keyframe in the foreground layer. To do this, select frame 1 of the background layer and choose Copy Frames (CTRL/CMD+ALT/OPT+C) from the Edit menu. Finally, click on the first blank keyframe in the foreground layer and choose Edit > Paste Frames (CTRL/CMD+ALT/OPT+V).

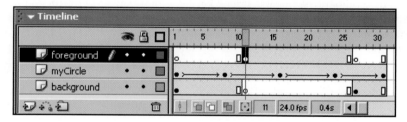

Test out the movie and you should see that the smaller circle now rotates around the larger one in a realistic fashion. The finished effect can be seen in `basic_tweened_rotate_around.swf`, available with the downloaded sample files. All we did was copy the larger circle to a higher layer for those frames where the smaller circle was supposed to be behind it. Doing this gave the larger circle a higher z-order and led to it obstructing the smaller circle. This is the simplest way of creating the effect of one object rotating around another. Another way to create the same effect uses motion paths and is the topic of our next effect.

3D rotation using a motion guide

In your original 3D rotation effect using scaling, you used multiple keyframes and tweens (alongside changes in scale) to achieve the 3D rotation effect. Here you're going to create the same effect using a motion guide. Most animation programs allow you to draw a path that an object should follow in a given amount of frames. Using a motion guide, or motion path as it is also known, can greatly cut down development time when you need your object to follow an irregular path that has lots of twists and turns. In Flash, you draw a motion path in a special type of guide layer called the motion guide. Motion paths are very powerful animation tools and can easily allow you to create complex animations that would otherwise take many keyframes and lots of tweaking.

1. Follow steps 1 to 4 from the basic 3D rotation using scaling effect so that you have a `myCircle` movie clip centered on the stage (alternatively, you could use the movie clip featured in `basic_tweened_rotate.fla` as a starting point for this example).

2. You'll right away add the motion path to your circle: with the `myCircle` layer selected, choose Insert > Motion Guide. You should see a motion guide layer called Guide: myCircle appear above the `myCircle` layer.

    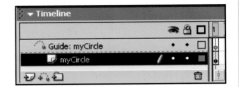

3. Using the Oval Tool (O) with a stroke color that is different from the color of the circle (so you can see it easily) and no fill, draw a large, flat oval on the motion guide layer. This is going to be the path that your circle follows:

    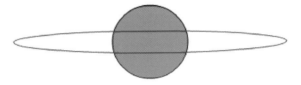

4. It's a good idea at this point to lock your `myCircle` layer so that you can easily work with the motion path layer without selecting the circle by mistake. Once you've locked the layer, select a tiny portion of the upper arc of the motion path, toward the middle, and delete it to create a small hole (zooming in helps). The important point is that motion paths cannot be closed shapes—they need a beginning and an end.

    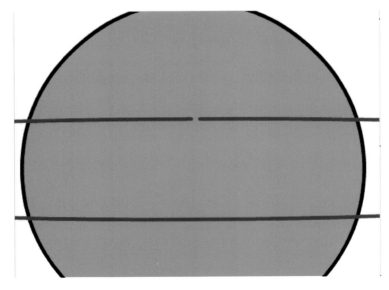

5. You're done with the motion guide layer itself, so lock it and unlock the `myCircle` layer since you're going to be manipulating that next. Click on frame 32 of the motion guide layer and select Insert > Frame (F5) to extend the motion path all the way to frame 32.

6. Now click on frame 32 of the myCircle layer and add a keyframe (Insert > KeyFrame or F6). Your timeline should now resemble the one below:

7. Zoom in so that you can see both sides of the motion path at either side of the hole. Click on frame 1 of the myCircle layer to move the playhead there. Then click on the registration point (center) of the `myCircle` movie clip and drag it to one of the ends of the motion path. It should snap into place—if it doesn't, make sure Snap to Objects is turned on under the View menu (CRTL/CMD+SHIFT+/).

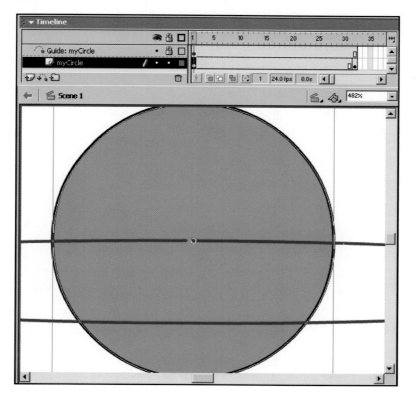

8. Click on frame 32 of the myCircle layer to move the playhead and snap the `myCircle` movie clip to the other end of the motion path.

9. Click on frame 1 of the myCircle layer and select Insert > Create Motion Tween to create the animation.

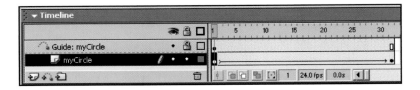

10. Play the movie by pressing ENTER, and you should see that the circle follows the motion guide.

11. Now let's add the scaling effects. Click on frame 1 of the myCircle layer. Scale the myCircle clip to 33% of its normal size using Modify > Transform > Scale and Rotate... (CTRL/CMD+ALT/OPT+S).

12. Starting with frame 2, use the Control > Step Forward (.) command to move the playhead forward until your myCircle clip reaches the first horizontal extreme of its motion path. Create a keyframe here (F6) and scale the myCircle clip to 66%.

13. Repeat the previous step for when the circle reaches the other horizontal extreme.

14. Continue scrubbing the timeline until you reach the end of the motion path and scale the myCircle clip to 33%. When you're done, your timeline should resemble the one below:

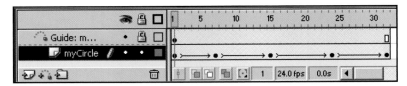

15. Test the movie to see the 3D motion path rotation.

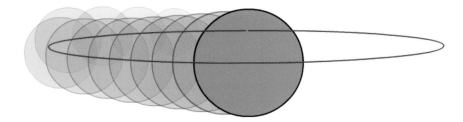

16. If you tried out the first basic 3D rotation effect in this chapter, you should notice that this effect too is plagued by the two issues mentioned there in step 12, so following steps 13 to 17 of that effect will fix those issues for this one too; no more abrupt stopping and easing at key points will help create the illusion of motion in 3D. Additionally, feel free to adapt the "3D rotation around another object" effect to use the motion path animation instead of the version using basic 3D rotation with scaling.

3D rotation effect variations

You can modify the 3D rotation effects presented here in many ways to create variations and combinations. To do this, create the effects inside a movie clip so you can apply transformations to the whole animation. Turning the animation and scaling it, as well as using multiple instances of it will allow you to create more complex scenes. For a simple example of what is possible, take a look at the sample file `sphere_variation.fla` from this chapter's examples:

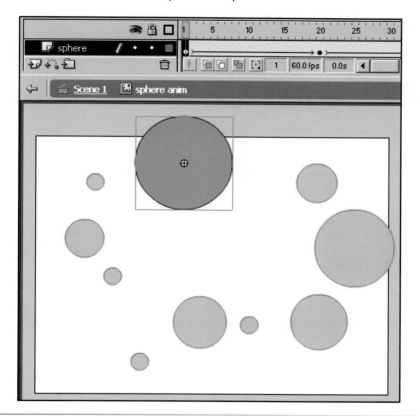

Scripted motion

Now we'll turn our attention to the easy way to produce mock-3D motion effects using ActionScript. Having worked through the relatively straightforward tweened effects presented earlier in this chapter, you may be excused for doing a double-take at that last line. Can I really be implying that using ActionScript to create motion is easier than tweening? After all, ActionScript is supposed to be hard as hell and anyone who understands a word of it is a genius, right? Well, not really—especially since I've already done all the hard work for you!

During the past year or so, I've been working on creating an open-source ActionScript framework for Flash MX called the Moose ActionScript Library. By the time this book hits the shelves, Version 1.0

should have already been released over at SourceForge. Although there are many modules in the framework that do all sorts of different things, the one that concerns us here is a class called `Move`. Using this class, you can animate any property of a movie clip over time using any movement function you like—for example, ease in, ease out, and so on.

For instance, if you want to scale in a movie clip from 0% to 100%, just set its `_xscale` and `_yscale` properties to 0 and create an instance of the `Move` class where you specify that the `_xscale` and `_yscale` properties should be increased by 100%. Do you want to also make it fade in from 0% to 100% simultaneous with the scaling? Easy, just set the `_alpha` of the clip to 0% and tell the same instance of the `Move` class that you'd like the `_alpha` property of the clip increased by 100% at the same time. How would you like that movement, with ease in, ease out, or both? Just pass the movement function you'd like to use as a parameter when instantiating the class. The class comes with quadratic ease in, ease out, and ease in/out functions by default, thanks to Robert Penner, but there's no reason why you can't plug any movement function in there instead (for example, a circular motion function).

To demonstrate just how much simpler this way of doing things is, let's jump in and re-create the atmospheric perspective effect that you created earlier, now using the `Move` class. This time, instead of text, you're going to scale in a window. Before starting, make sure you've downloaded this chapter's sample files from www.friendsofed.com, which include the Moose ActionScript Library files for this project (`init.as`, `frame_event.as`, `chronos.as`, and `move.as`).

1. Open a new movie (CTRL/CMD+N), set the stage size to 500x400, and set the frame rate to 120. Since you're going to be using time-based instead of frame-based motion, setting your frame rate to the maximum will allow you to get the smoothest motion. We may never reach 120 fps, but you'll take whatever Flash can dish out!

   As a side note, it's worth noting that there has always been controversy on the "ideal frame rate" for Flash. In truth, there isn't one: it's application-specific. When I write my applications, I usually keep the frame rate at 120 since all of my code is time-based. I use scripted routines even for frame-based animations, giving me complete control over the frame rate I want to play them back at (independent of the actual Flash frame rate). Thus, the higher the frame rate, the more precise my time-based calculations will be since they are recalculated every time an `enterFrame` event occurs. The side effect of this on slower systems is that Flash might slow down the whole system as it tries to deliver on your request for 120 frame refreshes per second. The only real solution is to test your application out on all supported platforms and on your minimum supported system specifications for each platform. If you find that 120 fps slows down the system unacceptably, then by all means lower the frame rate.

2. Draw a largish window. You can choose to make this as elaborate or simple as you please. We created the following window, which is 400x250px and has a ScrollPane component, from the Flash UI Components Set 1 with its content set to a movie clip that contains the picture of an adorable little kid (well, of a little kid in any case!). You can check out our version of this example, `my_window.fla`, in the sample files. If you want, you can very easily follow these steps with a 400x250 rectangle.

3. Convert your window graphic to a movie clip symbol and call the symbol `my window`. Using the Property Inspector, give it an instance name of `win_mc`.

4. Create a new layer (Insert > Layer), label it `actions` and enter the following script into its first frame:

```
// Include necessary Moose ActionScript Library modules
// These modules must be saved in the same directory as your SWF
#include "init.as"
#include "frame_event.as"
#include "chronos.as"
#include "move.as"

// Set the window's opacity to be completely transparent
win_mc._alpha = 0;

// Set the window's scale to 0%
win_mc._xscale = win_mc._yscale = 0;

// Create new instance of the Move class, telling it to increase
// the _alpha, _xscale, and y_scale of the movie clip by 100%
// and to move the movie clip up (_y) by 50 pixels in 1 second.
var move1 = new Moose.Move(Math.easeOutQuad, this, "win_mc", 2,{_alpha:
100, _xscale: 100, _yscale: 100, _y:-50}, true);
```

5. That's it! Test the movie to see the window fade in, scale up to 100%, and move up by 50 pixels. So in five simple steps you've accomplished what took over twice as many steps to do using tweens.

As you start to build more complicated applications, you will notice that more often than not, using a well-written script will save you lots of work over tweening in the long run (especially when it comes to customizing an animation or effect). At this point, you may be wondering what the four external ActionScript files you loaded in contain. Here's a brief explanation of each:

> `init.as`—*Contains code that initializes the Moose ActionScript framework. This is mostly boring stuff that you never have to worry about unless you start writing your own modules for the Library.*
>
> `frame_event.as`—*A frame-event engine. The one thing they left out of Flash MX was a good frame event engine (for creating frame event listeners—functions that get called every time the playhead enters a new frame). This is a simple class that fills this void.*
>
> `chronos.as`—*Contains time-related functions. For example, for calling a certain function every so many seconds.*
>
> `move.as`—*Contains the* `Move` *class we used to animate our window. More often than not, modules in the Moose framework are made up of single classes that each have their own external* `.as` *file.*

Although we've outlined what these files do, you really don't have to worry about it (at least about the first three). All you need to do is learn the interface for creating an instance of the `Move` class. Here's the part of the signature (or definition) of the `Move` class constructor that concerns us currently:

```
moose.Move = function(movementFn, theTimeline, theClip, theDuration,
 deltaProps, run, nextMove, ...)
```

Let's analyze what this means. First off, we have `moose.Move`, which just tells Flash to look in the `moose` namespace for the `Move` class. All modules in the Moose framework are located under the `moose` namespace so that they don't accidentally conflict with built-in classes or classes from other frameworks (Moose tries, as much as possible, to play nice with other frameworks!). All you really need to know is that to create a new `Move` instance, you begin your statement with `new moose.Move`. This gives Flash all the information it needs to find the `Move` class and create an instance of it. Of course, you also need to pass it some parameters so that it knows details of the animation. Some of these parameters will benefit from a little further explanation:

- The `movementFn` parameter is a reference to the function that will define how the initial properties (for example, `_x`, `_y`, `_xscale`, `_alpha`, and so on) of a movie clip are animated. There are three movement functions that come with the Moose Library, and this number will surely increase in time; they are the famous Robert Penner easing equations `Math.easeInQuad`, `Math.easeOutQuad` and `Math.easeInOutQuad`.

- `deltaProps` is an object that contains the movie clip properties that you want to animate and the amount by which you want the properties changed (in math, delta represents "change in"). For example, to move a certain clip 50 pixels to the right, you would pass `{_x: 50}` as the `deltaProps` parameter. To move it 65 pixels to the left, you would pass `{_x: -65}`. You can pass any valid movie clip property using the `deltaProps` object, including, but not limited to, `_x`, `_y`, `_xscale`, `_yscale`, `_width`, `_height`, and `_alpha`.

- `run` is a Boolean (`true`/`false` value) that determines whether the move/animation will run immediately. If you choose not to run the move immediately, you can run it at a later time by calling the `startMove()` method of the returned `Move` instance (which, in the preceding example, you save in the `move1` variable. Thus, you would call `move1.startMove();`). Logically, you can also call the `stopMove()` method to stop an animation at any time.

- The `nextMove` parameter provides a simple way of chaining together multiple moves to create a larger animation. For example, if you have another move defined as `move2` that you wish to run after `move1` is complete, create a `Move` instance called `move2` and pass it as the `nextMove` parameter when creating `move1`.

The Moose framework provides an even better way of creating complex scripted animations called `MoveScript`, and even the `Move` class constructor can accept additional arguments that we haven't covered here, but those topics are beyond the scope of this book. For those of you who are interested in finding out more, be sure to check out the final version of the Library when it is released at http://sourceforge.net/projects/moose/.

Summary

Our eyes can be tricked into seeing three-dimensional perspective even when there is none by the careful **scaling** and **placement** of objects on a two-dimensional screen. All the effects in this chapter have used the same few principles that filmmakers have been using and perfecting for over a hundred years (and painters for thousands before) to accentuate the three-dimensional realism of images projected onto a two-dimensional format. Although, for simplicity's sake, we have used basic shapes in our examples, there's no reason why you can't re-create the effects using fancier artwork, such as 3D animations imported from Swift 3D.

We rounded off the chapter by introducing a powerful way of creating scripted animations using a class from the Moose ActionScript Library. In the next chapter, we will add another facet to our faux-3D scaling effects by introducing interactivity and delving further into the benefits of ActionScript.

Want more?

If you want to take these techniques further, you'll be interested to hear that we've produced a bonus chapter on interactive scaling. You can download this chapter absolutely free of charge from the friends of ED website at www.friendsofed.com. In the chapter you'll learn how to design 3D interfaces and you'll take a crack at creating the Windows 3000 operating system.

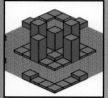  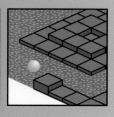

Isometric 3D

After so much work with perspective in the scaling chapter, it may seem odd that in this chapter we're going to abandon perspective entirely. That's right, we're going to explore 3D without perspective. If you've grown up in a Western country, you may be thinking that the previous sentence is an oxymoron. Isn't 3D all about perspective? Well, not really.

As we mentioned in the earlier chapter on scaling, what we commonly call perspective (more precisely, **linear perspective**) is not a natural phenomenon—it was developed as part of the Renaissance movement in Europe. Linear perspective, based on a model relying on the existence of vanishing points where all lines in a scene converge and a single point of gaze for the user, was embraced, further developed, and grew ubiquitous in the West. In the East, however, the Chinese were using a very different method of pictorial representation. Their pictures were not snapshots in time like Western pictures were; instead, they were *stories*. Drawn on huge scrolls, "reading" them would be a journey in time through a narrative.

> *Jan Krikke, in his excellent online essay "A Chinese Perspective for Cyberspace?" gives a wonderful example of such a scroll depicting life along a river: "Upon unrolling the opening sequence of the scroll, we may see people boarding a boat on a river. As we unroll the scroll further, we see the boat cross a lake, navigate rapids in the river, stop at a small harbour, and lastly arrive at its destination on the seashore. In other words, the scroll has taken the viewer through an experience in space and time."* (http://iias.leidenuniv.nl/iiasn/iiasn9/eastasia/krikke.html)

Instead of using vanishing points and relying on optical principles that would break the continuity of the story, the Chinese kept all lines along their "z-axis" parallel. In doing this, they developed **axonometric projection**. The term axonometric is the marriage of the Greek word *axon*, meaning axis, and the English word metric, meaning measure. Literally, it means *measure from the axis*, since you can calculate the true length of lines in an axonometric image by measuring them and applying the necessary transformations (something you cannot do with linear perspective).

> *Thiadmer Riemersma has written the definitive introduction to axonometric projections. You can read his whole paper at www.compuphase.com/axometr.htm.*

Isometric projection is one specific application of axonometric projection. If you break down the word isometric, you get *iso*, which means equal, and *metric*. This comes from the fact that if you were to draw a cube in an isometric universe, all of its sides would be the same length. Compare this to a cube drawn in linear perspective in the diagram below. Note how, as you travel from the front face to the back face of the cube with linear perspective, the diagonal lines converge and are foreshortened. However, as you can see below, all lines along the z-axis in an isometric projection are parallel. There is no foreshortening of diagonal lines and, if you know the angle of the projection used, you can calculate the actual length of a line by measuring it off the image and applying the correct calculation to it:

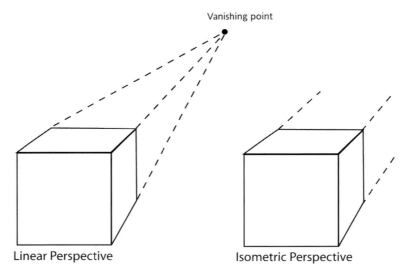

Linear Perspective   Isometric Perspective

As mentioned earlier, isometric 3D refers to an axonometric projection where unit distances on the x-, y-, and z-axes are equal. There can also be different types of isometric projections, depending on the angle made between the z- and x-axes of the isometric world and the x-axis of the 2D Cartesian plane. The latter corresponds to the stage coordinates of Flash.

> *Camillo Trevisan has an amazing freeware program called Cartesio that you can download from www.iuav.it/dpa/ricerche/trevisan/intern02.htm to see the difference between many types of axonometric, isometric, and other types of projections.*

The most common type of isometric projection uses a 30° angle. This angle of projection, first publicized by William Farish in 1822, is used extensively for architectural and technical drawings due to the fact that it is very easy to do calculations on it (since *sin* 30° = 0.5). However, another common version of isometric projection, especially with isometric computer games based on bitmap tiles, uses an angle of 25.56505° (approximately), or *arctangent* 0.5. This seemingly weird angle is used because it results in more aesthetically pleasing and proportional diagonal lines on a computer screen. This is a much bigger issue when graphics are not antialiased. In Flash, since both vectors and bitmaps can have antialiasing applied (where the edges are softened to remove jagged lines), you will see the 30° projection applied in isometric Flash games.

We're going to kick off this chapter with a look at the simplest type of parallel projection you can create in Flash: the 45° projection. It's especially easy to draw using this angle because Flash's Line Tool, when constrained using the SHIFT key, automatically snaps to 45° increments. Although this is an example of isometric projection, it is not what is commonly thought of when the term isometric is used in computer applications and games.

The 45° cheat

You can use 45° isometric projection when the floor details are more important than vertical details. For this reason, apparently, it's popular in military drawings—it's often even referred to as *military projection*. In Flash, we can easily draw an isometric projection using a 45° angle with the Line Tool. In this example (called `draw45.fla`) you're going to draw a basic 45° isometric cube and use it to discover some of the properties of axonometric projection and isometric 3D.

1. After you open a new Flash file, you need to draw the square that will constitute the base of your cube. Start out by drawing a line inclined at a 45° angle. Flash makes this very easy for you by constraining the Line Tool (N) to 45° increments when you hold down the SHIFT key while drawing. Do this now to draw a line as shown in the figure at right. Don't worry about the dimensions or position of the line while drawing it, just make sure that you snap it to a 45° angle.

2. Select the line and, using the Property Inspector, enter 50 (pixels) for the width, W, and 50 (pixels) for the height, H. For the x coordinate, enter 120 and for the y, 130:

3. Next, you're going to draw what will become the top edge of your square. You want to make all sides of your square equal, so instead of drawing the top line manually, you're going to duplicate the slanted line and rotate it. Click on the line you drew in step 1 and choose Edit > Duplicate (Ctrl/Cmd+D). This should create a copy of the line and place it 10 pixels to the left and down from the original line. The new line should be selected by default.

4. With the new line still selected, use the Free Transform Tool (Q) to rotate it 45° clockwise so that you end up with a horizontal line. By transforming the line, you are able to keep its length the

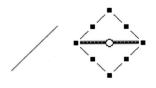

same. You could also calculate this by hand using the Pythagorean theorem. Since the height and width of the line are both 50, the length of the line (the *hypotenuse*—let's call it *h*) will be equal to the sum of the squares of its height and width projections. Thus, $h = 50^2 + 50^2 = \sqrt{5000} = 70.7$. If you look at the Property Inspector, you will see the length of your rotated line is indeed 70.7 pixels.

5. Although you could keep the length of your horizontal line at 70.7, it will make it very difficult for you to position your isometric cube and to use it as a tile. So, instead, you're going to forgo a little accuracy in favor of ease of use. Using the Property Inspector, set the width of the line to 70 pixels. Set its x-coordinate to `170` and its y-coordinate to `130` to make it align with the top of your diagonal line:

6. Well, you've got half of your square base, and since a square is symmetrical, you can create the other half very easily. Using the Arrow Tool (V), click on the diagonal line, then SHIFT-click on the horizontal line to select them both. With both lines selected, duplicate them using Edit > Duplicate (CTRL/CMD+D).

7. With both lines still selected, use Modify > Transform > Flip Horizontal followed by Modify > Transform > Flip Vertical.

8. Without deselecting, use the Property Inspector to set the x-coordinate of the lines to `120` and the y-coordinate to `130`. There you are, your isometric square base is ready (it's shown opposite with the duplicated lines still selected).

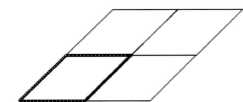

9. Use Edit > Select All (CTRL/CMD+A) to select all four lines, and then use CTRL/CMD+D to create a copy of the square. Position this flush left with the original square. It will be easy to do this if you use the arrow keys to move the square while you hold down SHIFT to constrain your movements to 10-pixel increments. This was the reason you made sure that the tile had whole-number dimensions divisible by 10. Repeat twice more to create a four-square grid, as shown in the image opposite.

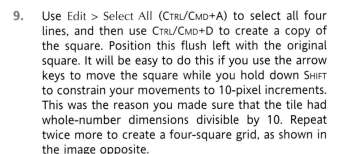

10. Use three lines to connect the edges of two of the diagonal square tiles to create the frame of an isometric cube, as shown opposite.

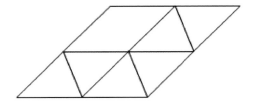

11. Remove the extra lines from the grid to leave just the cube. Use the image at right as a guide, where we've selected the lines that need to be removed from the grid, and then press DELETE.

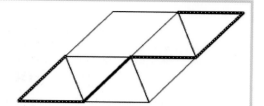

12. Now that you have your wire-frame cube, you'll shade it in. Fill in the top and sides of the cube with two similar colors (we used #0099FF for the sides and #0099CC for the top) using the Paint Bucket Tool (K).

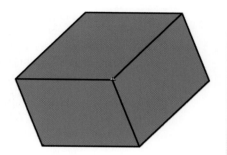

13. Next, use Edit > Select All (CTRL/CMD+A) to select all the lines and fills that make up the cube and use Insert > Convert To Symbol... (F8) to convert it to a movie clip. Call the movie clip iso cube and click OK.

14. Make duplicates of the cube using Edit > Duplication (CTRL/CMD+D) and play around with arranging the cubes to create a sculpture. Do you notice how the z-order of the clips is important in creating a believable tile-based isometric 3D representation?

You will be tackling z-order (or the stacking order) of movie clips a little later when you learn about true isometric graphics. For the moment, it's important to realize that z-ordering is a critical part of isometrics (to brush up on the basics of z-ordering, refer to the section on Z-Ordering in Flash in Chapter 3).

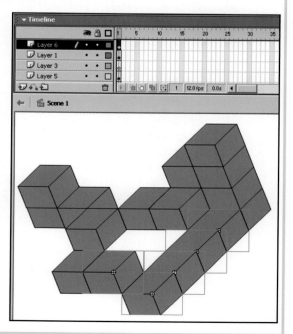

With a little patience, you can create some really great effects using just a simple isometric cube as a building block. In `draw45.fla` (see the image below), we scaled down the cubes to fit the stage. Also note that we had to use multiple layers when arranging the cubes to artificially handle the z-ordering. Although we could have used the Bring Forward (Ctrl-Up) and Send to Back (Ctrl-Down) options under the Modify > Arrange options, keeping each object on a separate layer is generally a preferred "best practice" technique that increases the scalability and maintainability of your movies. Since layers don't add anything to the file size of your movies, you really don't have any excuse not to keep objects in separate well-labeled layers!

Well, that's it—you've made your first foray into the realm of isometric 3D. Although Flash makes it easy for you to create isometric 3D using a 45° angle, this is not the type of isometric drawing that immediately comes to mind when the phrase is used. Instead, isometric graphics on computer screens are usually drawn using a 25.56505° (or 30°) angle. This creates much more pleasing and balanced compositions, and this is exactly what we're going to look into next.

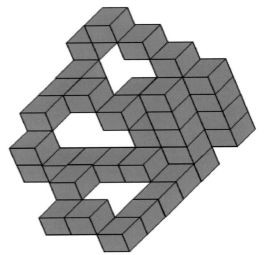

Trigonometry-free zone

Now that you've seen how to draw a military perspective isometric scene and learned some of the core concepts, you'll now learn how you can draw the most common type of isometric projection: that which is used most often in computer games. We are going to be using an angle of 25.56505° (or, even more precisely, arctangent 0.5). The reason we use arctangent 0.5 for the angle is because a line at an angle where the tangent is 0.5 has a nice, regular pixel pattern consisting of two steps to the right and one step up. It also means that our tile will be twice as wide as it is high. To make the edges of the tiles match, the width of the tile has to be a multiple of 4 pixels, and the height should be one less than half the width (in our examples, we use 32x15 tiles, which satisfy the rule). Knowing these three rules, you can easily draw perfect isometric tiles using arctangent 0.5. If you're getting worried that this is about to lead into a full-blown trig-fest, you can relax—we're not going to be using a single trigonometric equation in the rest of the chapter. This is partly because our heads have always been too thick when it comes to trigonometry, but also because it's just not necessary when using isometric 3D. In fact, this is why isometric graphics became so popular: they are less processor-intensive since you don't have to use computationally-heavy trigonometric functions.

The method that we're going to use is the one that is traditionally used in bitmap-based game programming. One of the advantages of using isometric projection is that you don't need to use real 3D math and it makes applications such as isometric games run faster. There's a really great introduction to the technique we're going to be using by Jim Adams over at GameDev called "Isometric Views" (www.gamedev.net/reference/articles/article744.asp). In fact, you would do well to bookmark GameDev since they have many interesting articles that, although they focus mostly on C or Delphi programming, can be applied to ActionScript with some work once you understand the concepts being presented.

Although we're going to sneakily avoid the use of trig in our examples, to get the full picture we encourage you to get a good book on trigonometry and read it through carefully. Trig will pop up in everything you do, especially if you're creating games or scripted animations in Flash. Learn it, and learn it well!

Staggered isometric grid

In this next example, you're going to create an isometric grid by laying out a basic floor tile. The particular arrangement that you're going to be using is called a **staggered layout**.

1. Start a new movie (File > New; CTRL/CMD+N) and set your stage to 500x300 pixels using the Document Properties dialog box. You can keep your frame rate at 12 fps since you're not going to be animating anything in this example. Save the file as `grid_staggered.fla` (also available in this chapter's source files).

2. Create a new movie clip using Insert > New Symbol... (CTRL/CMD+F8) and call it `grid tile`. You should then be presented with the empty timeline and stage for the new symbol.

You'll start out by creating a basic floor tile that you'll duplicate and lay out using ActionScript to form a staggered isometric grid. Your tiles will be 32 pixels wide and 15 pixels tall. These dimensions allow you to achieve the unwieldy 25.56505° angle we were talking about earlier and create diagonals that look beautiful and tile perfectly. To help you draw the floor tile precisely, you're first going to draw a **guide**. The guide will be made up of a rectangle divided up into four smaller and equal-sized rectangles.

Using the Rectangle Tool (R) with a stroke color of black (#000000) and no fill color, draw a small rectangle of arbitrary size. Since you're going to be working with small dimensions, it will help to zoom in on the rectangle so it takes up a little less than a quarter of the stage. This rectangle marks out the horizontal halfway point for your tile.

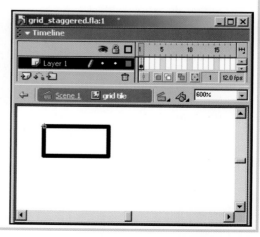

3. Double-click on one of the sides of the rectangle to select all sides and, using the Property Inspector, set its width to 16, its height to 7.5, x to 0, and y to 0.

4. With the rectangle still selected, use Edit > Duplicate (CTRL/CMD+D) to create a copy of the rectangle.

5. With the duplicate of the rectangle still selected, use the Property Inspector to set its x-coordinate to 16 and its y-coordinate to 0.

6. Without deselecting the second rectangle, use CTRL/CMD+D to make a third rectangle.

7. With the third rectangle still selected, use the Property Inspector to set its x-coordinate to 0 and its y-coordinate to 7.5.

8. To make the fourth and final rectangle, use CTRL/CMD+D with the third rectangle still selected and, using the Property Inspector, set its x-coordinate to 16 and its y-coordinate to 7.5. That's it—you're done with the guide. Now use it to draw the ground tile.

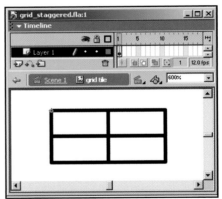

9. Without exiting the edit mode for the grid tile symbol, right-click (CMD-click on a Mac) on Layer 1 in the timeline and select Guide from the context-sensitive menu to convert Layer 1 into a Guide layer. A small hammer icon will appear to denote that the layer is indeed a guide. Turning a layer into a guide means that it will not show up when you export the movie. Finally, double-click on the layer name to edit it and rename it guide, and then lock this layer.

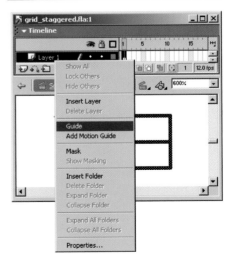

10. Next up, use Insert > Layer (or use the Insert Layer icon at the bottom of the timeline) to create a new layer. Double-click on it to rename it and call it tile. When you're done, your timeline should resemble the one opposite.

11. Making sure that Snap To Objects is active (checked) under the View menu (CTRL+SHIFT+/ on a PC, CMD+SHIFT+/ on a Mac), use the Line Tool (N) and a light gray Stroke Color (we used #999999) to connect the edges of the cross formed by the intersection of the four rectangles into a diamond shape as shown below. You should notice that the Line Tool automatically snaps to the points where the cross intersects the larger rectangle. Since the smaller rectangles are equal in size, these intersection points mark the horizontal and vertical midpoints of the larger rectangle. They also allow you to draw a symmetric isometric tile that adheres perfectly to the 25.56505° angle. Here's what the isometric tile looks like with the guide rectangles still visible:

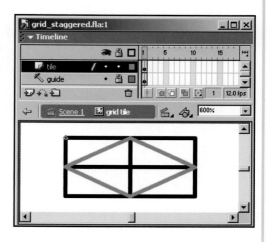

12. You're done with our grid tile movie clip. Return to the main timeline by clicking on the Scene 1 link underneath the timeline.

13. Since you're going to be using ActionScript to create our staggered isometric grid, you need to give the tile movie clip a Linkage ID (also known as a Symbol ID or Linkage Properties Identifier). Open the Library using Window > Library (F11), right-click (CMD-click on a Mac) on the grid tile movie clip, and select Linkage... from the context-sensitive menu.

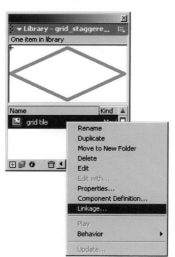

14. In the Linkage Properties window, check the Export for ActionScript checkbox and make sure Export in first frame is also checked (it should become checked by default). Also make sure that the Identifier name is `grid tile` (again, it should default to it since it is the symbol's name).

15. Double-click on Layer 1 in the timeline to edit it and rename it actions. Click on frame 1 of this layer to select it and enter the following script in the Actions panel:

```
// the starting stage x-coordinate for the isometric 3D world
WORLD_X = 90;
// the starting stage y-coordinate for the isometric 3D world
WORLD_Y = 30;

// the width of a floor tile in our world
TILE_W = 32;
// the height of a floor tile in our world
TILE_H = 15;

// movie clip stacking depth
var depth = 1000;

// create the rows
for (var gridY = 0; gridY<31; gridY++) {
 // handle odd and even rows differently
 if (gridY%2) {
   // even row

   // offset even rows, 16 pixels to the left
   xOffset = 16;
   // draw one additional tile for even rows
   numTiles = 11;
 } else {
   // odd row
   xOffset = 0;
   numTiles = 10;
 }
 // create the columns
 for (var gridX = 0; gridX<numTiles; gridX++) {

   // symbol ID of the tile
   var tileID = "grid tile";

   // attach a copy of the tile movie clip to the stage
   _root.attachMovie(tileID, "gridTile"+depth+"_mc", depth++);

   // calculate the stage x- and y-coordinates to place the tile
   // based on its grid coordinates (gridX, gridY)
   var stageX = WORLD_X+(gridX*TILE_W-xOffset);
   var stageY = WORLD_Y+(gridY*TILE_H/2);
```

```
        // short-cut reference to the tile movie clip
        var theTile_mc = _root["gridTile"+depth+"_mc"];

        // position the tile to by setting its _x and _y properties
        theTile_mc._x = stageX;
        theTile_mc._y = stageY;
    }
}
```

The preceding simple script demonstrates the most important foundations of any tile-based world. We start off the code by setting up some initial constants to hold the top left coordinates of the world in stage coordinates, the dimensions of our tile movie clip and a counter to keep track of the depths of attached movie clips. We then come to the heart of the script: the nested loop that lays out the grid.

Here, we tell Flash that we want to create 31 rows. Depending on whether it is an odd- or even-numbered row, the rows have either 10 or 11 tiles in them. We do this so that if we were to mask the screen to a rectangular window (as is usually the case when the staggered layout is used), we wouldn't end up with gaps at the end of the even rows due to the horizontal offset toward the left.

Since the loop used to create the columns (that is, lay out the tiles horizontally) is executed within the loop used to create the rows (that is, lay out the tiles vertically), it is said to be a **nested loop**. The diagram below shows the order in which the tiles are laid out and how we arrived at the equations used to position the tiles:

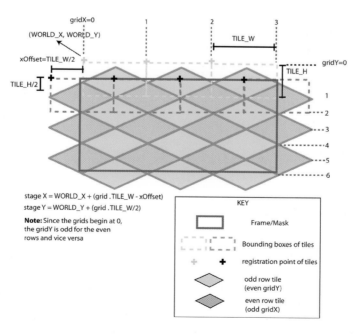

stage X = WORLD_X + (grid .TILE_W - xOffset)
stage Y = WORLD_Y + (grid .TILE_W/2)

Note: Since the grids begin at 0, the gridY is odd for the even rows and vice versa

KEY

Frame/Mask

Bounding boxes of tiles

registration point of tiles

odd row tile (even gridY)

even row tile (odd gridX)

If our tiles had been regular, 2D rectangles, we could have laid them out very simply using the following code:

```
var stageX = WORLD_X + (gridX * TILE_W);
var stageY = WORLD_Y + (gridY * TILE_H);
```

Basically, this means start with the origin we defined for our 3D world on the Flash stage (WORLD_X, WORLD_Y) and place each tile as far away from the origin horizontally as its horizontal position in the current row (gridY) multiplied by its width (TILE_W) and as far away from the origin vertically as its vertical position in the current column (gridX) multiplied by its height (TILE_H). Refer again to the preceding diagram to see this represented visually.

However, since our tiles are in fact not rectangular but are diamond-like in shape, we use the following code to lay the grid out:

```
var stageX = WORLD_X + (gridX * TILE_W - xOffset);
var stageY = WORLD_Y + (gridY * TILE_H / 2);
```

These calculations create a staggered isometric layout.

To see what this looks like, test out the movie using Control > Test Movie (CTRL+ENTER):

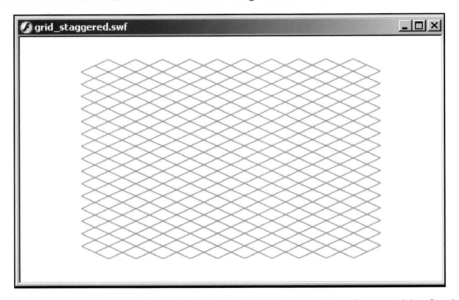

Creating a staggered isometric grid didn't do it for you? OK, so at this point you'd be forgiven for thinking that our design isn't exactly a prizewinner! But there's a reason for this: we need to cover the basics first. The isometric grid may not be much to look at, but it forms the basis on which isometric worlds are built. Carry right on to the next example, where you will create a new tile (a cube this time) and randomly attach it to your grid to create isometric cube structures. By the time you get to the end of this chapter, you'll know how to create a map-based isometric world and how to make a sprite to traverse the world using the keyboard.

Laying out isometric tiles with ActionScript

Now that you know how to create a staggered isometric grid, you'll create a tile with a little more substance (or should we say, *volume*). You'll expand the code to attach a new tile randomly to create dynamic isometric cube sculptures. Although you saw in the earlier example on military projection that you can lay out your isometric tiles by hand in the authoring environment, you'll now learn how to use ActionScript to do this, and how this dynamic technique gives you far greater freedom. Eventually it will allow you to create worlds that you can move around in. Here you're going to see how to lay out an isometric world using ActionScript. Along the way, we touch upon the subject of z-ordering as it pertains to isometric tiles.

1. You're continuing where you left off in the previous example. If you haven't been following in order, you'll find `grid_staggered.fla` in this chapter's source files. Open it and follow along with this exercise. If you'd like a sneak peek at the finished effect that you're going to create here, take a look at `staggered_sculptures.fla`.

2. OK, first off you're going to need a little extra space for this movie since you're going to be stacking isometric cubes on top of one another. Go into the Document Properties dialog box and expand the stage dimensions to 500x400 pixels.

3. Open up the Library if it isn't already showing using Window > Library (F11), right-click (CMD-click) on the `grid tile` movie clip, and select Duplicate to create a copy of the symbol. Call the new symbol `cube` and make sure its Behavior is set to Movie Clip.

4. Double-click on the new `cube` movie clip in the Library to open it up for editing, and zoom in on the tile to make it easier to work with. Unlock the guide layer and lock the tile layer.

5. Click once in an empty area of the stage to make sure you've deselected everything, and then double-click anywhere on the black rectangle to select it all.

6. With the guide rectangle selected, use the Property Inspector to set its y-coordinate to −10. This will place it 10 pixels higher than it was. When we're working on a real project and playing with the positions of objects and we don't necessarily know exactly where they're going to end up, we find it easier to position them using the arrow keys on the keyboard. You can hold down SHIFT while using the arrow keys to move objects in larger increments.

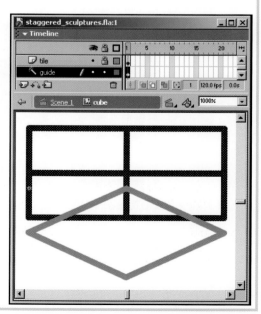

7. Now lock the guide layer and create a new layer using Insert > Layer (or the Insert Layer icon underneath the timeline) and call it tile top.

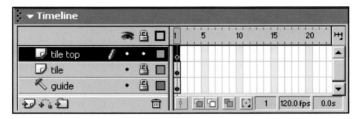

8. With the first frame of the tile top layer selected and using the same stroke color as for the grid/floor tile, use the Line Tool (N) to create a second diamond, identical to the first one, by joining the edges of the cross at the center of the rectangular guide.

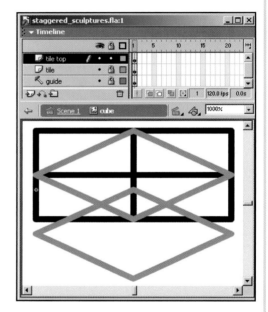

9. Join the lower three vertices (corners) of the two diamonds together using the Line Tool (N) as shown in the image below. You will find it easier to draw the perfectly vertical lines if you hold down SHIFT while drawing them to constrain the Line Tool to 45° increments.

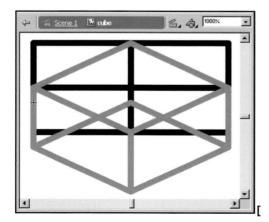

10. Since you will eventually want to fill in the faces of the cube with color, you need to merge the tile and tile top layers. Flash combines strokes that are of the same color on the same layer, so instead of a top tile with vertical extensions and bottom tile, you will end up with a single shape. To do this, start out by unlocking the tile layer and then click on frame 1 of the tile top layer to select all of its contents.

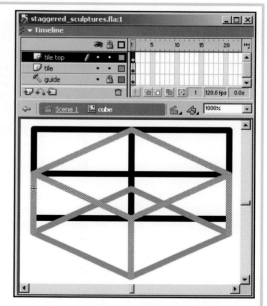

11. Use Edit > Cut (CTRL/CMD+X) to transfer the selected lines to the clipboard.

12. Click on the first frame of the tile layer and use Edit > Paste in Place (CTRL/CMD+SHIFT+V) to paste the contents of the clipboard onto the layer.

13. Click on a free area of the stage to deselect everything. Now if you double-click on any of the lines that make up the cube, you will see that the whole cube gets selected. The two diamonds and vertical beams have merged into a single shape. You'll also notice if you try selecting different parts of the cube that, at the points where two lines of the same color intersect, the lines have been broken up into two segments (in general, when two lines intersect on the same layer, the lines each get broken up into two segments around the intersection point).

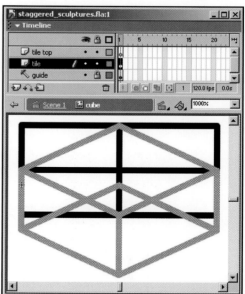

14. Now let's remove those lines that should be hidden from view (in traditional 3D jargon, this is called—perhaps none too inventively—*hidden line removal*). Select the back face of the lower diamond by holding down SHIFT and clicking on the unwanted line segments. Use the DELETE key to remove the back face of the lower diamond.

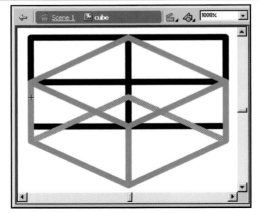

15. Next, using two colors of your choice, fill in the sides and top face of the cube (we used #0066FF for the sides and #0099FF for the top).

16. Then change the stroke color of the lines to black. Double-click on the border of the cube to select all the lines and use the Stroke Color selector on the Property Inspector to change the color to black (#000000).

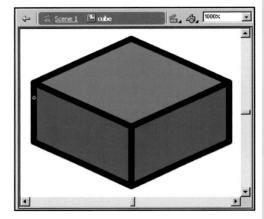

17. While you're at it, you'll do a little housekeeping to keep your movie tidy. Right-click (CMD-click) on the now empty tile top layer and click on the trash can icon to remove the layer. Also, you can hide your guide layer now if you wish since you don't need it any more for this tile:

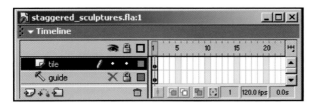

18. All right, now that you have your new cube tile ready, you can get to the good stuff and modify the logic for the movie to randomly disperse these cubes around your grid. Before you do that, however, you need to set a Linkage ID for your new movie clip. Open your Library if it isn't already showing (F11), right-click (CMD-click) on the cube symbol, and select Linkage... from the context-sensitive menu. In the Linkage Properties dialog box that opens, enter cube in the Identifier box and click on the Export for ActionScript checkbox to activate it (as usual, Export in first frame automatically gets checked when you check Export for ActionScript, so just leave it checked), and then click the OK button to exit out of the dialog box.

19. Now you're ready to write some code. Click on the Scene 1 link to exit out of editing the cube symbol and modify the script in frame 1 of the actions layer (in the main timeline) according to the listing below. New and changed code has been highlighted for you.

```
// the starting stage x-coordinate for the isometric 3D world
WORLD_X = 90;
// the starting stage y-coordinate for the isometric 3D world
WORLD_Y = 90;

// the width of a floor tile in our world
TILE_W = 32;
// the height of a floor tile in our world
TILE_H = 15;

// movie clip stacking depth
var depth = 1000;

// create the rows
for (var gridY = 0; gridY < 31; gridY++) {

 // handle odd and even rows differently
 if (gridY % 2) {
   // even row

   // offset even rows, 16 pixels to the left
   xOffset = 16 ;
   // draw one additional tile for even rows
   numTiles = 11;
 } else {
   // odd row
   xOffset = 0;
   numTiles = 10;
 };

 // create the columns
 for (var gridX = 0; gridX < numTiles; gridX++) {

   // the tile added will either be a grid tile or a cube
   // there's a 20% chance that it will be a cube
   var tileID = (Math.random()*10 < 2) ? "cube" : "grid tile";

   // attach the chosen symbol
   _root.attachMovie(tileID, "gridTile"+depth+"_mc", depth++);

   // calculate the stage x- and y-coordinates to place the tile
   // based on its grid coordinates (gridX, gridY)
   var stageX = WORLD_X + (gridX * TILE_W - xOffset);
   var stageY = WORLD_Y + (gridY * TILE_H / 2);
```

continues overleaf

```
        // short-cut reference to the tile movie clip
        var theTile_mc = _root["gridTile"+depth+"_mc"];

        // position the tile to by setting its _x and _y properties
        theTile_mc._x = stageX;
        theTile_mc._y = stageY;

        // randomly stack cubes
        if (tileID == "cube") {
          // select a random number of cubes to stack
          num = Math.abs(Math.random()*4);
          if (num >= 1) {
              for (var tileY = 1; tileY <= num; tileY++) {
                  // attach a new cube to the stage
                  _root.attachMovie(tileID, "gridTile"+depth+"_mc",
➡depth++);
                  // short-cut reference to the tile movie clip
                  var theTile_mc = _root["gridTile"+depth+"_mc"];
                  // calculate the new tile's position
                  theTile_mc._x = stageX;
                  // stack
                  theTile_mc._y = stageY - tileY *
➡(theTile_mc._height/2 - 3);
              }
          }
        }
      }
    }
```

Let's now concentrate on what you changed and what you added. First, you modified the value of the constant that determines where on the stage vertically that you start drawing the isometric world (WORLD_Y). Simple enough. Next, you added the following line that sets the value of a variable called tileID based on whether or not a random number you generate between 0 and 10 is less than 2. If it is, the value of tileID is set to cube (the symbolID of the cube symbol); otherwise, it is set to grid tile (the linkage ID of our regular grid/floor tile).

```
        var tileID = (Math.random()*10 < 2) ? "cube" : "grid tile";
```

If you haven't seen the ? operator (called a ternary operator) in use before, the preceding line may look very cryptic to you. Actually, it has a very simple syntax. The parentheses around the condition we're checking for are not mandatory, but we use them all the time to make the statements easier to read. The general form of this statement is as follows:

```
        myVar = (some condition) ? valueOfMyVarIfConditionIsTrue :
➡valueOfMyVarIfConditionIsFalse;
```

Next, you attach the chosen movie clip (either the cube or the grid tile, depending on the value of the `tileID` variable). Everything else is the same as before (and involves placing the chosen grid tile at the correct grid location) until you get to the following new code:

```
if (tileID == "cube") {
  // select a random number of cubes to stack
  num = Math.abs(Math.random()*4);
  if (num >= 1) {
    for (var tileY = 1; tileY <= num; tileY++) {
        // attach a new cube to the stage
        _root.attachMovie(tileID, "gridTile"+depth+"_mc", depth++);
        // short-cut reference to the tile movie clip
        var theTile_mc = _root["gridTile"+depth+"_mc"];
        // calculate the new tile's position
        theTile_mc._x = stageX;
        // stack
        theTile_mc._y = stageY - tileY * (theTile_mc._height/2 - 3);
    }
  }
}
```

To see the effect of this code, test your movie (CTRL/CMD+ENTER), and then comment out this section of code (surround it with `/*` and `*/`, like so: `/* code block */`) and test out the movie again. You should see that with the code in place, you get stacked columns of cubes, whereas without the code, you get single cubes:

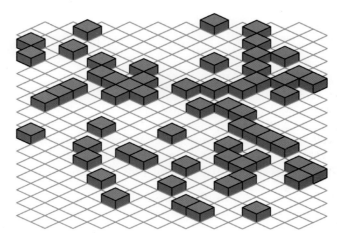

So what you do here is find how many extra cubes to stack on top of a cube (if, and only if, the tile you've just added is a cube). Then, you go through a loop, attach the extra cube movie clips, and position them on top of the base cube. The actual code that carries out the positioning is thus:

```
theTile_mc._x = stageX;
theTile_mc._y = stageY - tileY * (theTile_mc._height/2 - 3);
```

As you can see, you're setting the x-coordinate of the stacked cubes equal to the x-coordinate of the base cube. This makes sense when you think about it, since you're putting them on top of one another; thus, only the y-coordinate should be different. To calculate the y-coordinate, you start with the y-coordinate of the base cube and move upward.

20. Go ahead and test the movie again (`staggered_sculptures.swf`) a couple more times to restart the movie and see the random placement of the cubes in action. Note how cubes that should appear in front of other cubes do so automatically. This is because they are automatically assigned the correct z-order due to the way in which you draw the grid (from left to right and top to bottom). This greatly simplifies your job since you do not have to worry about z-order explicitly. It will also make your life easier when it does come time to take control of the z-order manually in the last example of the chapter. There, you'll make a sprite to move around your 3D world.

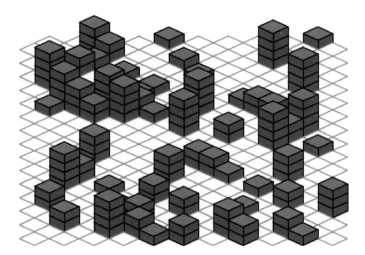

In this example, you created a staggered isometric layout and dynamically populated it with some cube-shaped tiles. You did *not* make the heights of the cubes equal to or a multiple of the height of the floor tile on purpose to escape from the rigidity of the grid.

Going forward, instead of creating random blocks, wouldn't it be nice if you could have various types of tiles and create your worlds based on maps? That's exactly what you're going to do in the next example, where you'll see the more common layout model for isometric maps: the diamond-shaped or rotated model. You'll also see how you can use a tile map to create your worlds with precisely placed tiles.

Diamond-shaped isometric grids and tile maps

In this example, you're going to create some new tiles, look at a different layout scheme, and use a map to lay out your tiles in exactly the manner you want.

1. You're going to start off by creating some new tiles. Specifically, you're going to create a grass floor tile to use in place of the boring and unrealistic grid floor tile that you were using previously, and you'll create a variant of your blue cube to use as a wall. We're not going to go

through the specifics of how to create the tiles in great detail, since we covered the general techniques you'll need in the previous example. If you would rather not create the tiles yourself, just open up `diamond_map_start.fla` from this chapter's sample files folder, available for download with all the examples in this book from www.friendsofed.com, skip the following early steps, and start at step 10.

2. The first tile you're going to create is the grass tile. You will base all of your tiles on the grid tile you used in the previous example. If you haven't been following in order, you can simply use `staggered_sculptures.fla` from the downloaded source files and follow these steps (alternatively, this example can be found as `diamond_map.fla` in the source files).

3. Make a duplicate of the `grid tile` movie clip symbol and name it `grass`.

4. Right-click (CMD-click) on the `grass` movie clip symbol in your Library and choose Linkage... from the context-sensitive menu. In the Linkage Properties dialog box, call its identifier `grass`.

5. Double-click on the `grass` movie clip symbol in the Library to open it up for editing.

6. Modify the original grid tile by filling it in with a shade of green (#009933).

7. Select the outline of the tile by double-clicking on the gray line, and use the DELETE key to remove it. If you click on the green fill now, you'll see that its dimensions are still 32x15. Flash is weird like that! The reason we deleted the outline instead of keeping it and making it the same green as the fill is because Flash has issues with outlines sometimes, especially when you need them to

be placed at exactly the pixel locations you specify—something that is very important for tile-based graphics. The image at right shows your grass tile with the outline removed. In what is no doubt a miracle of modern mathematics, its dimensions are not affected. Making a cameo appearance is your guide, which can be seen in the background.

> For other oddities with outlines, see the post titled "Deeper into the sizing issues" in the Flash Bugs & Workarounds category of onRelease (www.onrelease.org/index.php?m=200210#12).

8. Next, use the Line Tool with your stroke color set to a light shade of green or cyan to create a small horizontal highlight. Click on the line and convert it to a movie clip symbol using F8. Give it the symbol name `grass spot`. Use Edit > Duplicate with your instance of the `grass spot` movie clip selected to create about 20 copies of it and sprinkle them around the grass tile. These will be your grass highlights, giving the grass ground tile some texture. If you like, you can place these grass highlight movie clips in their own layer called `grass` to make it easier to select them en masse.

Here's the final `grass` tile, showing the tiny highlights that you added. Make sure you keep all highlights within the green area—you don't want any accidents while you're tiling!

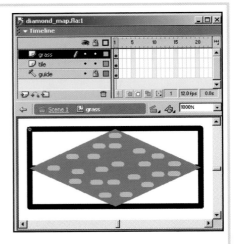

9. Next, you're going to create a variant (basically a shorter version) of the cube movie clip you made in the last example. In fact, to create it, you can follow steps 3 to 17 in the previous example, with the only difference being that in step 3, you should give it the symbol name `short wall`, and in step 6, you should move the guide layer up by 4 pixels only, so that its y-coordinate is at `-4` (instead of `-10`). That should result in a shorter version of the blue wall tile, as shown. Using the Linkage Properties dialog box, give your new symbol a symbol ID of `short wall`.

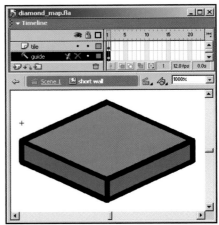

10. Great! With these two new tiles in your arsenal, let's get cracking with a new type of isometric layout. Instead of staggering your tiles as you did in the previous example, you're going to lay them out in a neat diamond shape. Modify the script in frame 1 of the actions layer using the listing below. As usual, we've highlighted the changes and additions for clarity:

```
// the starting stage x-coordinate for the isometric 3D world
WORLD_X = 225;
// the starting stage y-coordinate for the isometric 3D world
WORLD_Y = 75;

// the width of a floor tile in our world
TILE_W = 32;
// the height of a floor tile in our world
TILE_H = 15;

// the world map (hey, it's a small world!)
map_array = [
```

```
    [1, 1, 1, 1, 1, 1, 1, 1, 1, 1],
    [1, 0, 0, 0, 0, 0, 0, 0, 0, 1],
    [1, 0, 0, 1, 0, 0, 1, 0, 0, 1],
    [1, 0, 1, 1, 0, 0, 1, 1, 0, 1],
    [1, 0, 0, 0, 0, 0, 0, 0, 0, 1],
    [1, 0, 0, 0, 1, 1, 0, 0, 0, 1],
    [1, 0, 1, 0, 0, 0, 0, 1, 0, 1],
    [1, 0, 0, 1, 1, 1, 1, 0, 0, 1],
    [1, 0, 0, 0, 0, 0, 0, 0, 0, 1],
    [1, 1, 1, 1, 1, 1, 1, 1, 1, 1]
];

// movie clip stacking depth
var depth = 1000;

for (var gridY = 0; gridY < map.length; gridY++) {
 for (var gridX = 0; gridX < map[gridY].length; gridX++) {

    var tileID = (map_array[gridY][gridX]) ? "short wall" : "grass";

    _root.attachMovie(tileID, "gridTile"+depth+"_mc", depth++);

    var stageX = WORLD_X - gridY * 0.5 * TILE_W + gridX * 0.5 * TILE_W;
    var stageY = WORLD_Y + gridY * 0.5 * TILE_H + gridX * 0.5 * TILE_H;

    var theTile_mc = _root["gridTile"+depth+"_mc"];

    theTile_mc._x = stageX;
    theTile_mc._y = stageY;
  }
 }
```

Looking through the new script, you should notice that the structure of the loops that lay out the tiles has not changed. We have, however, introduced a very important new construct called the `map_array`. This is a two-dimensional array that shows which tile should be used in which grid position in your isometric world. Look at the array in the listing and mentally replace the 1s and 0s with little graphics tiles.

This is exactly what you're doing in the code. In the inner layout loop, you set `tileID` equal to the linkage ID of the `short wall` movie clip if the map contains a 1 for a certain grid/map position. If a map position contains 0, you set `tileID` equal to the linkage ID of the `grass` tile. You do this using the ternary operator that you learned about in the previous example:

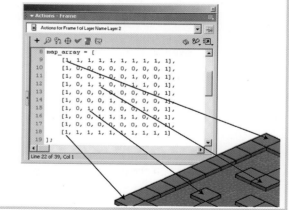

```
var tileID =
(map_array[gridY][gridX]) ?
"short wall" : "grass";
```

Another major change is that you are now using a new formula to decide the stage coordinates at which to place your isometric tiles:

```
var stageX = WORLD_X - gridY * 0.5 * TILE_W + gridX * 0.5 * TILE_W;
var stageY = WORLD_Y + gridY * 0.5 * TILE_H + gridX * 0.5 * TILE_H;
```

You no longer have a horizontal offset to calculate since you are not staggering the tiles, but you are placing them in a diamond pattern. Look at the diagram below to see how we arrived at those equations for the rotated isometric projection:

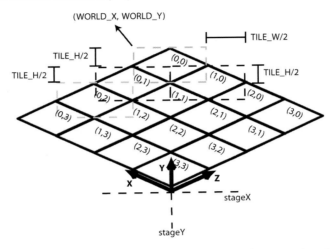

11. Can you guess what the output will look like by looking at the map alone? Test out the movie (CTRL/CMD+ENTER) to see if you were right!

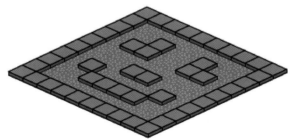

It's an isometric smiley face! Using a tile map allows you to place tiles in exact locations and easily use various types of tiles. Play around with the map array, switching the position of the 1s and 0s to create new grass and wall patterns.

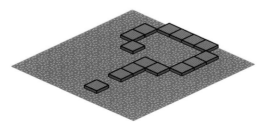

In the next example, you're going to add some more tiles and even create an animated tile. You're going to see how the layout scheme automatically handles z-order, even for animated tiles when they change height.

Isometric terra-forming and animated tiles

We're not going to go into detail about how best to draw isometric tiles here, but we will show you how you can create interesting virtual worlds even with the simplest of tiles. You're also going to see how you can create an animated tile.

1. You'll continue with the framework built up in the previous example (`diamond_map.fla`). This extension is called `diamond_terra.fla`, which you'll find in this chapter's samples folder, available for download from www.friendsofed.com as usual.

2. In addition to the `short wall` movie clip symbol that's already in the Library, you're going to create two new blue blocks called `tall wall` and `really tall wall`. Again, those interested can follow the instructions in steps 3 to 17 of the *Laying out isometric tiles with ActionScript* example to create both movie clip symbols. For the `tall wall`, move the guide 10 pixels up from its original position (`y = -10`), and for the `really tall wall`, move it 40 pixels up (`y = -40`) in step 6. Make sure that you give them linkage IDs that match their movie clip symbol names (`tall wall` and `really tall wall`, respectively).

3. Now that you've got more than two tiles to manage, it makes sense to keep track of the linkage IDs of the tiles in an array. So, you're going to add a `tiles_array` to your script, just before the section where you define the `map_array`, and you're going to modify your map to use these new tiles you have at your disposal.

    So, first off, add the following code above the `map_array` definition:

    ```
    // an array to hold tile symbol IDs
    tiles_array = [
     "grass",
     "short wall",
     "tall wall",
     "really tall wall"
    ];
    ```

4. Next up, modify the `map_array` so that it now looks like this:

    ```
    // map of our lovely garden
    map_array = [
     [1, 1, 1, 2, 0, 0, 0, 2, 1, 1, 1],
     [1, 0, 0, 0, 0, 0, 0, 0, 0, 0, 1],
     [1, 0, 0, 0, 0, 0, 0, 0, 0, 0, 1],
     [2, 0, 0, 1, 1, 1, 1, 1, 0, 0, 2],
     [0, 0, 0, 1, 2, 2, 2, 1, 0, 0, 0],
     [0, 0, 0, 1, 2, 3, 2, 1, 0, 0, 0],
    ```

```
       [0, 0, 0, 1, 2, 2, 2, 1, 0, 0, 0],
       [2, 0, 0, 1, 1, 1, 1, 1, 0, 0, 2],
       [1, 0, 0, 0, 0, 0, 0, 0, 0, 0, 1],
       [1, 0, 0, 0, 0, 0, 0, 0, 0, 0, 1],
       [1, 1, 1, 2, 0, 0, 0, 2, 1, 1, 1]
   ];
```

5. Finally, replace the line in the inner loop where you decide the `tileID` of the tile to load in with the following one, so that it uses your new `tiles_array` when deciding which tile to display:

    ```
    var tileID = tiles_array[ map_array[ gridY ][ gridX] ];
    ```

6. Now take a look at your new isometric garden. Test the movie with the usual CTRL/CMD+ENTER.

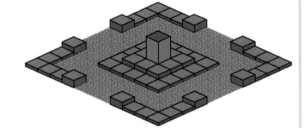

7. No, we haven't forgotten about the animated tile we promised you and, furthermore, it's going to be very simple to create and add to your movie since you now have a `tiles_array` and `map_array` to work with. Start out by creating the animated tile. Create a new movie clip symbol using Insert > New Symbol (CTRL/CMD+F8) and call it `anim wall`.

8. Rename Layer 1 as tiles.

9. Using the timeline below as a guide, place new keyframes at the 1st, 6th, 11th, 26th, and 32nd frames by clicking on the frames and pressing F6. Now you can drag the movie clips from the Library onto specific frames (specified below) and set their x- and y-coordinates using the Property Inspector:

Frame	Movie Clip Symbol	x-coordinate	y-coordinate
1	short wall	0	−4
6	tall wall	0	−10
11	really tall wall	0	−45
26	tall wall	0	−10
32	short wall	0	−4

10. Finally, click on frame 36 and select Insert > Frame (F5) to extend the timeline to that frame. Your timeline should now look like this:

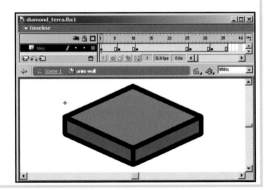

11. Your animated tile is nearly finished. Click on the Scene 1 link to return to the main timeline. Right-click (CMD-click) on your newly created anim wall movie clip in the Library and select Linkage... from the context-sensitive menu. Give it the linkage ID anim wall.

12. Next, you need to add this linkage ID reference to your tiles_array near the start of the code:

```
tiles_array = [
 "grass",
 "short wall",
 "tall wall",
 "really tall wall",
 "anim wall"
 ];
```

13. Then you can modify the map to use the new animated tiles. Replace the map_array definition with the one below:

```
map_array = [
 [1, 1, 1, 2, 0, 0, 0, 2, 1, 1, 1],
 [1, 0, 0, 0, 0, 0, 0, 0, 0, 0, 1],
 [1, 0, 0, 0, 0, 0, 0, 0, 0, 0, 1],
 [2, 0, 0, 1, 1, 4, 1, 1, 0, 0, 2],
 [0, 0, 0, 1, 2, 2, 2, 1, 0, 0, 0],
 [0, 0, 0, 4, 2, 4, 2, 4, 0, 0, 0],
 [0, 0, 0, 1, 2, 2, 2, 1, 0, 0, 0],
 [2, 0, 0, 1, 1, 4, 1, 1, 0, 0, 2],
 [1, 0, 0, 0, 0, 0, 0, 0, 0, 0, 1],
 [1, 0, 0, 0, 0, 0, 0, 0, 0, 0, 1],
 [1, 1, 1, 2, 0, 0, 0, 2, 1, 1, 1]
 ];
```

14. Finally, test the movie (CTRL/CMD+ENTER). Notice how even the taller, animated tiles display properly with regard to the z-order. This is, again, due to the order in which you draw the tiles.

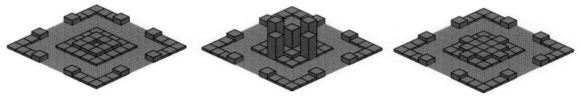

The richness and realism of a tile-based isometric world is very much dependent on the quality of its tiles. If you want to take your isometric tile drawing skills further than the techniques described in this chapter, take a look at the wonderful tutorial by Zoggles over at www.indie-rpg.net/pixel-zone/shtml/tut-isometric.shtml.

In the final example, coming up next, you'll place an interactive character in your isometric world (in this case, your beloved sphere from the scaling chapters). There, you will need to take control of the z-order manually. Don't worry, though—it's not complicated.

Interactive landscape

What use is an isometric 3D world if you can't play in it? In this example, your old friend the sphere will be making a comeback to take a stroll around the isometric world that you just created. Having an interactive character brings up a few more issues you need to handle when it comes to z-ordering, as you'll see in the exercise.

1. As usual, you're going to be building upon the previous effect, so open `diamond_terra.fla` from the previous exercise. The finished version of this example is available in the sample files as `diamond_walk.fla`.

2. The major addition to your isometric world in this example comes in the form of a sphere that you can move around the grassy areas of your isometric world using the keyboard. To start, duplicate the `grid tile` movie clip by right-clicking (CMD-clicking on a Mac) on this symbol in the Library and selecting Duplicate from the context-sensitive menu. Call the new movie clip symbol `sprite`, and give it the linkage ID `sprite`.

3. Double-click on the newly created `sprite` movie clip to open it up for editing. Make the guide layer invisible by clicking on its Show/Hide bullet in the timeline (it's the one underneath the eye icon). Also, make the `tile` layer a guide by double-clicking on the layer icon in the timeline and selecting Guide from the Layer Properties window.

4. Lock both the `tile` and `guide` layers, create a new layer for the sphere, and move it to the top of the stack. On this layer, draw a sphere of arbitrary size using the Oval Tool (O) and constraining it to a circle by holding down the SHIFT key as you drag. Click on the sphere to select it and set its dimensions to 14 pixels by 14 pixels, its x-coordinate to 9, and its y-coordinate to −3 (we found these values by trial and error, using the tile grid as a guide). Note that if you place the sphere too high, at some point it will appear to float.

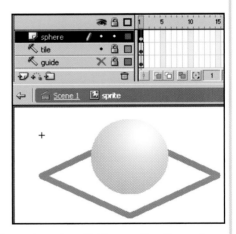

5. That's it—you've created your sphere! Exit out of editing the sphere by clicking on the Scene 1 link in the timeline to return to the main stage.

6. Modify the script in frame 1 of the `actions` layer using the listing below. Although the organization of the script has changed considerably, we haven't bothered to highlight sections that have merely moved to new places in the listing below if the code itself has not changed (for example, some chunks of code have now been placed within a function). This should make it easier for you to see how we've moved things around.

```
// define global constants
with (_global) {
```

```
    // the starting stage x-coordinate for the isometric 3D world
    WORLD_X = 225;
    // the starting stage y-coordinate for the isometric 3D world
    WORLD_Y = 75;

    // the width of a floor tile in our world
    TILE_W = 32;
    // the height of a floor tile in our world
    TILE_H = 15;

    // an array to hold tile symbol IDs
    tiles_array = [
      "grass",
      "short wall",
      "tall wall",
      "really tall wall",
      "anim wall"
    ];

    // map of our lovely garden
    map_array = [
      [1, 1, 1, 2, 0, 0, 0, 2, 1, 1, 1],
      [1, 0, 0, 0, 0, 0, 0, 0, 0, 0, 1],
      [1, 0, 0, 0, 0, 0, 0, 0, 0, 0, 1],
      [2, 0, 0, 1, 1, 4, 1, 1, 0, 0, 2],
      [0, 0, 0, 1, 2, 2, 2, 1, 0, 0, 0],
      [0, 0, 0, 4, 2, 4, 2, 4, 0, 0, 0],
      [0, 0, 0, 1, 2, 2, 2, 1, 0, 0, 0],
      [2, 0, 0, 1, 1, 4, 1, 1, 0, 0, 2],
      [1, 0, 0, 0, 0, 0, 0, 0, 0, 0, 1],
      [1, 0, 0, 0, 0, 0, 0, 0, 0, 0, 1],
      [1, 1, 1, 2, 0, 0, 0, 2, 1, 1, 1]
    ];

}

// calculates the depth of a tile given its grid coordinates
function getTileDepth ( gX, gY ) {
 // the minimum depth to start attaching movie clips
 var MIN_DEPTH = 1000;
 // spacing between consecutive depths
 var DEPTH_SPACING = 10;

 return MIN_DEPTH + map_array.length * gY * DEPTH_SPACING + gX *
➥DEPTH_SPACING;
}

// calculates the stage x- and y-coordinates, given grid coordinates
```

continues overleaf

```
function gridToStage ( gX, gY ) {
 var stageCoor = new Object();
 stageCoor.x = WORLD_X - gY * 0.5 * TILE_W + gX * 0.5 * TILE_W;
 stageCoor.y = WORLD_Y + gY * 0.5 * TILE_H + gX * 0.5 * TILE_H;

 // return the stage coordinates object
 return stageCoor;
}
// draws the isometric map using the map and tiles arrays
function drawMap() {
 // iterate through the rows of the map array
 for (var gridY = 0; gridY < map_array.length; gridY++) {
   // iterate through the columns of the map array
   for (var gridX = 0; gridX < map_array[gridY].length; gridX++) {
     // find the tile ID for the current tile from the array
     var currentTile = map_array[gridY][gridX];
     var tileID = tiles_array[currentTile];

     // calculate the depth to assign to the tile
     var tileDepth = getTileDepth ( gridX, gridY );

     // attach the tile movie clip movie clip to the stage
     _root.attachMovie(tileID, "gridTile"+tileDepth+"_mc", tileDepth);

     // calculate the stage x- and y-coordinate of the tile
     var stageCoordinates = gridToStage( gridX, gridY );

     // short-cut reference to tile
     var theTile = _root["gridTile"+tileDepth+"_mc"];

     // position the tile
     theTile._x = stageCoordinates.x;
     theTile._y = stageCoordinates.y;
   }
 }
}

// attaches and initializes the sprite movie clip
function createSprite() {
 // set initial starting coordinates for sprite
 spriteXGrid = 5;
 spriteYGrid = 0;
 spriteDepth = getTileDepth( spriteXGrid, spriteYGrid ) + 1;

 // attach the sprite movie clip
 _root.attachMovie("sprite", "sprite_mc", spriteDepth);

 // calculate the sprite's coordinates
```

```
        spriteCoordinates = gridToStage( spriteXGrid, spriteYGrid );
        sprite_mc._x = spriteCoordinates.x;
        sprite_mc._y = spriteCoordinates.y;
}


// places the sprite at a specified grid/map location
function placeSprite ( spriteXGrid, spriteYGrid ) {
 // calculate the sprite's coordinates and depth
 spriteCoordinates = gridToStage( spriteXGrid, spriteYGrid );
 sprite_mc._x = spriteCoordinates.x;
 sprite_mc._y = spriteCoordinates.y;
 spriteDepth = getTileDepth( spriteXGrid, spriteYGrid ) + 1;
 sprite_mc.swapDepths(spriteDepth);
}


// checks that the destination tile is a ground tile (tileID = 0)
// returns true if it is, false if it is not
function checkDestination ( spriteXGrid, spriteYGrid ) {
 return !map_array[spriteYGrid][spriteXGrid];
}


function createKeyListener() {
 // Create a new object. We will make this a key listener
 // so it gets notified of keyboard events.
 keyListener = new Object();

 // onKeyDown handler: Gets called whenever the user presses a key
 keyListener.onKeyDown = function() {

   // user wants to move up the z-axis using the Up Arrow key
   if ( Key.isDown(Key.UP) ) {
     if ( spriteYGrid > 0 ) {
         // bound check ok - user has not reached the top of the map
         if ( checkDestination ( spriteXGrid, spriteYGrid - 1) ) {
             // decrement the Y map/grid position
             spriteYGrid--;
             // place the sprite at the new location
             placeSprite( spriteXGrid, spriteYGrid );
         }
     }
   }

   // user wants to move down the Z axis using the Down Arrow key
   if ( Key.isDown(Key.DOWN) ) {

     // find the vertical limit of the grid (number of rows - 1)
     var gridYLimit = map_array.length - 1;
```

continues overleaf

```
        if ( spriteYGrid < gridYLimit ) {
            // bound check ok - user has not reached the bottom of the map
            if ( checkDestination ( spriteXGrid, spriteYGrid + 1) ) {
                // destination ok - tile is a ground tile

                // increment the Y map/grid position
                spriteYGrid++;
                // place the sprite at the new location
                placeSprite( spriteXGrid, spriteYGrid );
            }
        }
    }

    // user wants to move left along the x-axis using Left Arrow key
    if ( Key.isDown(Key.LEFT) ) {
      if (spriteXGrid > 0) {
            // bound check ok - user has not reached left edge of map
            if ( checkDestination ( spriteXGrid - 1, spriteYGrid) ) {
                // destination ok - tile is a ground tile

                // decrement the X map/grid position
                spriteXGrid--;
                // place the sprite at the new location
                placeSprite( spriteXGrid, spriteYGrid );
            }
        }
    }

    // user wants to move right along the x-axis using Right Arrow key
    if ( Key.isDown(Key.RIGHT) ) {
    // find the horizontal limit of the grid (number of colums - 1)
      var gridXLimit = map_array[spriteYGrid].length - 1;

      if ( spriteXGrid < gridXLimit ) {
            // bound check ok - user has not reached right edge of map
            if ( checkDestination ( spriteXGrid + 1, spriteYGrid) ) {
                // increment the X map/grid position
                spriteXGrid++;
                // place the sprite at the new location
                placeSprite( spriteXGrid, spriteYGrid );
            }
        }
    }
};
// add the key listener object as a key listener
Key.addListener(keyListener);
}
```

```
/*
 Main
*/
// draw the isometric map
drawMap();
// create the sprite
createSprite();
// start listening for keyboard events
createKeyListener();
```

Phew! Although you've added quite a bit of code and moved things around a bit, you haven't actually changed anything about how the isometric world is drawn. The biggest organizational change you've made is to split up your code into functions. This is a much better way of organizing your movie (especially larger ones) than having all your code together in one huge mess (or, even worse, scattered all around the place attached to movie clips). Going one step beyond this is to use object-oriented programming (OOP) techniques and classes to organize your code. In fact, we use classes in Chapters 3 and 4, but a detailed study of the intricacies of OOP and a demonstration of how to create classes are beyond the scope of this book.

Starting from the top, you'll notice that you're defining your constants on the `_global` namespace now so that they can be accessed easily from everywhere within your movie (any timeline or object). Next, you have the `getTileDepth` function which, when passed the grid x- and y-coordinates for the `map_array`, returns the depth that you should use when attaching a tile on the stage for that position. Take a look at the math behind it:

$$MIN\_DEPTH + map\_array.length * gY * DEPTH\_SPACING + gX * DEPTH\_SPACING$$

This formula is responsible for assigning individual depths to each tile, and the depth between tiles essentially increases in tens because of the `DEPTH_SPACING` variable. For instance, a sphere placed on the tile whose depth is `1400` receives a depth that is equal to one more than the tile it is on. And, since you have set aside nine depth positions between any two tiles that appear next to each other along the x-axis, you could theoretically have nine sprites on a tile at the same time with correct z-order. The z-order for the sprite is handled by the `placeSprite` function:

```
function placeSprite ( spriteXGrid, spriteYGrid ) {
  // calculate the sprite's coordinates and depth
  spriteCoordinates = gridToStage( spriteXGrid, spriteYGrid );
  sprite_mc._x = spriteCoordinates.x;
  sprite_mc._y = spriteCoordinates.y;
  spriteDepth = getTileDepth( spriteXGrid, spriteYGrid ) + 1;
  sprite_mc.swapDepths(spriteDepth);
}
```

There, you find the sprite's coordinates using the `gridToStage` function (which contains the same code you were using to find the coordinates of tiles in the earlier example). Based on these coordinates, you calculate what the depth of the tile at that position is and add one to the result to arrive at the depth you will use for your sprite.

The `createSprite` function is very similar to the `placeSprite` function but it is called just once, when the sprite's movie clip is being attached to the stage for the first time.

The next important addition you make is to create an object to act as a *key listener*. A listener is an object that has methods that get called when specific events occur. The `keyListener` object you create is a plain old empty object with functions in it until you make it a key listener by adding it as a listener to the built-in `Key` object of Flash. To do this, you use the `addListener` method of the `Key` object.

Your `keyListener` object listens for just one event: the `onKeyDown` event, which occurs when the user presses down on a key. By adding the `keyListener` object as a listener to the `Key` object, you tell it that you want to receive keyboard events when they happen. Although the `Key` object broadcasts one other message (`onKeyUp`), you only want to know when a user pressed *down* on a key so you only create an `onKeyDown` handler. The `Key` object will still broadcast `onKeyUp` messages to your `keyListener` object, but since you haven't set up an `onKeyUp` handler to listen for these events, you won't hear them.

In the `onKeyDown` handler, you have separate checks to see which of the arrow keys are currently down. You respond to each accordingly by first checking if the sphere has reached a boundary in the direction it wants to move and, if it hasn't, the tile that the sphere wants to travel to is a grass tile (your sphere has an aversion to walls!). If both conditions are met, you update the map location of the sphere and place it there. During placement, the z-ordering is again handled automatically by the `placeSprite` function. Refer to the diagram below to see how the sprite responds to the arrow keys:

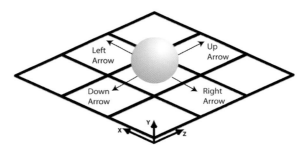

Well, that's it—you've come to the end of a long road! Test the movie (CTRL/CMD+ENTER) and use the arrow keys to move the sphere around the isometric world.

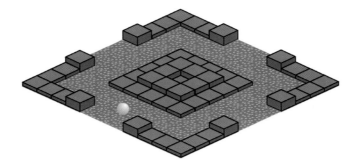

To get a solid introduction to object-oriented programming, we suggest that you start out with the excellent Flash MX Upgrade Essentials *by Sham Bhangal (friends of ED, ISBN: 1-903450-76-4), and then continue on to* Object-Oriented Programming with ActionScript *by Branden Hall and Samuel Wan (New Riders, ISBN: 0-7357-1183-6). To polish off your ActionScript experience, don't forget to get a copy of* ActionScript for Flash MX: The Definitive Guide, Second Edition *by Colin Moock (O'Reilly, ISBN: 0-596-00396-X) and* Flash MX Designer's ActionScript Reference *(friends of ED, ISBN: 1-903450-58-6). You'd be wise to keep these books near you at all times!*

Summary

In the span of one chapter, you learned how to create a tile-based isometric world that you can traverse with a keyboard-controlled sprite. That's pretty impressive! You should now have the essential theory and tools you need to create an isometric game or a multiuser world (or even an experimental site interface) using Flash. We've sprinkled the chapter with quite a few links and references to some truly amazing resources relating to isometrics. With these resources, you'll find an abundance of information and guidance on the topics that we didn't have time to cover here—perhaps the most important one being *scrolling* an isometric map.

In fact, there are many ways to implement a scrolling isometric map, ranging from redrawing the visible portion of the map every time to laying out the world in an empty movie clip and allowing the user to drag the movie clip along (this will create the appearance of scrolling the map if you apply a mask to the visible portion). You can also implement scrolling independent of the keyboard control of your character (for example, the user could be allowed to scroll using the mouse), or scroll automatically when the character approaches the edges of the visible world window (if you are old enough to remember them, the *King's Quest* games from Sierra used this approach, although they didn't use an isometric viewpoint).

So what are you waiting for? You now have all the knowledge, tools, and resources you need—go forth and create! And be sure to send us a link to your wonderful isometric creations.

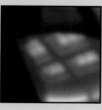

Focus and Depth of Field

So far we have explored several different depth cues, such as size, occlusion, perspective, and light and shadow. In this chapter we'll turn our attention to the concepts of focus and depth of field. The notion of establishing depth in a scene has its origins in art, but the specific term *depth of field* has found broad usage in photography. Depth of field as defined in photography is the distance from the camera within which objects remain in focus.

One way of visualizing how depth of field works is to imagine a plane at some point in front of the camera where objects are perfectly in focus. As an object moves farther from this plane, it becomes less sharp. The rate at which this sharp to blurry transition occurs is determined by the aperture and speed of the camera's shutter. Photographers often use this effect to emphasize a certain part of a scene in a photograph. In cinematography, depth of field is often used to move the viewer's attention from one part of a scene to another.

Depth of field and focus are essentially depth-based camera artifacts that we can exploit to build more convincing 3D scenes—so let's get started!

Stay focused...

Our first example will demonstrate the impact that focus has in a scene. Consider the two images below. The first is sharp and clear, whereas the second is blurry and less distinct. In this exercise, you'll create a lens icon that can be dragged over the blurry image to pull the focused image forward.

1. Select File > New (CTRL/CMD+N) to create a new movie. Next, click on the Size button in the Property Inspector to edit the movie properties. Set the movie dimensions to the dimensions of the two source images. In this particular example, called `focus1.fla` in the sample files, you'll be working with two 400x300 images.

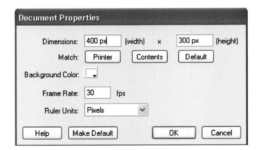

2. Create four layers. Select the bottom layer and import your blurred image by selecting File > Import... or by pressing CTRL/CMD+R (you can use `focus1_blurred.jpg` from the sample files). The image should be centered on the stage by default.

3. Select the second layer from the bottom and import your clear image (`focus1_clear.jpg`) by pressing CTRL/CMD+R again.

4. On the third layer from the bottom, create a solid black circle. Select this circle and convert it to a movie clip symbol with Insert > Convert to Symbol (F8). Name the symbol c1, and then in the Property Inspector give it the instance name c1.

5. Convert the third layer from the bottom into a mask layer by choosing Mask from the timeline layer menu (right-click/CMD-click).

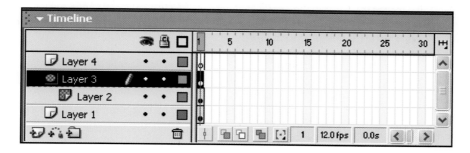

6. On the top layer, create a circle the same size of the circle in step 4 but with a thick black border and a clear fill color. Select the circle, convert it to a symbol (F8), and name the symbol c2. Then in the Property Inspector, name the instance c2.

7.   Select frame 1 on the timeline. Open the Actions panel by selecting Window > Actions (F9) and insert the following code:

```
this.onEnterFrame = function () {
 c1._x = _xmouse;
 c1._y = _ymouse;
 c2._x = _xmouse;
 c2._y = _ymouse;
};
```

This code defines a method for the onEnterFrame event that will be invoked continuously at the frame rate of the movie. Each time this function is invoked, you will change the position of the mask, c1, and the outline of the mask, c2, so that they follow the mouse's position.

8.   Now test the movie by selecting Control > Test Movie (CTRL/CMD+ENTER). As you move the mouse, notice how the clear portion of the scene really seems to be pulled forward. Even in this very simple example, focus creates a sense of depth and dimensionality.

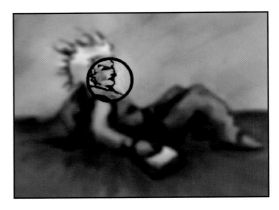

9.   One obvious enhancement to this example would be to magnify the contents of the circular lens. Accordingly, scale the image on the second layer from the bottom so that it is 50% larger. For best results, create a larger version of the image in a graphics manipulation application, such as Adobe Photoshop, rather than scaling it in Flash. Select the image and convert it to a symbol (F8). Name the instance i1.

10.   Add the following ActionScript to your existing code from step 7:

```
this.onEnterFrame = function () {
 c1._x = _xmouse;
 c1._y = _ymouse;
 c2._x = _xmouse;
 c2._y = _ymouse;
 i1._x = _xmouse - (_xmouse/400)*i1._width + i1._width/2;
 i1._y = _ymouse - (_ymouse/300)*i1._height + i1._height/2;
};
```

11.   This new code changes the position of the clear image, i1, so that the mouse's relative position in the blurry image corresponds to the same relative position in the clear image.

12. This time when you test the movie (found as `focus1b.fla` in the sample files), the circle really does magnify the blurry image. It appears that the circular lens you created really is focusing the picture.

Approaching the plane of focus

The simplest example of a depth of field effect is when the focus is fixed. In the following examples, you will move an object that is far away closer to the viewer. As the object moves forward, it will become sharper and thus will seem to approach the depth of field.

Atmospheric perspective

Here we're returning to what is referred to as atmospheric perspective. We introduced this concept in Chapter 3 when we started to look at scaling for 3D. Atmospheric perspective is an effect created by the environment. For example, photos with mountains in the horizon often look slightly bluish and hazy. The reason for this is that there are dust and water particles in the air between the camera and the mountains, so the farther away the object, the hazier it may look. Changing the opacity of an object or moving the object's overall color toward an atmospheric color changes our perception of the object's sharpness and depth. The overall effect is similar to that of depth of field when the plane of focus is near. Thus, it is often useful to use these effects together. You'll find this example in the support files as `focus2.fla`. Let's see how it was constructed:

1. Press CTRL/CMD+N to create a new movie, and then click on the Size button in the Property Inspector to edit the movie properties. Set the frame rate to 20 fps.

2. Next, you need to create the object or character that you can use to demonstrate the idea of approaching the plane of focus. You should exercise some care in creating your character so that when the character's overall opacity is changed it doesn't show undesirable construction lines or artifacts. You can see an example of what *not* to do by opening the `focus2_poor_opacity.swf` animation from this book's website. Taking a little more care than you see in the poor-opacity example, we've created a simple UFO and named the corresponding Flash symbol `ufo` (pretty logical, huh?):

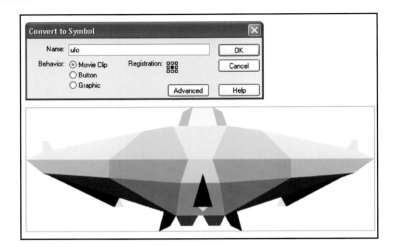

3. After you've designed the main character, you'll need to create an animation of that character showing a transition from a blurry state to a sharp state. Select Insert > New Symbol... (CTRL/CMD+F8) to create a new movie clip, and name it `ufo_blur`.

4. Within the `ufo_blur` movie clip, drag the `ufo` symbol from the Library (F11) onto the center of the stage. Give it an opacity of 15% by setting the Alpha value accordingly in the Property Inspector.

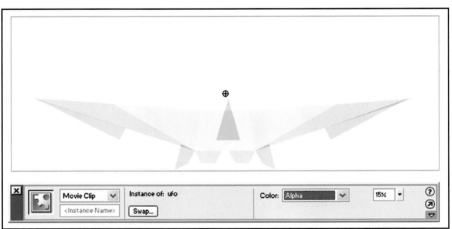

5.   Create seven new layers in the timeline window. Remember, you're still within the timeline of the `ufo_blur` movie clip. Click on the single frame that you created on the first layer when you dragged the `ufo` movie clip onto the stage, and then select Edit > Copy Frames (CTRL+ALT+C/CMD+OPT+C). Paste this frame to the seven new layers (CTRL+ALT+V/ CMD+OPT+V).

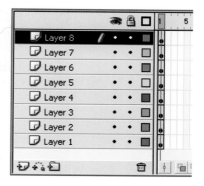

6.   Create a keyframe (Insert > Keyframe, or press F6) on frame 45 of each layer, and extend the animation to frame 60. Frame 45 is where the character will be sharp, or in focus, and it will remain in focus until the last frame. By clicking on the layer names, we've given them names that will be useful in the next step.

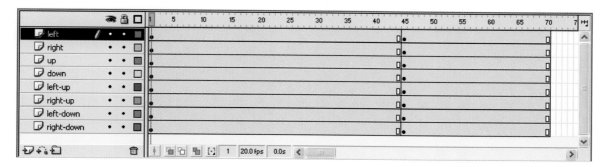

7.   On frame 1 of each layer, you need to offset the UFO in eight different directions. Start by clicking the first frame of the first layer. Then use the arrow keys to nudge it over a little to the left. Next, click the frame 1 of the right layer and nudge that UFO a little to the right. Nudge the UFOs on the other layers (from top to bottom) upward, downward, left-upward, right-upward, left-downward, and right-downward. Don't worry about being too precise—messing up a little probably won't hurt the overall effect. The completed blur effect should look something like this:

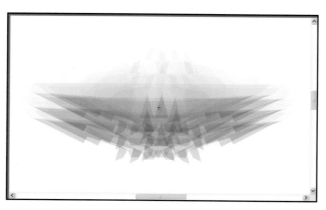

8. Click on frame 1 of each layer and then select Insert > Create Motion Tween (of course, you can also create the tween by selecting each frame and choosing Motion from the Tween option in the Property Inspector).

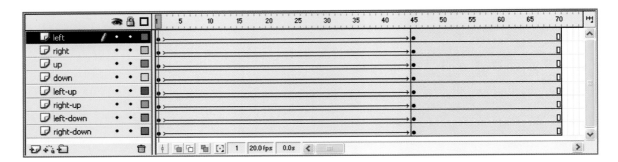

You should now have a fairly convincing transition (from fuzzy to clear) as you move from frame 1 to frame 45. So let's now put this effect into context. Return to the main timeline and drag a copy of the ufo_blur symbol that you just created from the Library onto the stage. Position the UFO in its initial position in the upper left of the stage, and scale it so that it is relatively small. You can also add a more suitable background at this point. Check out the Martian landscape we've used in focus2.fla.

9. Next, add a keyframe (F6) on frame 45 and move the UFO to the position it will be in when it is hovering in front of you. Scale the UFO so that it is much bigger than it was on the first frame.

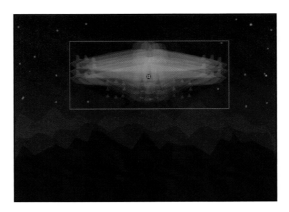

10. Add a keyframe on frame 55 and then another on frame 70. On frame 70, position the UFO slightly above the upper edge of the canvas.

11. Create a couple of motion tweens by selecting frames 1 and 55 and choosing Motion from the Tween option in the Property Inspector.

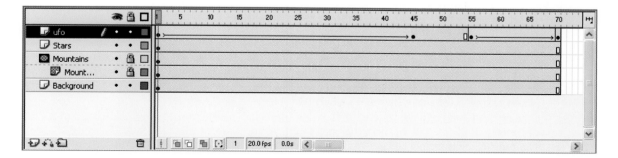

12. Finally, when you play the movie, the UFO will initially be fuzzy and then it will seem to sharpen as it approaches the plane of focus. This is essentially because you've synchronized the main timeline with the timeline of the ufo_blur movie clip. This movie clip becomes fully focused in frame 45, at which point it is also at the forefront of the main movie.

In this example, you've used eight copies of the ufo to simulate a blur effect. Because doing tweens in Flash can be computationally expensive, you could apply this same technique to fewer instances of the UFO. In the next example, you will be working with more than one object, and you'll accomplish the blur effect with only four duplicates per object in order to keep the movie fast.

Marble madness

In this example we'll again examine the concept of approaching the plane of focus, but this time we'll come at it from a programmatic angle and use ActionScript to create some neat pseudo-3D effects. The source file for this example is `focus3.fla`.

1. Select File > New to create a new movie, and then choose Modify > Document to edit the movie properties. Set the Dimensions to 400x300 and the Frame Rate to 30 fps.

2. In this movie, you will animate a series of balls. Your ball is made up of three circles. The first circle uses a gradient so that it looks like light is striking it from one side (if you haven't already done so, it's worth taking a look at Chapter 2, where we examine the use of shading and highlighting to create faux-3D effects). The second circle is a duplicate of the first that has been mirrored vertically. The third circle is simply a black circle that represents a shadow. Set the alpha on the second and third balls so that the background will show through. Save this graphic as a movie clip named `sphere`.

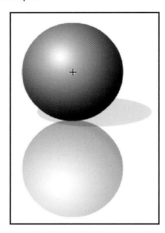

3. Now create another movie clip. On the main timeline, select Insert > New Symbol (CTRL/CMD+F8) and name the new symbol `blurred_sphere`.

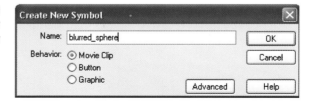

4. Drag an instance of `sphere` from the Library (F11) onto the stage of `blurred_sphere` and name the instance `s1`.

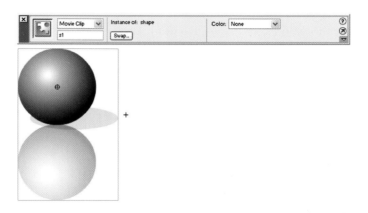

5. On frame 1 of the `blurred_sphere` movie clip, add the following ActionScript:

```
for (i=2; i<=4; i++) {
 s1.duplicateMovieClip("s"+i, i);
}
ar = s1._width/s1._height;
function set_blur(blur) {
 o = (blur/100)*4;
 for (i=1; i<=4; i++) {
   eval("s"+i)._x = o*Math.cos(i*1.57);
   eval("s"+i)._y = o*Math.sin(i*1.57);
   eval("s"+i)._alpha = 10+(50*(100-blur)/100);
   eval("s"+i)._width = ar*(20+(70*(100-blur)/100));
   eval("s"+i)._height = (20+(70*(100-blur)/100));
 }
}
```

The first line in this code segment creates three more copies of the sphere movie clip that will be named s2, s3, and s4. On the second line, we note the width to height ratio of the sphere movie clip in the variable ar. We then define the set_blur function, which performs three important operations on each of the four sphere instances. First, set_blur adjusts the position of each sphere so that as the blur variable increases, each instance moves farther from the center of the movie. Second, set_blur adjusts the _alpha so that as the blur variable increases, the _alpha decreases. And third, set_blur adjusts the _width and the _height so that the size is also dependent on the blur value.

6. Return to the main timeline. At this point, you need to create a surface that your spheres can glide across. The surface should be sharp in the foreground and indistinct in the distance. In the demonstration file, focus3.fla, we've created an image in Photoshop by performing a perspective transformation on a checkerboard pattern and then adding a linear gradient from the top of the image to the bottom, which we used as a selection mask for the Gaussian Blur filter. This has the effect of blurring the top of the image more than the bottom. We then applied a black-to-transparent gradient from the top of the image to the bottom to make the background seem darker.

7. Now drag an instance of the blurred_sphere symbol from the Library window onto the stage, and name this instance bs1.

8. On frame 1 of the top layer, add the following ActionScript:

```
t = 0;
n = 6;
for (i=2; i<=n; i++) {
 bs1.duplicateMovieClip("bs"+i, i);
}
this.onEnterFrame = function() {
 // increment the position along the path
 t += (.1745/4);
 // Keep values in the range 0 to 2*pi
```

```
if (t>6.283) {
  t -= 6.283;
}
// Iterate over all n (6) balls
for (i=1; i<=n; i++) {
  // Reference a particular ball bs1 .. m6
  bs = eval("bs"+i);
  // offset each ball by .785 radians or 45 degrees
  u = t+i*.785;
  // Calculate how much blur to apply based on position
  blur = Math.abs(Math.sin((u/2)-.785)*100);
  bs.set_blur(blur);
  // The width of the ellipse is 150*2 pixels
  bs._x = 150*Math.cos(u)+200;
  // The height of the ellipse is 70*2 pixels
  bs._y = 70*Math.sin(u)+150;
}
};
```

The position along the elliptical path is determined by the variable t, where t = 0 corresponds to the beginning of the path and t= 6.283 (or approximately 2 times π) corresponds to the point where the ball has come full circle. Thus, by changing how much we increment t, we can change the speed at which the balls travel. Within the onEnterFrame function, we use a second variable, u, which has an offset dependent on the index of the sphere. So, for example, m2 will arrive at the origin slightly after m1. In this way, we can increment a single variable t that can then be used to calculate the position of all of the spheres.

9. Test the movie. The final animation is swift and convincing. Spheres glide in an elliptical path in and out of focus. The shadows and reflections help establish the placement of the spheres on the floor, and the focus truly establishes the depth of each sphere in the scene.

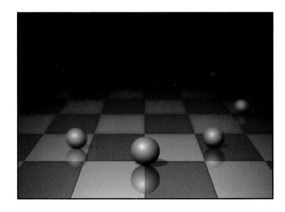

Text preloader

In this example, we use a variation of the programmatic technique we developed in the last example to animate the word LOADING, for use in a preloader. Preloaders are small animations that are placed at the very beginning of a Flash movie and typically animate until the movie is completely loaded. If you aren't already familiar with preloaders and how to check if a movie is completely loaded, you can refer to any solid introductory Flash text. Also, you'll find some highly creative examples of preloaders in *Flash MX Most Wanted: Effects and Movies* (friends of ED, ISBN:1-5959-224-7). To check out the finished version of this example, have a look at `focus4.fla`.

1. Press CTRL/CMD+N to create a new movie, and then set the document dimensions to 500x300 and the frame rate to 30 fps.

2. Use the Text Tool (T) to write the word LOADING in an attractive font. Select the LOADING text and then select Modify > Break Apart (CTRL/CMD+B) twice to convert the text into vector representations (once to break the word into individual characters, and then once again to break the letters down into vector graphics). Convert each character into a different movie clip by pressing F8. The symbol names are not important, but you do need to be able to control them from ActionScript, so the instance names are crucial. Use the Property Inspector (CTRL/CMD+F3) to name the letters in order: `m1b1`, `m2b1`, `m3b1`, `m4b1`, `m5b1`, `m6b1`, and `m7b1`.

3. In the previous example, you created a `set_blur` function that manipulated four copies of a sphere to make the sphere look fuzzy. Duplicating that code for each letter in the loading animation could be a lot of work, so you are going to move that functionality to the root movie. You can accomplish this by creating four copies of each letter. The three extra copies of letter `m1b1` will be called `m1b2`, `m1b3`, and `m1b4`. The naming convention is actually very important because it lets you iterate over each unique movie clip and each duplicated movie clip.

Add the following ActionScript code to frame 1:

```
t = 0;
// The number of characters
n = 7;
// The number of character copies
b = 4;
// Create three additional copies of each character
depth = 100;
for (i=1; i<=n; i++) {
 for (j=2; j<=b; j++) {
   eval("m"+i+"b1").duplicateMovieClip("m"+i+"b"+j, depth);
```

continues overleaf

```
        depth++;
  }
}
this.onEnterFrame = function() {
  // increment the position along the path
  t += .0582;
  // Keep values in the range 0 to 2*pi
  if (t>6.283) {
    t -= 6.283;
  }
  // Iterate over all n (7) characters
  for (i=1; i<=n; i++) {
    // offset each character by .2617 radians or 15 degrees
    u = (t+i*.2617);
    // v is used for scale as it corresponds to when u is
    // farthest from the viewer
    v = Math.abs(Math.cos(u/2));
    c = Math.cos(u);

    // dx, dy is the position of the character
    dx = 50*c+35;
    dy = 100*Math.sin(u)+150;
    // Iterate over each copy of a particular character
    for (j=1; j<=4; j++) {
      // Reference a particular character copy
      m = eval("m"+i+"b"+j);
      // We offset each copy of the character and adjust
      // the scale and alpha appropriately
      offset = (1-v)*4;
      m._yscale = c*100+100*v;
      m._xscale = 200*v;
      m._alpha = 10+90*v;
      m._x = dx+offset*Math.cos(j*1.57)+50*(n+1-i);
      m._y = dy+offset*Math.sin(j*1.57);
    }
  }
};
```

4. When you test this movie, CTRL/CMD+ENTER, you'll see that the letters really do seem to come forward from a fuzzy state to crisp clarity in this simple text effect.

Changing the plane of focus

In the examples of the previous section, you were essentially moving a single character toward the plane of focus. In this section, you will work with several characters and shift the plane of focus between them. You'll use bitmaps with prerendered blurs, but you could easily combine the techniques in this example with the blurring technique you used in the last example.

1. You'll find this example in the chapter's source files as `focus5.fla`. As usual, create a new movie by pressing CTRL/CMD+N. The first thing you must do here is import four source images. You can do this by selecting File > Import (CTRL/CMD+R) and then browsing to find your required images.

2. First, import the background images:

   `focus5_bg_clear.jpg` – The sharper of the two background images (below left)
   `focus5_bg_blurred.jpg` – The out-of-focus version of the background image (below right)

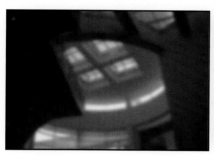 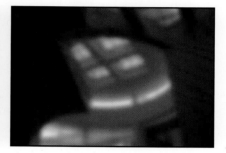

3. Next, import the foreground images:

   `focus5_ufo_clear.png` – The sharp version of the UFO (below left)
   `focus5_ufo_blurred.png` – The blurry version of the UFO (below right)

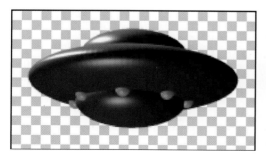 

It's worth noting at this point that the sharper background image isn't nearly as sharp as the sharper foreground image. In this example, you will only focus on the foreground objects. Thus, the background will never *really* be completely in focus.

4. Convert each image to a movie clip (F8) and name them `bg_sharp`, `bg_blurry`, `ufo_sharp`, and `ufo_blurry`, respectively.

5. Select Insert > New Symbol... (CTRL/CMD+F8) and create a new movie clip named `background`.

6. In the `background` movie clip, create an additional layer and then select the bottom layer. Drag the `bg_sharp` image from the Library window (F11) onto the stage. Name this instance `sharp` in the Property Inspector.

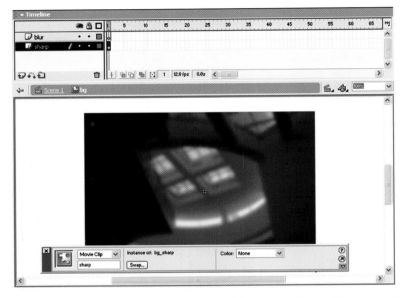

7. Select the top layer and drag the `bg_blur` symbol from the Library (F11) onto the stage. Name this instance `blur` in the Property Inspector. Make sure that both the `sharp` and `blur` movie clips are centered on the stage. If they aren't in the exact same position, there will be an unnatural shift when the effect occurs.

8. Now go back to the main timeline, select Insert > New Symbol..., and name the symbol `ufo`.

9. In the `ufo` movie clip, create an additional layer and then select the bottom layer. Drag the `ufo_sharp` image from the Library onto the stage and give it an instance name of `sharp`.

10. Now drag the `ufo_blur` symbol from the Library onto the top layer and name it `blur`. Again, remember to center both the `sharp` and `blur` movie clips on the stage.

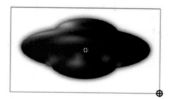

11. Return to the main timeline and drag one instance of the `bg` movie clip to the scene and three instances of the `ufo` movie clip to the scene from the Library window (Window > Library). Name the instances of these movies `background`, `ufo1`, `ufo2`, and `ufo3`.

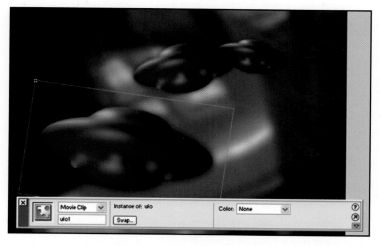

12. The primary motivation in this effect is making the characters closer to the plane of focus sharp and those farther away from this plane less sharp. You will accomplish this with some ActionScript. On the main timeline, select frame 1 of the first layer. Then open the Actions panel (Window > Actions or F9) and insert the following code:

```
function set_depth(movie, movie_depth, radius, current_depth) {
  // x is the distance between the current depth and this object's
  depth.
   x = current_depth-movie_depth;
   blur_amount = Math.min(100, Math.max(0, Math.abs((-
  100/radius)*x), 100));
   if (x<=0) {
     sharp_amount = (100/(.5*radius))*x+150/.5;
```

continues overleaf **117**

```
    } else if (x>=0) {
      sharp_amount = (-100/(.5*radius))*x+150/.5;
    }
    sharp_amount = Math.min(Math.max(0, sharp_amount), 100);
    movie.blur._alpha = blur_amount;
    movie.sharp._alpha = sharp_amount;
  }
```

Here, `blur_amount` decreases as x (the distance between the current depth and the depth of the object) tends toward 0. When x is equal to `radius`, it achieves its maximum value of 100. The `sharp_amount` has a value of 100 when x is less than `radius` and tends toward 0 as you leave the radius. It is exactly 0 when x=1.5*radius. In this way, the `sharp` and `blur` movie clips make their transitions in two phases: `blur` fades in as x changes from 0 to radius, and `sharp` fades out as x changes from `radius` to 1.5*radius.

If you had simply faded `blur` in as you faded `sharp` out, the `_alpha` value of each movie would be 50% at the midpoint of the transition and you would be able to see through them. When two objects at 50% opacity overlap, you might think that together they will be completely opaque. Color is actually computed according to this formula:

```
color = background*(1-alpha) + foreground*alpha
```

So, if the background color is black (0), the foreground color is white (1), and alpha is 50%, then `0+1*0.5 = 0.5`, or 50% white, which is what you would expect. If you apply this operation again with another white layer at 50% opacity, you find `0.5*0.5+1*0.5=0.75`, or 75% white and not 100% white.

If the background had been a solid color, perhaps 75% opacity would be good enough, but it would look odd if you could see the background through the UFO in this particular example.

13. You'll continue your script with the `evaluate_depth` function:

```
function evaluate_depth() {
 current_depth = depth_scroll.getScrollPosition();
 set_depth(ufo1, 0, 30, current_depth);
 set_depth(ufo2, 50, 30, current_depth);
 set_depth(ufo3, 100, 30, current_depth);
 set_depth(bg, 100, 50, current_depth);
}
```

What you are doing here is making the blur instance of each character have less alpha value as you approach that character. The sharp instance of each character has more alpha value as you approach it. We have written the `set_depth` function in such a way that the sharp transition and the blur transition do not overlap. Instead, it happens in stages. First we change the sharp symbol and then we change the blur symbol. If we changed the alpha value of the sharp and blur symbols at the same time, you would be able to see through them as they changed.

If you weren't interested in making this example interactive, you could do this example manually on the timeline using a transition as described to get the same effect.

In the `evaluate_depth()` function, each character is assigned a different depth. An object at depth `0` is closest to the observer, and an object at depth `100` is farthest. Each time `set_depth()` is called with a different current depth, the alpha values of the blur and sharp instances in the corresponding movie are adjusted.

14. You've completed the core functionality of this piece, but nothing will happen if you run the movie at this point, because there is no way to change the current depth. You need to add some mechanism to play with the depth values. Let's add a ScrollBar component to the movie. When you drag the ScrollBar from the Components panel (Window > Components or CTRL/CMD+F7) onto the stage, it will automatically try to snap to the nearest movie. In this particular case, such behavior is undesirable. To make working with the ScrollBar easier, create a new layer and lock the other layers before you drag the ScrollBar onto the stage. Once it's on the stage, set the instance name to `depth_scroll` and set the Horizontal attribute to `true` in the Property Inspector.

15. Now you need to add the final few lines of code to your chunk of ActionScript that sets the `ChangeHandler` of your `depth_scroll` ScrollBar to your `evaluate_depth` function defined earlier. This will give you complete control of the focus of your UFO movie:

```
depth_scroll.setScrollProperties(5, 0, 100);
depth_scroll.setChangeHandler("evaluate_depth");
evaluate_depth();
```

16. Finally, test the movie (CTRL/CMD+ENTER) and use the ScrollBar to alter the plane of focus.

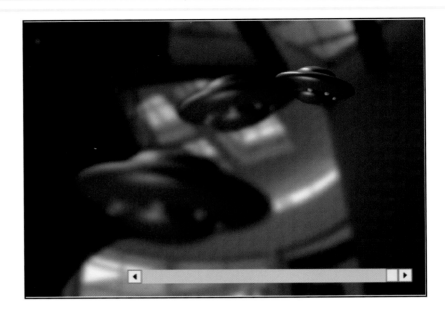

Summary

The examples in this chapter demonstrated how powerful focus and depth of field can be as three-dimensional cues in a scene. In the first section, you designed a magnifying lens that illustrated how focus can be used to pull an image forward. You used a prerendered Gaussian Blur to simulate a lack of focus.

In the second section, we described how to move an object toward the plane of focus. We presented a couple of different techniques: a *manual* approach and a *programmatic* version. With the manual approach, you animated by hand a UFO that emerges from distance and then disappears into the sky. You then used two variations of the programmatic approach to guide spheres in an elliptical path on a checkerboard and make text dance in an elegant preloading animation. In these examples, we showed how to simulate a blur in Flash using multiple instances of a movie clip.

In the final section you explored some more advanced techniques and learned how the plane of focus itself can be changed and used to travel through a scene along the imaginary z-axis.

This chapter emphasized how focus, opacity, and blurring techniques can be used together to create a variety of effects that establish depth and help move an animated element to and from a plane of focus. These techniques are powerful tools that help add dimensionality and realism to a scene.

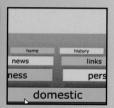

Parallax Scrolling

There is a wonderful Halloween episode of *The Simpsons* that parodies a classic *Twilight Zone* episode in which a young girl passes through a wall and is trapped in the fourth dimension. In the *The Simpsons* variant (episode 706, "Treehouse of Horror VI," for all you *The Simpsons* fans), Homer stumbles into a dimensional portal and ends up in a reality that has *three* dimensions (amusingly rendered with 3D software by Pacific Data Images). His two-dimensional family and friends are shocked to discover the existence of such a place, while Homer is surprised to discover how his body bulges out in front and behind him. What makes this idea even more amusing is the fact that we as an audience never really thought of Homer's Springfield as a two-dimensional place and consequently never thought that Springfield inhabitants were conscious of being two-dimensional. Of course, in the back of our minds we knew that what we were watching on our television screens consisted of two-dimensional drawings, but the animators always succeeded in making those drawings *seem* three-dimensional.

One technique used frequently in most 2D animation to help simulate a three-dimensional feeling is **parallax scrolling**, where different planes of graphics and/or animation scroll at different rates depending on their relation (or supposed relation) to the viewer and camera, creating an illusion of depth as the nearer planes scroll at a faster rate than the farther planes.

To better understand what parallax scrolling is, you can first think of it in terms of your own three-dimensional reality. Imagine you're looking straight down on three different-colored balls. As you watch, each ball moves in the same direction 50 meters. From your vantage point high above, each ball appears to move the same distance:

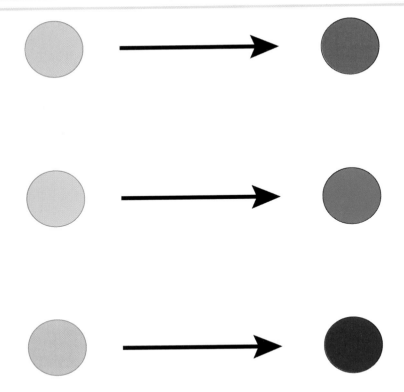

Now let's take the same situation and reposition your vantage point. Imagine you are on the ground looking at the three balls as each moves that same distance of 50 meters. Because of your new vantage point and the depth of the balls, the ball that is farthest from you *appears* to be moving less of a distance, while the ball that is nearest to you seems to move the most distance (each ball would be scaled differently as well, which is a related concept):

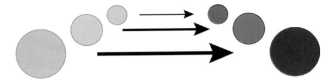

From this you can conclude that the farther an object is away from the viewer, the less it will appear to be moving *in relation* to objects closer to the viewer.

Another classic example you should be familiar with from the world around you is the movement of the landscape as you view it from a moving vehicle. If there are mountains in the distance, they will appear almost stationary while the roadside trees fly by, even though you are moving the same rate past these two sets of stationary objects. So how would you re-create this 3D effect on a 2D screen? Parallax scrolling is the answer.

Scrolling in animation: Wyvern's Claw

In this first example, we'll step through the technique of manually tweening your animation planes to simulate depth. The main idea of this method, and with parallax scrolling in general, is that you separate your animation into distinct planes (typically housed in movie clips) that you tween at separate rates. Each plane should consist of whatever elements exist at that particular depth in your animated world. For this exercise, the drawings have all been completed for you (they are available for download along with the rest of this book's examples from www.friendsofed.com), so you can concentrate on the camera movement and how you can use parallax scrolling to give your animated world more dimension.

What you will be creating are the opening shots for an episodic animation entitled *Wyvern's Claw*, which is a Philip Marlowe/Sam Spade–type film-noir detective story transplanted to a fantasy setting. Imagine this setup: the camera is fixed on the nighttime sky as a voiceover begins ("*There are a million stories in the naked city...*"—you get the general idea). Slowly, the camera tilts and pans down on the town where our tale takes place. Cut to a typical street in the town as the camera is dollied forward, down the street. The final establishing shot of the opening voiceover will be of the inn where our hero resides, which we'll slowly move toward before cutting to the interior of his room.

Look to the storyboard below to get a better idea of our task, and then, as a teaser, open up `WyvernsClaw_end.swf` to see the completed project:

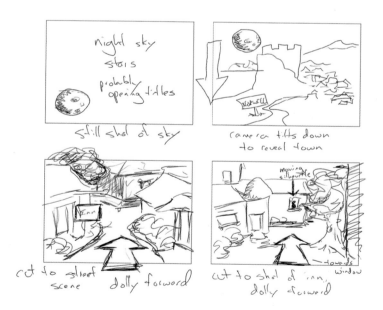

Often with animations, you will see scrolling that is parallel to the viewing plane (think of the repeating backgrounds in a Hanna-Barbera cartoon such as *Scooby Doo* or *The Flintstones*). This is pretty easy to achieve, and the next two examples explore this. For manual tweening, though, you can be a bit more adventurous. The only thing you need to remember is that objects farther from the camera will move less than objects nearer to the camera.

Shot 1: Over town

1. Open the file `WyvernsClaw_start.fla`. This file contains all of the drawings for this animation. The timeline has a single top-level folder named scene 1 – through town. Inside this folder are three additional folders for each shot in the scene: over town, down street, and toward inn. Expand each of these folders to see the layer structure for each shot in the scene (and note that the Library contains a similar structure for all the featured symbols). The initial graphics have been placed in their appropriate layers, all ready for you to start tweening.

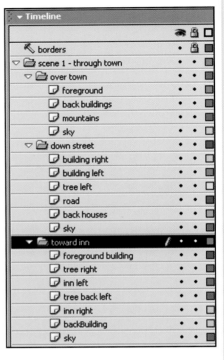

2. Expand the over town folder and look at frame 1. This is actually the *end* position of each of your planes for the first shot. We usually lay out our shots by placing the clips where we want them to end up when the "camera" stops moving rather than where they are at the start of the shot (especially here, since all of the elements will be offstage). Since this is how you want the shot to end, you need to add an ending keyframe for each layer. Select frame 208 in all four over town layers (foreground, back buildings, mountains, and sky). Now press F6 or use the menu command Insert > Keyframe.

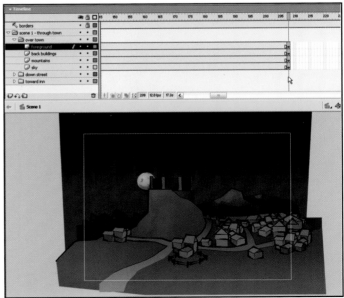

3. Return to frame 1 and alter the properties of the movie clips in the four layers using the following values. Use the Property Inspector and the Info and Transform panels for the most accuracy, but play with the values if you wish to tweak (you'll need to deselect the Constrain option in the Transform panel in order to scale the clips disproportionately, which we do for a slightly more organic effect):

Movie Clip	_xscale	_yscale	_x	_y
foreground	46.7%	45.4%	-17.1	225.2
back buildings	46.7%	45.4%	270.6	274.3
mountains	48.3%	47.0%	-15.4	194.6
sky	no change	no change	-67.6	-343.1

These values were all determined by fervent tweaking until we saw the desired effect. Each project will have different values, so just work to find what's right for you. You will notice, though, that the planes that are farthest from the viewer move the least. The sky (which doesn't scale at all) moves only a small distance, as do the mountains, whereas the foreground graphic scales and moves more than any of the others.

Note that you must scale the movie clips first before you adjust their positions, since scaling the clips repositions them on the stage.

4. To add to the effect, you're going to tween the brightness of your two nearest foreground planes, so that they may "come into the light." Select the foreground movie clip at frame 1 and set its brightness value in the Property Inspector to -75% (select Brightness from the Color drop-down menu, and then move the corresponding slider down to -75). Next, select the back buildings clip at frame 1 and set its brightness value to -66%.

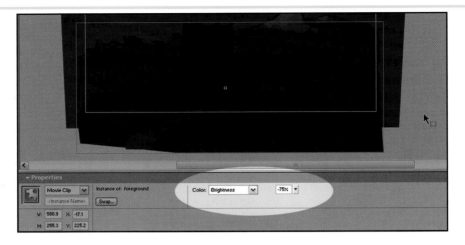

5. So you can check what you currently have, select all four layers at frame 1. You should see animation options appear in the Property Inspector. Select Motion from the Tween drop-down menu, and then test your movie to see where you are. You have a nice zoom-in movement toward the town. The sky and mountains barely move, while the foreground moves and scales quite a bit.

6. Now you're going to add a bit of camera tilt at the start, so that the camera is initially focused on an empty sky. To do this, you first need to get rid of the motion tween you added in the last step by using Undo (CTRL+Z). Alternatively, so you may see how easy it is to remove a tween, select frame 1 in all four layers and change the Tween option in the Property Inspector to None.

7. Add a new keyframe in each layer at frame 110 by pressing F6 (note that if you had not removed the tween in the previous step, the values in this new keyframe would be off). Now head back to frame 1 and change the properties of each graphic using the following values:

Movie Clip	_y	Brightness
foreground	517.1	-100%
back buildings	570.1	-100%
mountains	481.9	—
sky	-73.8	—

As you can see, you are only changing the _y value as the camera tilts (plus the Brightness to affect the foreground and back buildings).

8. Create motion tweens at frame 1 and at frame 110 for all four layers by first selecting the frames and then selecting the Motion option in the Tween drop-down of the Property Inspector (you can also right-click/CMD-click the layers and select Create Motion Tween from the Insert menu).

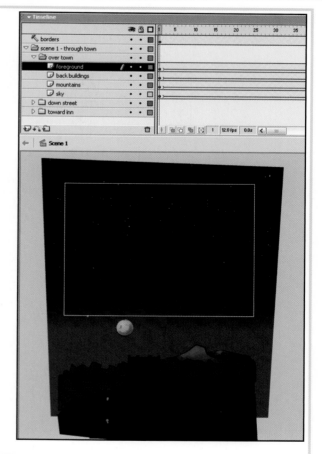

9. Now select frame 79 in all four layers and create a new keyframe in each. Adjust the values of each layer's movie clip as follows:

Movie Clip	_y	Brightness
foreground	297.1	-100%
back buildings	350.1	-100%
mountains	261.9	—
sky	-293.8	—

10. You will keep the camera still at the start of your shot. To do that, drag the keyframes in frame 1 for all four layers to frame 28. That should leave the first 27 frames blank. Now copy the `sky` movie clip at frame 28, and use Edit > Paste in Place (CTRL/CMD+SHIFT+V) at frame 1 of the `sky` layer. Test your movie now to see the results.

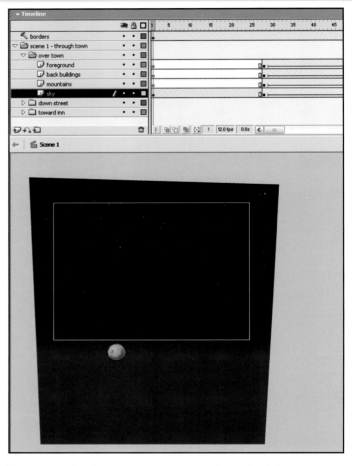

11. The final step to finish this shot is to add some easing to your camera moves to make things seem less mechanical. Easing creates acceleration and deceleration in your animation. Easing in values will cause clips to accelerate through a tween, whereas easing out values will cause clips to slow down during a tween.

Set the easing values for each keyframe by selecting it and then adjusting the Ease value in the Property Inspector to the following:

- Frame 28 (all layers) – Ease: -10 (In)
- Frame 79 (all layers) – Ease: 60 (Out)
- Frame 110 (all layers) – Ease: -40 (In)

Not bad for a first shot!

Shot 2: Down street

The next shot of our camera moving forward down a street will only require two keyframes at the start and end of the sequence.

1. Close the over town folder and open the down street folder to see the new layers. Go to frame 209, which is the first frame of the sequence, to see how the shot will start out. Then go to frame 300 (the last frame) of each layer in this folder and create a new keyframe (F6). You don't have to create a keyframe for the sky layer, as you will not be tweening it in this shot and it will remain static.

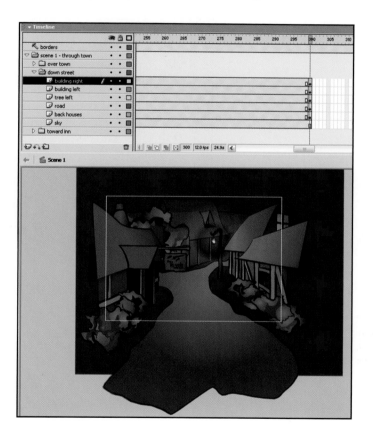

2. Set the values for the properties of the movie clips in frame 300 to the following:

Movie Clip	_xscale	_yscale	_x	_y
building right	102.0%	88.2%	172.3	6.4
building left	102.3%	92.3%	-226.8	3.0
tree left	80.4%	80.4%	-72.9	25.8
road	91.0%	72.5%	-91.9	245.3
back houses	65.2%	65.2%	-8.4	16.4

3. You move the buildings at the right and left foreground more of a distance off the stage since they are nearest to the viewing plane. The back buildings, being central in the viewing plane, hardly move at all to the right or left. We've also added some scale distortion by not keeping the _xscale and _yscale values proportionate on a movie clip to aid in the illusion of having the side buildings in the viewer's peripheral vision.

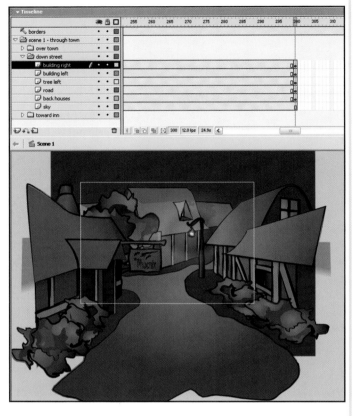

4. Select the five keyframes at frame 209 (all excluding the sky layer) and create a motion tween in the Property Inspector. Test your movie to see the results.

Shot 3: Toward inn

The final shot moves the camera around a building and toward the inn, which houses the hero of our piece. Keep an eye on how the building in the foreground right moves more than any other movie clip on the stage, while the buildings behind the inn remain fairly still. This all goes to aid in the illusion of depth for our 2D drawings.

1. Close the down street folder and open the toward inn folder in the timeline layers. Again, you will have two keyframes for each layer, excluding the sky layer, which will remain static. Go to frame 352 for all layers in the toward inn folder (except sky) and create a new keyframe in each (F6).

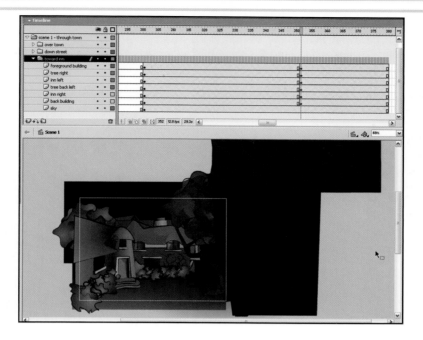

2. The movie clips are currently set for the ending of the shot, so you need to adjust the first keyframes' values. Go to frame 301 and set each movie clip's properties to the following:

Movie Clip	_xscale	_yscale	_x	_y	Brightness
foreground building	41.9%	41.9%	277.4	-61.0 0%	(None)
tree right	47.9%	47.9%	83.9	24.1	13%
inn left	47.9%	47.9%	-23.3	153.1	-40%
tree back left	47.9%	47.9%	-81.8	84.1	-70%
inn right	47.9%	47.9%	120.0 1	56.6	-55%
back building	47.9%	47.9%	65.8	116.3	-80%

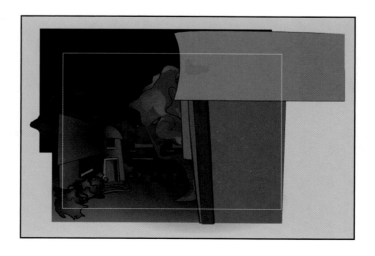

3. Select the same five layers at frame 301 (excluding sky) and create a motion tween in the Property Inspector. Set the Ease value for these tweens to 30 (ease out). Now test your movie to see the final result.

In this demonstration, you have successfully used manual tweening of multiple animation planes to simulate depth, plus you've made a pretty cool animation in the process!

Next, we will look at how we can incorporate parallax scrolling into Flash games to enhance the pseudo-3D feel.

Scrolling in games: Mars Patrol

When we were first considering content for a chapter on parallax scrolling, the example we thought of right away was the 1980s arcade hit *Moon Patrol*. This game featured a multilevel scrolling background as the moon buggy remained fairly static in the foreground, giving a nice 3D feeling of the vehicle moving over a lunar landscape. We thought we could create a similar setup here—though transplanted to the Red Planet this time.

This tutorial will focus on explaining the ActionScript that is necessary to move the background landscape planes across the screen. You will constantly assess locations of the planes as they move so that you may remove clips once they leave the left side of the stage (they will be moving left, simulating movement of your vehicle to the right), and then attach new clips when needed off the right side of the stage, thus creating a seamless landscape scroll. As you code, keep in mind that for the effect to work, you need to move the landscape planes at different rates depending on their relation to the foreground—more specifically, the planes farthest away from the viewer will move the least.

The file `marsPatrol_start.fla` has already been set up for you with all of the graphics prepared in its Library, though you will be attaching all of the clips and adding the necessary code for the scrolling effect. Note, however, that the finished project will *not* be a complete game, but merely the framework to build upon. Take a look at `marsPatrol_end.swf` to see how far we're going to take this project. Pay particular attention to the different levels of scrolling mountains (also, see what happens when you press the left, right, and up cursor keys).

Setting the stage

1. On the main timeline of the file `marsPatrol_start.fla`, create a new layer folder below the border guide layer (the border layer is there so you can see the stage borders in the authoring environment). Name the new layer folder graphics.

2. Create three new layers and name them, from top to bottom, rover, ground, and sky. Drag all three folders into the graphics folder you created in step 1.

3. Open up the Library (CTRL/CMD+L or F11) and find the `sky` movie clip in the `level1 assets` folder. Drag the movie clip onto the stage in the `sky` layer and position it at x: `-11.7`, y: `-10.7` using either the Info panel or the Property Inspector. Look at all that Martian dust!

 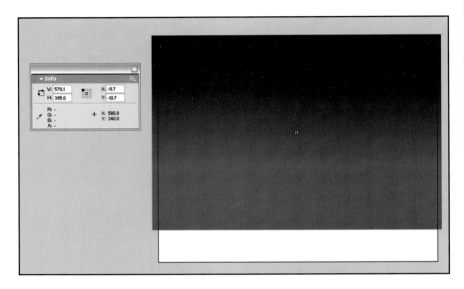

4. Now find the `ground` movie clip in the `level 1 assets` folder in the Library. Drag two instances of this clip onto the stage in the `ground` layer and name them (using the <Instance Name> field in the Property Inspector) `groundA` and `groundB`, respectively. Still using the Property Inspector, position them at (groundA) x: `-331.8`, y: `352.5` and (groundB) x: `279.0`, y: `352.5`. This should line the two identical ground instances right up against each other.

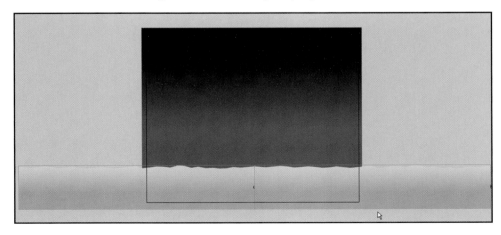

5. In a moment we'll show you how to move both instances to the left by a few pixels each frame using ActionScript. As soon as one instance completely moves off the left side of the stage, it will reposition itself directly to the right of the other ground clip, almost like a game of leapfrog. This

will ensure that the ground continues scrolling seamlessly throughout the game, and it is a common technique for creating seamless scrolling backgrounds. Note that to make this work (as with a lot of seamless backgrounds), the left and right side of the ground movie clip are at the same height, so when two clips are set next to each other, you are unable to tell where the break is.

6. Finally, drag a `rover` movie clip instance from the rover assets folder in the Library onto the stage in the rover layer. Using the Info panel or Property Inspector, position the `rover` instance at x: `213.7`, y: `275.6`. Name this instance `rover` so that you may reference it later in your code.

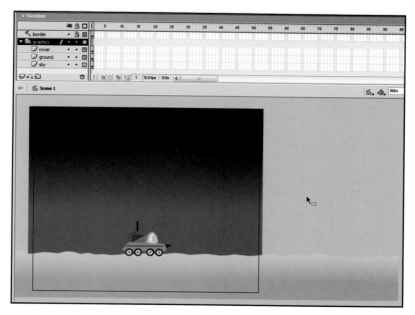

Test your movie to see what you have set up, though right now there's not much to look at. We've already preprogrammed the bouncing of the wheels (though they don't as yet rotate) with the following code, which you can find inside the `wheel` instance in the Library:

```
this.onEnterFrame = function() {
    this._rotation += this._parent.wheelRotSpeed*this._parent.speed;
    this._y = Math.random()*4 - 2;
};
```

Since the wheels would continue moving throughout the entire game, we thought taking care of it using an `onEnterFrame` for each wheel would be the best way to go about it. As you can see, every frame the wheels will rotate a little based on two variables: the constant value of the rover's `wheelRotSpeed` variable and the changing value of the rover's `speed` variable. You will set both of these variables later in this tutorial. The `_y` position of each wheel is also set generating a random number between −2 and 2.

You'll see the wheels working in just a few steps. First, let's work on making the ground move beneath the rover to get the game rolling (sorry about the pun!).

Hitting the ground running

1. Create a new layer folder above the graphics folder on the main timeline and name it code. Create a new layer named landscape code and drag this new layer into the code folder.

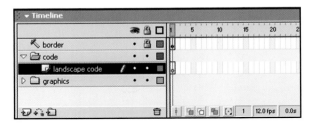

2. With the landscape code layer's first frame selected, type the following ActionScript into the Actions panel (F9):

```
// rate each plane moves at
scrollSpeeds = {};
scrollSpeeds.ground = 10;
```

Here we have created an object called scrollSpeeds that will hold the rate that each landscape plane will move at. Each plane will be represented by a separate property of the scrollSpeeds object. This is just a nice way to contain all of the movement rates in one package, instead of having individual variables for each plane. As a side note, the following lines will yield identical results to those preceding:

```
scrollSpeeds = new Object();
scrollSpeeds.ground = 10;

scrollSpeeds = {ground:10};
```

3. Type the following lines after the previous object declaration:

```
// moves and swaps out ground clips
moveGround = function() {
  this._x -= scrollSpeeds.ground;
  // if clip is off stage left...
  if (this._x <= -5) {
    // places clip off stage right
    this._x += (this._width*2);
  }
};
groundA.onEnterFrame = groundB.onEnterFrame = moveGround;
```

This covers all of the movement for your ground plane (with a few tweaks you'll add in a moment). moveGround is a function that moves a movie clip this (which is whatever movie clip calls the function) a little to the left each time it is called. It then checks to see if the clip has gone off the left of the stage. If so, the clip is moved to the right by twice its _width, which should place it directly to the right of the next ground plane (since both instances are the same width). The final line sets the onEnterFrame event handler for both ground clips to call the moveGround function each frame.

Test your movie now to see the results. Not bad! But, as you will notice, you have a small gap between the two clips—you'll fix that next.

4. Add the following lines of code *before* the moveGround function:

    ```
    // x pixel overlap for each clip in plane
    groundA.xOffset = groundB.xOffset = 2;
    ```

    This adds a new property to both ground clips with a value of 2. You will use this as a pixel overlap buffer to ensure that the clip always meets up with (or possibly overlaps) the other, making a seamless landscape.

5. Modify the moveGround function by adding the code in bold below:

    ```
    moveGround = function() {
      this._x -= scrollSpeeds.ground;
      // if clip is off stage left...
      if (this._x <= -5) {
        // places clip off stage right
        this._x += (this._width*2) - this.xOffset;
      }
    };
    ```

    Notice that you can also reference the xOffset value using this since you set it as a property of the movie clip. Test your movie again to see that the gap has been fixed.

This method of *leapfrogging* the clips is an effective way to seamlessly scroll a background. Perhaps it's not ideal for a game situation (or at least *this* game), since the ground plane will need to display different characteristics at different stages, such as craters to jump over, but it serves our purpose as a simple demonstration of scrolling. We will explore another, perhaps more useful, form of attaching and removing scrolling clips in the next section.

Scrolling mesas

The next step is to add the second landscape plane to your stage, the mesas. You will do this completely dynamically using an empty movie clip, so you will only see the completed effect in the published file. The movie clip itself will hold all of the code to move the mesas, so it makes sense to place all of the graphics for that plane inside that movie clip. This technique will allow you to add multiple planes to your game with the confidence that each plane will act independently of all other planes, making things more modular and easier to alter and update.

1. Use the menu command Insert > New Symbol… (CTRL/CMD+F8) to create a new movie clip symbol named mesas. Once you click OK in the dialog box to create the symbol, you will be taken to symbol editing mode for the new symbol.

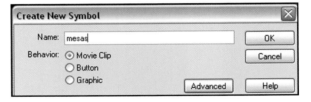

Go ahead and exit this mode and return to the main timeline by clicking the Scene 1 button at the bottom left of the timeline. With your Library open, drag the new mesas symbol into the level 1 assets folder.

2. Create a new layer on the main timeline within the graphics folder between the sky and ground layers. Name this new layer mesas.

3. Drag an instance of the empty mesas movie clip from your Library onto your stage in the mesas layer that you just created. Place it at x: 0, y: 392.5, using the Info panel or Property Inspector and name the instance mesas. This will place the movie clip, which is pretty small to begin with (being empty), underneath the ground plane. Don't worry, you haven't lost it!

In the upcoming code, you will attach the individual mesa movie clips to the empty clip you just placed on the stage. Keeping these inside a clip allows for a nice container for both the code and the graphics, as you will see.

4.   Go to frame 1 of the landscape code layer and open your Actions panel. Add the following lines to your previous code (new lines are shown in bold):

```
// rate each plane moves at
scrollSpeeds = {};
scrollSpeeds.ground = 10;
scrollSpeeds.mesas = 2;

// x pixel overlap for each clip in plane
groundA.xOffset = groundB.xOffset = 2;
mesas.xOffset = 30;
```

Here you are simply adding values for the movement of the mesas in the same way you added them for the ground planes. However, you will create a different method for controlling the mesas' (and eventually the mountains') movement.

5.   Add the following function after the moveGround function you entered earlier:

```
// adds initial landscape planes
makeLandscape = function() {
  // array to hold clip references
  this.mcs = [];
  this.mcs.push(this.attachMovie(this._name +
  ➥Math.floor(Math.random()*3), this._name + "0", 0));
  this.mcs.push(this.attachMovie(this._name +
  ➥Math.floor(Math.random()*3), this._name + "1", 1));
  this.mcs[0]._x = -this.xOffset;
  this.mcs[1]._x = this.mcs[1]._width - this.xOffset*2;
  this.onEnterFrame = moveLandscape;
};
```

This function is more complex than moveGround, but it sets up quite a bit as well. In this function, you first create a new array named mcs in which you will store references to the movie clips you will add to the stage. The next two lines attach two random mesa movie clips. You see, the three mesa symbols in the Library are exported as mesas0, mesas1, and mesas2—you can verify this by right-clicking (or CMD-clicking on a Mac) any of these symbols in the Library and selecting Linkage…. So, finding a random integer between 0 and 2, inclusive (which is accomplished with Math.floor(Math.random()*3)), and tacking that onto the end of the name of this particular holder movie clip (which you named mesas back in step 3) will return the identifier of one of the three mesa symbols in the Library. In addition to attaching the clips, you also push references to these new clips into the mcs array at the same time.

On the next two lines of the function, you set each clip's _x position based on the clip's _width and the xOffset value. The final line of the function sets the movie clip's onEnterFrame handler to equal a new function that you will write in a moment, although the purpose of the function, named `moveLandscape`, should be obvious.

Now how do you apply this function to your empty `mesas` movie clip that you placed on stage? Read on!

6. Add the following line of code after the `makeLandscape` function:

```
makeLandscape.apply(mesas);
```

Pretty easy, huh? What `apply` does in this context is run the function as if it was called by the specified movie clip. That means that every time `this` is used inside the function, it will be referring to the movie clip `mesas`. It's a pretty handy feature that allows you to write a single generic function and then apply it to numerous movie clips.

Test your movie now to see the mesa graphics added to the stage. Now all you need to do is get them moving.

Add the following function *before* the `makeLandscape` function that you just completed:

```
// moves and attaches/removes other landscape planes
moveLandscape = function() {
    // should always be 2 clips on stage
    for (var i in this.mcs) {
        this.mcs[i]._x -= scrollSpeeds[this._name];
        // if clip is off the left of stage, remove it
        // and add another off stage right
        if (this.mcs[i]._x < -this.mcs[i]._width) {
            // stores depth to place next clip at
            var depth = this.mcs[i].getDepth();
            this.mcs[i].removeMovieClip();
            // removes clip reference from array
            this.mcs.splice(i, 1);
```

```
            var newClip = this.attachMovie(this._name +
➥Math.floor(Math.random()*3), this._name + depth, depth);
            // stores clip reference
            this.mcs.push(newClip);
            // places clip off stage right
            newClip._x = this.mcs[0]._x + this.mcs[0]._width - this.xOffset;
        }
    }
};
```

So what does this function do exactly? Well, it loops through all movie clips that are stored in the mcs array and moves them slightly to the left each frame, based on the scrollSpeeds variable. The way you grab this variable is by using the movie clip's name to find the property in scrollSpeeds. So for the holder movie clip mesas, the following three lines are equivalent:

```
scrollSpeeds[this._name]
```

```
scrollSpeeds["mesas"]
```

```
scrollSpeeds.mesas
```

Accessing the property in the way you have, you can use this moveLandscape function for your mountain clips as well.

Once you have moved a mesa movie clip inside the holder clip, you check to see if it has gone off the left side of the stage. If it has, you first store that clip's depth, and then remove the clip from the stage, as well as its reference in the mcs array. Next, you attach another mesa symbol using the stored depth value, store the new clip's reference, and then place the new clip off the right of the stage, ready to be scrolled on.

Test your movie now to see the mesas moving and the parallax scrolling really adding to the depth of the animation.

Moving mountains

The process for adding and moving the mountain clips is the exact same as for adding and moving the mesa clips, so we'll cruise through this next section.

1. Create a new symbol (CTRL/CMD+F8) named `mountains`. Exit the editing mode for the symbol and return to the main timeline, but in the Library, drag the newly created symbol into the level 1 assets folder.

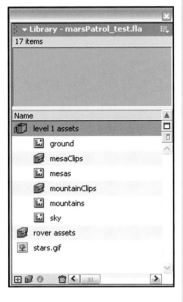

2. Create a new layer in the graphics folder on the main timeline. Place this new layer between the sky and mesas layers and name it mountains.

3. Drag a `mountains` instance from your Library and place it in the mountains layer. Name the instance `mountains` and place it at x: 0, y: 377.3.

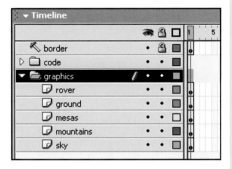

4. Add the following three bolded lines of code to the landscape code layer:

```
// rate each plane moves at
scrollSpeeds = {};
scrollSpeeds.ground = 10;
scrollSpeeds.mesas = 2;
scrollSpeeds.mountains = .5;
```

```
// x pixel overlap for each clip in plane
groundA.xOffset = groundB.xOffset = 2;
mesas.xOffset = 30;
mountains.xOffset = 250;

/*
CODE REMAINS UNCHANGED FOR moveGround, moveLandscape, and makeLandscape
functions
*/

makeLandscape.apply(mesas);
makeLandscape.apply(mountains);
```

It's pretty easy to add further planes, isn't it? That's what you get for modular programming! Test your movie now to see the results. Notice that the stars in the sky don't move at all since they are so far away that their movement is negligible to the viewer. The mountains move at a fairly slow rate compared to the mesas in front of them, and the ground plane streams by at the fastest rate since it is the nearest to the viewer. All these different scroll rates (as set in scrollSpeeds) control this effect, so play around with the values to see how they alter the animation.

Patrol's controls

Now that you have your landscape moving, you need to take care of your user's sprite, which should be interactively included in the scrolling effect. First, you will add some code that will allow the rover to respond to keyboard input.

1.   In the code folder on the main timeline, create a new layer below the landscape code layer and name it rover code.

2. Select frame 1 of the rover code layer and type the following into the Actions panel:

```
// handles all keyboard input to control rover
rover.checkKeys = function() {
    // can't change direction in mid-air!
    if (!this.jumping) {
      if (Key.isDown(Key.RIGHT)) {
        this.moveRight();
      } else if (Key.isDown(Key.LEFT)) {
        this.moveLeft();
      }
      if (Key.isDown(Key.UP)) {
        this.jumping = 1;
      }
    }
    updateAfterEvent();
};
```

Here, checkKeys is a function that will look for keyboard input from the user. You will take care of left, right, and jumping movement in this tutorial. As you can see, the rover will only respond to the keys as long as it is not currently jumping. If the rover is not jumping, it looks to see if the right or left arrow is down, and calls functions to handle the movement (which you will write next). If the up arrow is pressed, you will have the rover jump, though at this time all you do is set a variable flag to positive.

3. Add the following two functions after the checkKeys function:

```
rover.moveRight = function() {
    var moveAdj = this.jumping ? .5 : 1;
    if (this._x < this.maxX) {
      this._x += this.accel * moveAdj;
    }
};

rover.moveLeft = function() {
    var moveAdj = this.jumping ? .5 : 1;
    if (this._x > this.minX) {
      this._x -= this.accel * moveAdj;
    }
};
```

These functions, as indicated by their names, will move your rover to the left or right. First, you set an adjustment percentage based on whether the rover is currently jumping. Basically, if you are jumping, moveAdj will be 0.5 (50%). If not, it will be 1 (100%). So if the rover is currently in the air, its movement to the right or left will be half of its normal value.

Next, you check to see if your _x value is still less than the maximum x-position or more than the minimum x-position (you'll set these variables in a moment). If you have not exceeded the rover's _x range, you move its x-position based on an acceleration variable multiplied by your `moveAdj` variable. Let's now add these two new variables to the start of the code.

4. At the top of the rover code script, add the following lines:

```
stageWidth = 550;
stageMiddle = stageWidth/2;

// max and min x-positions on stage
rover.maxX = stageMiddle + stageMiddle/2;
rover.minX = stageMiddle - stageMiddle/2;
// rate rover can increase/decrease speed
rover.accel = 5;
rover.wheelRotSpeed = 30;
```

The first two variables correspond to the current width of the stage (550 pixels). You find the `maxX` and `minX` values based on the `stagewidth`. The `accel` property that you accessed in the `moveLeft` and `moveRight` functions is also set, as is a new property called `wheelRotSpeed`, which controls the rate at which the rover's wheels rotate.

Just one more line of code to get your rover reacting to user input!

5. Add the following line of code to the end of all the current rover code script:

```
moveInterval = setInterval(rover, "checkKeys", 40);
```

This line of code creates a new interval call for rover: every 40 milliseconds it will call its `checkKeys` method, which looks to see if the user is currently pressing any keys. Test your movie now to see the start of your rover actions. Using the left and right arrows should move the rover to the left and right on the screen. Pressing the up arrow will eventually cause the rover to jump, but at the present time it merely locks up the controls.

You say you want a revolution...

Everything is working fine to start, though your wheels are still are not turning, despite your new `wheelRotSpeed` variable. This is because the wheels are attempting to access a property of `rover` named `speed`, which you have yet to set. This property will be the perceived speed of the rover based on its position on the stage, so when the rover is on the right side of the stage it should appear to be going faster, and when it is on the left it should appear slower.

The way you will get this illusion to work is by altering the rate of rotation of the wheels as well as changing the scrolling speeds of each of the landscape planes. Since everything should be relative in a scrolling landscape, you can use a single variable that will return a percent that each plane (and the wheels) can look to. This is what is accomplished with the variable `speed`.

1. In the rover's `checkKeys` method, add the following bold line:

```
// handles all keyboard input to control rover
rover.checkKeys = function() {
    this.speed = this.getSpeed();
```

So `speed` will be recalculated every 40 milliseconds.

2. Now let's define the `getSpeed` method. At the end of all the rover code, after the `moveLeft` function but before `setInterval`, add the following lines:

```
rover.getSpeed = function() {
    return (this.accel + ((this._x - stageMiddle) *
➥this.speedFactor))/this.accel;
};
```

That looks pretty convoluted, so let's break it down. Basically, when the rover is at the middle of the stage, `this._x - stageMiddle` will evaluate to `0` and you will be left with `this.accel/this.accel`.

So, when the rover is centered on the stage you get `1`, or 100%. If the rover moves to the right or left of center, you get a value either below 100% (which will slow the rate down once it's multiplied with this value) or above 100% (which will increase rates). `speedFactor` is a variable that will bring the massive pixel size that might be returned by (`this._x - stageMiddle`) into a usable range. For instance, if the rover is at an x-position of `350`, then (`this._x - stageMiddle`) will return `75`. The value returned by this function then (without `speedFactor` included) would be 1600%. So let's take care of setting the `speedFactor` next.

3. Add the following bold line to the variable declarations at the top of the rover code:

```
// rate rover can increase/decrease speed
rover.accel = 5;
rover.speedFactor = 8/stageWidth;
rover.wheelRotSpeed = 30;
```

This will make sure the `speed` property stays within a healthy range. Go ahead and test your movie to see the wheel's spinning relative to the rover's placement on the stage. Next, you will look at altering the landscape scrolling rates based on the `speed` variable as well.

4. To change the scrolling rate of the ground based on the rover's speed variable you need to multiply the `scrollSpeed` by the value found in `rover.speed` (remember, this value will be less than `1` when the rover is on the left side of the screen, greater than `1` when the rover is on the right side of the screen, and exactly `1` when the rover is in the middle of the screen). Add the following bold code to the `moveGround` function in the landscape code layer:

```
// moves and swaps out ground clips
moveGround = function() {
    this._x -= scrollSpeeds.ground*rover.speed;
```

Piece of cake! Let's do the same thing for the other landscape planes.

5. Add the following bold code to the moveLandscape function in the landscape code layer:

```
moveLandscape = function() {
    // should always be 2 clips on stage
    for (var i in this.mcs) {
        this.mcs[i]._x -= scrollSpeeds[this._name]*rover.speed;
```

Test your movie now to see how the scrolling rate of the landscape as well as the rotation rate of the wheels changes based on the rover's position.

Jumpin' Jehoshaphat!

The final step in our parallax scrolling experiment is adding some bounce to the patrol vehicle.

1. Add the following bold lines to the rover's checkKeys function in the rover code layer:

```
if (Key.isDown(Key.UP)) {
  // ground plane
  this.startY = this._y;
  // how high and powerful
  this.jumpEnergy = 7;
  // works with friction to end bouncing
  this.bounceFactor = 1;
  // flag
  this.jumping = 1;
  this.jumpInterval = setInterval(this, "jump", 40);
}
```

Whenever the user presses the up arrow (if the rover is not already jumping), this code will run. After initializing three variables to control the jump, you create another setInterval call to handle the jumping action. As you can see, you will be calling a new function called jump every 40 milliseconds. Since the rover can't actually jump until that function is written, you'll write that function next.

2. Add the following new function after the rover's moveLeft function and before getSpeed:

```
rover.jump = function() {
    // moves rover up AND down
    this._y -= this.jumpEnergy--;
    // hitting ground plane
    if (this._y >= this.startY) {
      this._y = this.startY;
      this.jumpEnergy *= -this.bounceFactor;
    }
};
```

Every 40 milliseconds, you will change the rover's y-position based on its current `jumpEnergy` (which starts at `7`, then is subtracted from each iteration). When the rover hits the ground plane, it reverses direction. Test your movie now to see the result.

Notice the problem? Well, other than the fact that you haven't coded anything yet to *end* the jumping, the rover actually bounces higher each time it hits the ground. What you need to do is code it to *lose* energy each time it touches down. As soon as its energy is completely diminished, you will end the jump sequence.

3. Add the following bold lines to the jump function you just created:

```
rover.jump = function() {
    // moves rover up AND down
    this._y -= this.jumpEnergy--;
    // hitting ground plane
    if (this._y >= this.startY) {
      this._y = this.startY;
      // decreases each time ground is hit
      this.bounceFactor -= this.friction;
      this.jumpEnergy *= -this.bounceFactor;
      // bouncing ended
      if (this.bounceFactor <= 0) {
        delete this.jumpMove;
        this.jumping = 0;
        clearInterval(this.jumpInterval);
      }
    }
  }
};
```

So each time the rover hits the ground, you will subtract a `friction` amount from the `bounceFactor` (you'll set `friction` in the next step). Once `bounceFactor` hits 0, you clear the jumping interval and delete the unnecessary variables.

4. Add the following bold line to the initial variable declarations at the top of the rover code:

```
rover.accel = 5;
rover.speedFactor = 8/stageWidth;
rover.wheelRotSpeed = 30;
// how quickly rover bouncing will be dampened
rover.friction = .25;
```

Test your movie now to see the jumping made a bit more realistic. The only thing left to do is write the code that will keep the rover moving left or right (when necessary) while jumping through the air.

5. Add the following bold lines to rover's `checkKeys` function:

```
if (Key.isDown(Key.UP)) {
    // stores which way rover is currently moving
    // so that it will continue to do so while in the air
    if (Key.isDown(Key.RIGHT)) {
        this.jumpMove = this.moveRight;
    } else if (Key.isDown(Key.LEFT)) {
        this.jumpMove = this.moveLeft;
    }
    // ground plane
    this.startY = this._y;
    // how high and powerful
    this.jumpEnergy = 7;
    // works with friction to end bouncing
    this.bounceFactor = 1;
```

Here you check to see if the right or left arrow is also being pressed before the jump. If it is, you store the appropriate function in a new variable called `jumpMove`. This will allow you to call `this.jumpMove()` inside your `jump` method and the appropriate method (if any) will be called.

6. Add the following bold line to rover's `jump` method:

```
rover.jump = function() {
    // keeps rover moving in saved direction
    this.jumpMove();
    // moves rover up AND down
    this._y -= this.jumpEnergy--;
```

Now, if anything is stored in `jumpMove`, it will be called and the rover will move in the appropriate direction.

That's it! You have successfully completed a believable scrolling background system for a Flash game. Landscape planes move at different rates based on their relative distance from the user, as well as the relative speed of the foreground sprite. The way we have set it up, it's also fairly easy to add further planes of animation to your game. Now all you need are the hazards, enemies, and weapons.

Scrolling in navigation: A parallax menu

So far we have covered parallax scrolling through both manual tweening and ActionScript. Although the last example was somewhat dynamic, the scrolling wasn't completely controlled by user interaction; it was only affected by it. In this example, you will create a navigation system that scrolls based on the user's mouse position. As you delve further into the structure, top levels appear to recede on the stage, which should naturally affect their scrolling rate. Look at the file `parallaxMenu_end.swf` to see the final result.

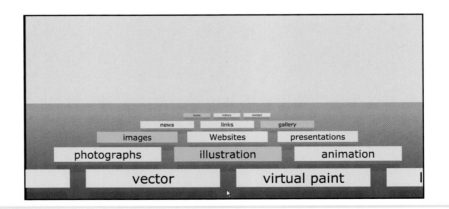

Setting up

1. Open the file `parallaxMenu_start.fla` and peruse its contents. Although you will be writing most of the code to create the ending navigation, there are a few pieces already prepared for you. First, the background gradient has been drawn on the locked background layer. Feel free to adjust these colors (and any other colors in this project) to your liking. The only other layer is the XML layer, which contains the code necessary to bring in and parse an XML file containing your menu information. XML, or eXtensible Markup Language, is a tagging language used to create structured documents, allowing data to be shared between applications. Since covering XML is beyond the scope of this chapter, we've taken care of all the code needed to deal with the XML file.

   Finally, the Library has a single symbol, `NavButton`, and this is the only symbol that will be used in this movie. This symbol doesn't contain much code, and the code has nothing to do with the scrolling effect, so it has also been prepared for you. All that the symbol does is draw a filled text field with a specified string of text, adds a faint trapezoidal shadow beneath the text field, and turns on the text field's border when the mouse rolls over it. The button's actions and its placement in the scrolling rows are controlled by the external script that you'll be writing in future steps.

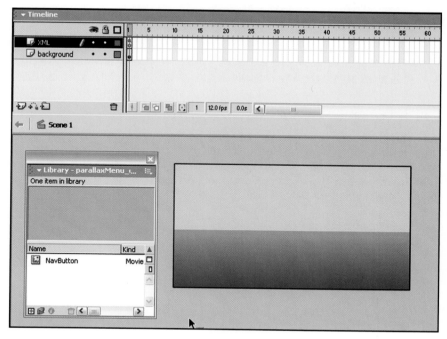

2. Open up the file `menus.xml` in your favorite text editor to see how the XML file is prepared with your menu information. Make sure this file is saved into the same directory as `parallaxMenu_start.fla`. Here's a truncated excerpt of the script:

```
<?xml version="1.0" encoding="iso-8859-1"?>
<menus>
  <level1 title="home">
    <level2 title="news">
      <level3 title="current" />
      <level3 title="archive" />
    </level2>
    <level2 title="links">
      <level3 title="business">
        <level4 title="domestic" />
        <level4 title="international" />
      </level3>
      <level3 title="personal" />
      <level3 title="others" />
    </level2>
        .
        .
        .
  </level1>
</menus>
```

The root node of the menus is appropriately named `<menus>`. Each nested node is named `<leveln>` and has at least one attribute, `title`. This is the name that will appear on the button. If a node does not have any children (such as home > news > current, above), then it should contain another attribute named `url` with a value that you want passed to the Flash movie, whether it be an actual URL, a Flash movie to load, or perhaps the identifer name of a symbol that you want to attach from the Library. It all depends on how you set up the navigation system in Flash (which you will do in a moment). For the purpose of this tutorial, we have left out the URL attribute since you're more interested in the scrolling of the system, rather than actually loading any content. But suppose you used this system to load a Flash movie into the Flash interface whenever you clicked a button at the bottom of the nested menu. In that case, you might write the home > news > current node as follows:

```
<level3 title="current" url="currentNews.swf" />
```

When the XML is loaded into your Flash movie, the code on the XML layer of the main timeline parses the file and places all the menus' information into an array named `sections`. To see this in action, and how `sections` is structured, you'll test the movie with the Flash MX Debugger.

3. Return to `parallaxMenu_start.fla` and create a new layer above the XML layer. Name it set up, then add this code to its first frame:

```
xmlFile = "menus.xml";
```

This lets the XML object created in the XML layer know which file to load into the movie.

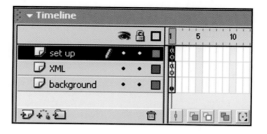

4. Test your movie with the Debugger window by using the menu command Control > Debug Movie (or by pressing CTRL/CMD+SHIFT+ENTER). When you enter the testing environment, click the green play button in the Debugger window. Your XML should load silently in the background. To see how it populated the sections array, select _level0 in the top left of the Debugger, and then click on the Variables tab in the center left of the Debugger panels.

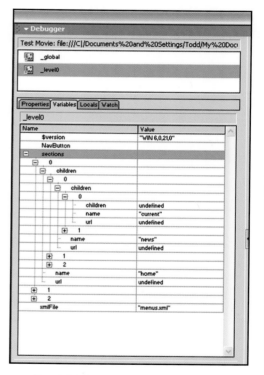

You should see $version, xmlFile, and NavButton listed in the Variables tab, along with sections, which has a plus sign next to it. Click on this plus sign to expand sections, and you should see nested indices (0, 1, 2) with plus signs next to each. You can expand each index to see what's inside. Basically, each index has three properties: name, url, and children. Its children property is another array that holds all of its children objects, or subsections. Each of these in turn has up to three properties. This continues down into sections until the bottom of the stack for each section is reached.

Phew! Now that you've had a glimpse of how you create your sections *outside* of Flash, as well as how you structure that information *inside* of Flash, it's time to actually do something with that information.

Button formatting

The first thing you need to do is decide on some parameters for your menu buttons. You will create some variables in the set up code layer that will allow you easy access to tweaking later on.

1. In the set up layer, add the following lines of code:

```
MovieClip.prototype.useHandCursor = 0;

stageWidth = 750;
xmlFile = "menus.xml";

buttonWidth = 250;
buttonHeight = 35;
unselectedColor = 0xDBEBCD;
selectedColor = 0xB3D396;
// space between each button
buffer = 30;

sectionTextFormat = new TextFormat();
sectionTextFormat.font = "Verdana";
sectionTextFormat.size = 25;
sectionTextFormat.align = "center";
```

The first line simply gets rid of the hand cursor as you mouse over a (movie clip) button. You then set a variable based on the width of the stage. After that, there are number of variables to affect the look of your buttons. Finally, you create a `TextFormat` object for the text on the buttons. We chose to use Verdana as the font, though you may change it to whatever you'd like (you might have to adjust the size).

2. Create a new layer above the background layer and name it textfield. With the layer selected, draw a *dynamic* text field off the left side of the stage. It doesn't matter too much where you place it since it will be invisible to the user (it has no text in it). You are adding the text field to the stage so you have control over the embedding of the font, which will allow for smoother animation and consistency of design for all users.

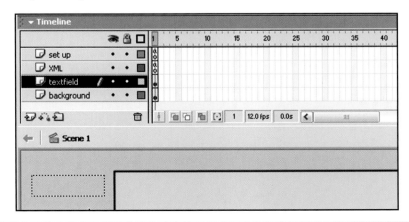

3. Deselect the new text field's Selectable option in the Property Inspector, and set its font to match the font you specified in the previous step's `TextFormat` (Verdana, in our case). To embed the font, click on the Character… button in the Property Inspector and select Only Uppercase Letters, Lowercase Letters, and Numerals. Then press Done. Again, you are embedding for two reasons: first, to keep your system visually consistent for all users, and second, because embedded fonts simply animate better on the stage.

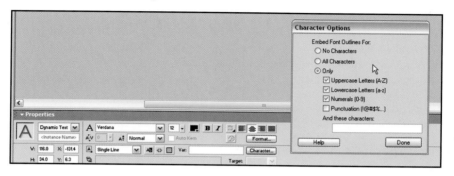

Adding rows

Now that you know what your buttons will look like, let's add your first row to the stage. In the XML layer, the parsing function (`parseXML`) calls another function once the `sections` array has been filled. The new function is called `drawRow`, and the top level of `sections` is sent to it initially so that the top level of buttons might be placed on the stage. Let's take care of that function now.

1. Create a new layer on the main timeline named row code and place it below the XML layer. On the first frame of row code, enter the following script:

```
// holds references to rows
rows = [];
currentRow = 0;
```

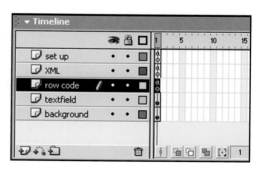

Before you write the `drawRow` function, you need to initialize some variables: `rows` will hold references to every row of buttons you place on the stage, and `currentRow` is the current index of that array, namely the first index.

2. Add the following function after the preceding code:

```
// draws row based on section sent
drawRow = function(sections) {
    // clip to hold row
    var r = this.createEmptyMovieClip("row" + currentRow, XcurrentRow++);
    rows.push(r);
    // holds references to all of row's buttons
    r.buttons = [];
    var sectionsLength = sections.length;
    // each button's _x based on width of entire row
    var totalButtonWidth = (buttonWidth*sectionsLength) +
➥(buffer*(sectionsLength-1));
    // attaches buttons for row
    for (var i = 0; i < sectionsLength; i++) {
      var b = r.attachMovie("NavButton", "btn" + i, i, Xsections[i]);
      r.buttons.push(b);
      b._x = -(totalButtonWidth/2) + (buttonWidth*i) + (buffer*i);
    }
};
```

That's pretty simple to start off with, though you will add more as you go along. The first lines create an empty movie clip to hold all of a row's buttons. A reference to this movie clip is stored in the `rows` array. Then, after creating a new array property named `buttons`, which will store reference to all of the row's buttons, you loop through all of the section's children and add a button for each to the row. The most interesting aspect in the preceding code is that you send an `initObject` in the `attachMovie()` call for the buttons. This sends a subsection's object (which includes `name`, `url`, and `children` as properties) to the newly created button. The button uses the `name` property to add to its text field, it will use the `url` property (if it has one) to load a page or a movie, and it will use the `children` property (if it has one) to create a subsection menu whenever it is pressed. All of that is done rather discreetly inside the `attachMovie()` call.

Test your movie now to see the first row added to the stage. You have a little way to go before this effect is complete, but what a nice start! We will next look at tweening the row into a desired position on the stage.

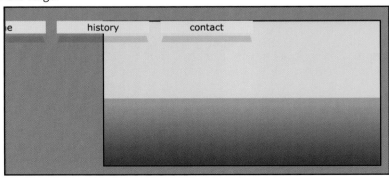

3.   Add the following bold lines to the set up code layer:

```
buttonWidth = 250;
buttonHeight = 35;
unselectedColor = 0xDBEBCD;
selectedColor = 0xB3D396;
// space between each button
buffer = 30;

// row attributes when first placed
startScale = 120;
startY = 400;

// factors for when a row moves up/back
yChange = 60;
yDiminish = .7;
scaleChange = 20;

sectionTextFormat = new TextFormat();
sectionTextFormat.font = "Verdana";
sectionTextFormat.size = 25;
sectionTextFormat.align = "center";
```

Here you are first positioning the row at the bottom of the stage (400) and at a scale of 120%. Then you will tween it into position—the next three variables handle the numbers you will tween to. Basically, every row will move up 60 pixels initially and will lose 20% in scale. The yDiminish variable will be used to lessen the yChange value each time a row moves up—this is a type of parallax scrolling. The rows that are closer in depth to the viewer will move more of a distance up the stage ("back") than the rows at the farther distances. This will go a long way to simulating a 3D menu system.

4. Returning to the row code layer, add the following bold lines to the drawRow function:

```
// draws row based on section sent
drawRow = function(sections) {
    // clip to hold row
    var r = this.createEmptyMovieClip("row" + currentRow, currentRow++);
    rows.push(r);
    // initial properties
    r._xscale = r._yscale = startScale;
    r.yMove = yChange;
    r._y = startY;
    // holds references to all of row's buttons
    r.buttons = [];
    var sectionsLength = sections.length;
    // each button's _x based on width of entire row
    var totalButtonWidth = (buttonWidth*sectionsLength) +
➥(buffer*(sectionsLength-1));
    // attaches buttons for row
    for (var i = 0; i < sectionsLength; i++) {
```

```
                var b = r.attachMovie("NavButton", "btn" + i, i, sections[i]);
                r.buttons.push(b);
                b._x = -(totalButtonWidth/2) + (buttonWidth*i) + (buffer*i);
            }
            // changes properties for each row to make room for new row
            for (var i in rows) {
                rows[i].newY = rows[i]._y - rows[i].yMove;
                rows[i].yMove *= yDiminish;
                rows[i].newScale = rows[i]._yscale - scaleChange;
                // each row set to tween into place
                rows[i].onEnterFrame = tweenToPosition;
            }
};
```

When a row is first created, you set its initial properties before adding its buttons. Then, at the end of the function, you loop through all rows currently on stage and set the properties that they will tween to (newY and newScale). Then you set their onEnterFrame handler to a function named tweenToPosition. You'll write that next.

5. Add the following function after the drawRow function:

```
// animates row into new position
tweenToPosition = function() {
    this._xscale = this._yscale -= (this._yscale - this.newScale)/5;
    this._y -= (this._y - this.newY)/5;
    // once close enough, ends animation
    if (Math.abs(this._yscale - this.newScale) < 1 && Math.abs(this.newY -
➥this._y) < 1) {
        this._y = this.newY;
        this._xscale = this._yscale = this.newScale;
        this.onEnterFrame = scroll;
    }
    // makes row invisible at low scales
    this._visible = this._xscale > 5;
};
```

This is a fairly standard easing function that moves and scales your row into position a little each frame. Once the row has reached its destination (or is close enough), its properties are set to its end values and the onEnterFrame handler is assigned a different function (which you'll tend to in a moment). You'll also notice that you make the row invisible if it is scaled to less than 5%.

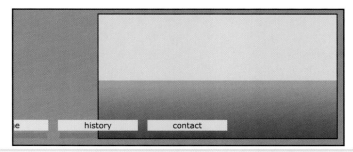

Test your movie now to see the tweening into position. It is working for _y, _xscale, and _yscale, but you need to get it working for _x. That, however, will always be controlled by the user's mouse position.

The sacred scroll

Now that you have successfully added your first row and tweened it into its starting position, you need to write the code that will control its scrolling. You have used these same concepts of parallax scrolling in the previous projects, where the foreground objects move at a faster rate than the background objects. But here you will build on it further by dynamically deciding the depth of a row (and thus its scrolling rate) based on its present scale.

1. Add the following new function to row code layer beneath the drawRow function (and above the tweenToPosition function):

```
// scrolls each row
scroll = function() {
    // amount diminishes the farther away row is
    // (thus at smaller scale)
    var scrollAmount = scrollFactor*this._xscale/100;
    // x-position changes based on _xmouse
    this._x = (stageWidth/2 - _root._xmouse)*scrollAmount + XstageWidth/2;
};
```

Just a couple lines of code take care of so much! Jumping to the end first, you will see that you set the x-position of the movie clip (which will be an individual row) based on where the mouse is in relation to the center of the stage. For instance, if the mouse was at center stage (375 pixels), then this._x will equal 375, placing the clip right in the center of the stage as well ((375–375)x + 375). The farther the mouse moves to the right, the more the row will move to the left based on its scrollAmount.

But what is scrollAmount? Well, as you can see, it is determined by the current _xscale of the row movie clip, so clips that are larger in scale (thus "closer" to the viewer) will have a larger scrollAmount and will scroll at a faster rate. We've also thrown in a new variable named scrollFactor to make it easy to change the relative scaling of the clips to affect the overall appearance of your menus. You'll set the variable in the next step.

2. Go to the set up code layer and add the following bold line of code:

```
// affects scrolling rate and distance
scrollFactor = 2;
// row attributes when first placed
startScale = 120;
startY = 400;
```

Now all you need to do is call the function when necessary. You've already set it to be called once a row is tweened into position, but you should also have it called *while* a row is being tweened, as well as when a row is first created.

3. Head back to the row code layer and add the following bold line to the end of the `tweenToPosition` function:

```
// makes row invisible at low scales
this._visible = this._xscale > 5;
// keeps scrolling the row as it animates
scroll.apply(this);
}
```

Here you use `apply` again (as you did in the Mars Patrol example) to apply the `scroll` function to an instance of a movie clip, meaning that the movie clip will be referenced by `this` inside the `scroll` function.

4. Next, add the following bold line of code to the `drawRow` function:

```
// initial properties
r._xscale = r._yscale = startScale;
r.yMove = yChange;
// _x set
scroll.apply(r);
r._y = startY;
```

You apply the `scroll` function here as well so that the row may be placed at the proper _x-position upon instantiation.

Test your movie now to see the tweening and scrolling working like a charm.

Spawning subs

This next, and final, function is probably the most complex that we've dealt with this chapter, but it's not so difficult to understand when broken down into parts. With it, you will enable your buttons to produce additional rows for their subsections. Once you do that, however, you'll have to move all previous sections up on the stage.

1. Add these lines of a new function right after the `drawRow` and `scroll` functions in the row code layer. Note that this is not the completed function (also note that many of the following lines are comments, so don't feel too intimidated!):

```
// called when a nav button is pressed
buttonScript = function() {
    // makes sure animation is occurring
    for (var i in rows) {
      if (rows[i].onEnterFrame == tweenToPosition) {return false};
    }
    // if this is front row
    if (this._parent == rows[rows.length - 1]) {
      // deselects all other buttons in row
      for (var i in this._parent.buttons) {
        this._parent.buttons[i].sectionName.backgroundColor =
➡unselectedColor;
      }
      // "selects" this button
      this.sectionName.backgroundColor = selectedColor;
      // if this section has no children, then it must
      // have content to load
      if (this.children == undefined) {
        // write code to load content
      } else {
        // draw this section's children to new row
        drawRow(this.children);
      }
    // this is a back row
    } else {
```

Don't test this just yet, as the preceding script is unfinished and so will generate errors. For clarity, let's break down this first part before you finish the function and get it working. This `buttonScript` will be called when any button in your navigation system is clicked, so it will need to know if the button clicked contains subsections, or information relating to a page or movie to load. The first thing you do in the function is run through all the current rows and make sure that none are currently animating. If any row is, then you exit this function. If, however, it is safe to proceed, you test to see if this row (the one with a button that was clicked) is the nearest row to the user by checking to see if this was the last row placed into the `rows` array. Only the nearest row can produce submenus, since any row farther back in the stack already has produced submenus.

OK, if you are indeed dealing with the front row of the stack, you deselect all of the buttons in the row (in case any are currently selected), and then select the button just clicked. Next, you look to see if this particular button doesn't have any children. If it doesn't, you know you've reached the bottom of the stack and you need to load a page or a movie. We haven't written the code that would do this, as it would change depending on the project, but this is where the code would be placed. If, however, children do exist for this button, then you need to add the new row by calling the `drawRow` function and sending it the array of children.

That's the brunt of it. Now you just need to take care of what happens when a button is clicked in a row *other* than the front.

2. Add these lines after the code from in the previous step. These lines will remove all rows *in front* of the row just clicked, leaving room for all the rows to move up:

```
// deselects all other buttons in row
for (var i in this._parent.buttons) {
    this._parent.buttons[i].sectionName.backgroundColor =
➥unselectedColor;
}
// finds this row number
for (var i = 0; i < rows.length; i++) {
  if (rows[i] == this._parent) {
    // row in front of this row
    var nextRowUp = i+1;
    break;
  }
}
// removes all rows in front of this row
for (var i = nextRowUp; i < rows.length; i++) {
  rows[i].removeMovieClip();
}
rows.splice(nextRowUp);
```

After deselecting all of the buttons in the clicked row, you loop through the `rows` array to find the reference to the row just clicked. Remember that the rows that are the farthest back will be lower indices in the `rows` array, so once you find the row index, you add 1 to it to get the next row in the stack. It will be this row and all subsequent rows referenced in the rows array that will need to be removed, which you do in the next lines. Once the clips are removed, you also remove the references (which no longer apply) from the `rows` array by using the `splice` method.

3. Here's the penultimate chunk of code. These next lines set the new positions for each of the rows based on each row's positions in the `rows` array. Add the following lines to the end of the `buttonSelect` function to finish it off:

```
// runs through all remaining rows and sets properties
// to tween to based on position in rows array
var rowNum = 0;
for (var i in rows) {
  rows[i].newScale = startScale;
  rows[i].newY = startY;
  rows[i].yMove = yChange;
  var rowPosition = rowNum;
  while (rowPosition > -1) {
    rows[i].newScale -= scaleChange;
    rows[i].newY -= rows[i].yMove;
    rows[i].yMove *= yDiminish;
```

```
            rowPosition--;
        }
        rows[i].onEnterFrame = tweenToPosition;
        rowNum++;
    }
}
};
```

After first reinitializing each position property for a row, you change each of these properties based on the row's index in the array. After the properties have been changed, you begin tweening into these new positions.

Almost there! You now have a beautiful button script for your menu buttons, but you haven't yet actually assigned it to your buttons. You can do this with a single additional line in the drawRow function.

4. Add the following bold line to the drawRow function to complete your scripting:

```
for (var i = 0; i < sectionsLength; i++) {
  var b = r.attachMovie("NavButton", "btn" + i, i, sections[i]);
  r.buttons.push(b);
  b._x = -(totalButtonWidth/2) + (buttonWidth*i) + (buffer*i);
  b.onRelease = buttonScript;
}
```

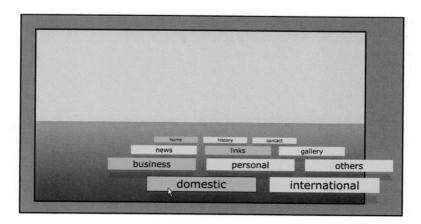

And you're done. Test your movie now (or take a look at parallaxMenu_end.fla) to see your beautiful finished effect. Notice how each row scrolls differently based on its placement in the stack. This, combined with the scaling of the clips and the graphical shadows, gives a wonderful 3D feel to a navigation system that doesn't contain a smidgen of 3D code—the ultimate 3D cheat!

Summary

Through three very different projects, we have looked at the uses of parallax scrolling to create unique, pseudo-3D experiences. The concept itself is a fairly simple one, so much so that it can almost be explained with a Tarzan-like simplicity.

"Things close move fast, things distant move slow!"

Although it is relatively simple in concept, the implementation of parallax scrolling can help to create some fantastic effects. By separating your content—whether it be in animations, games, or interfaces—into separate planes and animating movement of those planes at different rates, you can bring a wonderful 3D feeling to your Flash projects without having to ever leave the Flash authoring environment.

 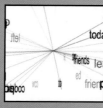 

Text Effects in 3D Space

Text is inherently difficult to render fast and accurately in a graphic environment; likewise, producing text in three-dimensional space is even more difficult and time consuming. However, all is not lost—we can use special techniques employing simple transformations to move text through an elegant and convincing third dimension. Accordingly, in this chapter we'll step through the construction and adaptation of three unique pseudo-3D text display systems:

- **Tornado text** – A chaotic rotational system that throws words around like cows in Oklahoma
- **Spherical text magnification** – An unusual method warping letters around an invisible spherical lens
- **Lost in text space** – A navigation system in 3D space using words as waypoints

All three systems render typography on the screen in such a way as to produce the effect of three-dimensionality. Although seemingly complex and computationally heavy, each system uses a series of transformations native to Flash MX, creating a robust, elegant display of spatial mastery using very little processor power.

Tornado text

The first system of three-dimensional space allows words to fly about in a seemingly chaotic vortex similar to the way ground debris is encaged within a tornado. Though wild in appearance, this system is actually rather constricted. As you will see during implementation, text within the tornado is not really free to do much more than spin about an axis, constrained within an imaginary cylinder. Still, the effect is rather stunning. Take a look at `textTornado.swf`.

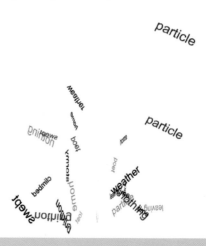

The construction of the tornado consists of three different movie clips. Open up `textTornado.fla`, available in this chapter's sample files from www.friendsofed.com, and look in the Library (F11). First we have `TextTornado` itself, the main container movie clip that holds the entire system together and watches the mouse for interactive prompts from the user. Inside `TextTornado` there is a chunk of ActionScript that dynamically attaches a collection of `TextTornadoRoto` movie clips. `TextTornadoRoto` produces the three-dimensional effect of the system through simple adjustment of scale. Attached within each `TextTornadoRoto` is a collection of independent `TextTornadoWord` movie clips. Graphically, the `TextTornadoWord` is a text box loaded with some random words. The `TextTornadoWord` moves itself independently using wind, gravitation, and periodic levitation.

Building the tornado

Let's build the tornado from the ground up, beginning with its most crucial elements. As an alternative to typing all this code into Flash, you can follow along using the `TextTornado.fla` file.

1. Within a new file (CTRL/CMD+N) or an existing project, create a new movie clip by selecting Insert > New Symbol... (CTRL/CMD+F8). Name it `TextTornadoWord`. Within the same Create New Symbol dialog box, enter advanced mode by clicking the Advanced button. This will provide access to the Linkage options. Link this movie clip by checking the Export for ActionScript and Export in first frame checkboxes. Give the new symbol the linkage identifier of `textTornadoWord` (note the lowercase t this time). Click on OK to create the new symbol. Later you will learn why it is critical that this movie clip be linked.

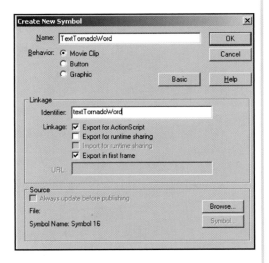

2. Name the first layer of your new movie clip definition, and create a new layer named word. The order of the two layers on this timeline is not important.

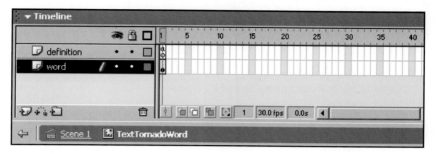

3. On the layer called word, use the Text Tool (T) to create a single **dynamic** text field. It might look something like this:

thinking tree

4. Make sure the text field is dynamic, and assign it the variable txtWord. You can assign the variable by selecting the text field and typing txtWord in the Var field of the Property Inspector. This will allow you to *dynamically* place any word you want into this text field at the time of the creation of the tornado.

5. To program this object, you will be prototyping the behavior of the TextTornadoWord so that it might be used in other places, at other times, for other purposes. For now, you are mainly interested in defining a word object that floats around randomly as if it is being affected by many disparate forces.

> *The behavior of all movie clips in this chapter are programmed using* prototype *functions. There are three advantages to using prototyped movie clips: they are* **transportable** *to other projects,* **extendable***, and easy to convert into Flash MX* **components***. It is also a great way to approach a programming exercise where there exist many similar objects.*

167

6. The entire code of the prototyped movie clip follows. This includes the skeleton of the prototype along with the two custom methods you will be using to give your movie clip behavior. For now, it is not important to concentrate on the syntax of the prototype. As the construction of this project continues, you will begin to notice similarities in design between the objects. Type this into frame 1 of the Definition layer of the TornadoTextWord movie clip:

```
#initclip
// constructor
function TextTornadoWord() {
 this.setup();
}

// allow TextTornadoWord class to inherit MovieClip properties
TextTornadoWord.prototype = new MovieClip();

// instance methods
TextTornadoWord.prototype.setup = function() {
 // allow the word to fade in
 this._alpha = 0;
 // self set the word
 this.txtWord =
Object.environment.wordlist[random(Object.environment.wordlist.length)];
 // set the word on a tumbling course
 this.onEnterFrame = this.tumble;
};

TextTornadoWord.prototype.tumble = function() {
 // tumbling consists of arbitrary gravity, rotation, and levitation

 // random levitation
 if (!random(500)) {
   this.vy = this.vy-random(5)-1;
 }
 // variable gravity
 this.vy -= this._y/(1000+random(500));
 // add vertical
 this._y += this.vy;
 // stop word from falling through ground
 if (this._y>50) {
   this._y = 50;
 }
 // random rotational velocity
 this.rv += (random(7)-3)/4;
 if (this.rv>4) {
   this.rv = 4;
 } else if (this.rv<-4) {
   this.rv = -4;
```

```
    }
    // add rotational velocity to rotation
    this._rotation = this._rotation + this.rv;
    // fade in if not at 100% opacity
    if (this._alpha<100) {
      this._alpha+=1;
    }
};


    // Connect the class with the linkage ID for this movie clip
    Object.registerClass("textTornadoWord", TextTornadoWord);
    #endinitclip
```

The entire code block begins with an `#initclip` and ends with an `#endinitclip`. These two keywords tell Flash MX to initialize this object before any others. Although this is not required, it is a good idea if the object is used within other prototyped objects.

The first step of the code block is very important: allowing the `TextTornadoWord` to inherit all the properties of the movie clip. Immediately afterward comes the `setup` function, which is executed each time an instance of this object is created. The `setup` function is a one-time event that sets the word up for its chaotic ride through the tornado.

The two instance functions, `setup` and `tumble`, are custom functions that give your `TextTornadoWord` its behavior. The `setup` function does three things: it sets the alpha, or opacity, of the movie clip to zero (so that it can fade in); it sets the display word (using an array at the root of the movie); and it sets the word on its tumbling course through the tornado (by mapping the `onEnterFrame` event to the `tumble` function).

The `tumble` function is what does most of the work in this project, so let's look at each section individually to understand how behavior is derived from code:

```
    // random levitation
    if (!random(500)) {
      this.vy = this.vy-random(5)-1;
    }
```

This random conditional statement occasionally gives the word an intense upward thrust. As it appears here, there is a 1 in 500 chance of this happening. To increase the frequency of the upward thrusts, change the number `500` to something smaller. The variable `vy` represents vertical velocity. For each upward thrust you subtract a random amount. For stronger thrusts, increase the amount that is subtracted.

```
    // variable gravity
    this.vy -= this._y/(1000+random(500));
```

You don't want your words to fly up and out of the screen, so with each frame, add some small amount of gravity to the word's vertical velocity. This method of variable gravity uses the word's current vertical position to determine how fast it should fall. Essentially, words higher up fall faster.

```
// add vertical
this._y += this.vy;
```

This simple step adds the word's vertical velocity to the word's vertical position. Note that you never adjust the horizontal position of the word—this is taken care of by the `TextTornadoRoto`, which you will build shortly.

```
// stop word from falling through ground
if (this._y>50) {
   this._y = 50;
}
```

Of course, you also do not want your words to fall through the bottom of the screen, so when the word is below a certain value, you set it to exactly that value. We have used a value of 50 pixels to give each word some clearance when rotating.

```
// random rotational velocity
this.rv += (random(7)-3)/4;
if (this.rv>4) {
   this.rv = 4;
} else if (this.rv<-4) {
   this.rv = -4;
}
```

Similar to the random adjustment of vertical velocity, you'll do the same thing for rotational velocity. The variable `rv` represents rotational velocity. The previous code both randomly modifies the rotational velocity (in either direction) and assures that the value does not become too large. Here, a maximum rotation speed of 4 degrees per frame is allowed. That's pretty fast, so you may want to slow this part down by using a number less than 4.

```
// add rotational velocity to rotation
this._rotation = this._rotation + this.rv;
```

This adds the rotational velocity to the word's rotation.

```
// fade in if not at 100% opacity
if (this._alpha<100) {
   this._alpha++;
}
```

This little hack increases the word's alpha if it's not at 100%. Keep in mind that you set the alpha of the word to zero in the `setup` function. This is an easy way to fade things in.

All the preceding functionality combined defines a movie clip that rises and falls while rotating randomly about its center. You may have noticed that when the `TextTornadoWord` is set up, it sets a display word from an array of words in some object called `environment`. Where does this value come from? Where is the `environment`? How do words get into the tornado? To answer these questions, you must keep building.

7. Create a new movie clip called `TextTornadoRoto` (CTRL/CMD+F8). Export it with the linkage identifier `textTornadoRoto` (again note the lowercase `t`) just as you did for the `TextTornadoWord`. Name the first layer definition (all code will be placed here) and create a new layer called words. This is going to be the layer where you will keep some instances of the `TextTornadoWord` you just created.

8. Drag a couple of instances of the `TextTornadoWord` from the Library onto the stage within the words layer. For the most accurate visual results, keep the words to the right of the `TextTornadoRoto` movie clip's registration point. You may also size and position the words as you desire. Remember that the vertical position of the word is not really important, since the word changes its own vertical position once the movie starts. Your `TextTornadoRoto` words layer might look something like this:

thinking tree

thinking tree

thinking tree

It's important that you do not place too many `TextTornadoWords` within the `TextTornadoRoto`. The total number of words in the tornado will be a multiple of how many words are placed here, as a fully assembled tornado consists of several `TextTornadoRotos`. If there are too many words, the Flash player will get bogged down in computation and frames will be lost.

The `TextTornadoRoto` movie clip can be thought of as a panel that spins about a vertical axis. Anything you put on the panel will spin along with it. Twice during the trip around the axis, the panel will momentarily disappear as it faces the user edge on, much like holding a piece of paper between your palms and looking at it straight on.

9. Now you'll program the behavior of your `TextTornadoRoto`. Again, place the following code for the prototype in frame 1 of the definition layer:

```
#initclip
// constructor
function TextTornadoRoto() {
 this.setup();
}


// allow ParticleClass to inherit MovieClip properties
TextTornadoRoto.prototype = new MovieClip();
```

continues overleaf

```
                    // instance methods
                    TextTornadoRoto.prototype.setup = function() {
                     this.onEnterFrame = this.spin;
                    };

                    TextTornadoRoto.prototype.spin = function() {
                     // increment rotation
                     this.theta = this.theta+this._parent.speed;
                     // keep theta reasonable
                     this.theta = this.theta%360;
                     // calculate spherical modifiers [-1..1]
                     var xbit = Math.sin(Math.PI/180*this.theta);
                     var ybit = Math.cos(Math.PI/180*this.theta);
                     // scale to show rotation
                     this._xscale = xbit*100;
                     // make word opaque when close, transparent when distant
                     this._alpha = 30+(ybit+1)*50;

                     //  this.swapDepths(Math.round(this._alpha*4));
                    };

                    // Connect the class with the linkage ID for this movie clip
                    Object.registerClass("textTornadoRoto", TextTornadoRoto);
                    #endinitclip
```

Just as in the first movie clip you prototyped, the `TextTornadoRoto` uses `#initclip` and `#endinitclip` to indicate initialization importance. You may also notice the similarities in the prototyping syntax, but here you are mostly interested in the functionality of the `TextTornadoRoto`, largely embodied by the `spin` function.

There are a few things going on in the `spin` function. Let's look at each section in more detail.

```
                    // increment rotation
                    this.theta = this.theta+this._parent.speed;
```

The variable `theta` keeps track of the angle used in the 3D computations. Here, the angle is being adjusted by the parental variable `speed`. We will discuss how `speed` is determined when you build the final component of the system, the `TextTornado`. For now, it is important to know that ultimately the user controls the angle of the `TextTornadoRoto`.

```
                    // keep theta reasonable
                    this.theta = this.theta%360;
```

As a user might sit hypnotized by your system for some hours, you must make sure that you do not let `theta` get too large or too small. A simple modulus operation keeps `theta` constrained within a reasonable range.

```
                    // calculate spherical modifiers [-1..1]
                    var xbit = Math.sin(Math.PI/180*this.theta);
```

```
var ybit = Math.cos(Math.PI/180*this.theta);
```

The mathematics of the system involve only these two serious computations: that of `xbit` and `ybit`. Both of these variables oscillate between –1 and 1, giving you nice sinusoidal modifiers for use in both scale and alpha. These two modifiers are key to the success of the text tornado effect. They are sinusoidal functions based on the angle `theta`. They are also the inverse of each other, such that when `xbit` is 1 or –1, `ybit` is 0, and when `ybit` is 1 or –1, `xbit` is 0. As demonstrated in the scaling and opacity statements below, you need both variables.

```
// scale to show rotation
this._xscale = xbit*100;
```

This is the essential transformation that produces the 3D effect. By simply changing the horizontal scale of your `TextTornadoRoto` panel (and consequently everything attached to it), you accurately and convincingly move the panel through three dimensions. Multiplying the value of `xbit` by 100 produces a smooth curve of values from –100 to 100.

```
// make word opaque when close, transparent when distant
this._alpha = 30+(ybit+1)*50;
```

Here, you want each panel to fade when it recedes into the distance. Just as you did with the scale, you can use the value of `ybit` to modify the `_alpha` of the movie clip. Negative values are not useful when talking about `_alpha`, so as a first step, you must add a constant of one. This shifts the range of `ybit` from 0 to 2. If you multiply this new value by 50, you get an effective `_alpha` range from 0 to 100. As we didn't want the words to ever disappear entirely, we simply added a constant of 30 to the computed `_alpha`.

This final statement is not necessarily required, so it has been commented out:

```
//  this.swapDepths(Math.round(this._alpha*4));
```

This is essentially a crude but effective way to sort the stacking order of the `TextTornadoRoto`s so that the movie clips that are closer to the user overlap those that are further behind. For black-and-white text, the overlapping is not obvious, so it's been commented out in this version of the tornado text to conserve precious processing power.

10. For the final object in your system, create a new movie clip and name it `TextTornado`. Again, export this movie clip with a linkage identifier of `textTornado`. The `TextTornado` is the hub of this 3D text effect. The tornado is self-building, self-operating, and self-contained, and this will allow you to easily drop and drag tornados wherever you want them.

11. Name the first layer of the `TextTornado` movie clip definition, and place the following code inside the first frame:

```
#initclip
// constructor
function TextTornado() {
 this.setup();
}
```

continues overleaf **173**

```
       // allow ParticleClass to inherit MovieClip properties
       TextTornado.prototype = new MovieClip();

       // instance methods
       TextTornado.prototype.setup = function() {
        // number of rotos
        this.numRotos = 13;
        // attach one rotational slice for each word
        for (n=0; n<this.numRotos; n++) {
          // give the rotational slice a name
          var nombre = "roto"+String(n);
          // distribute evenly around a circle
          var init = { theta : n*(360/this.numRotos) };
          // create and attach the new rotational slice
          neo = this.attachMovie("textTornadoRoto", nombre, n, init);
        }
        // set the tornado in motion by watching them mouse
        this.onEnterFrame = this.watchMouse;
       };

       TextTornado.prototype.watchMouse = function() {
        // rotational speed of text tornado is directly related
        // to horizontal mouse position
        this.speed=this._xmouse/30;
       };

       // Connect the class with the linkage ID for this movie clip
       Object.registerClass("textTornado", TextTornado);
       #endinitclip
```

When a new TextTornado is created, it immediately assembles itself and begins to watch the mouse. The function setup carries out the assembly process. A given number of TextTornadoRotos are attached inside the loop. Each TextTornadoRoto is assigned a unique theta, juxtaposing it within the tornado. The angle is a function of the total number of TextTornadoRotos and the current TextTornadoRoto being attached.

The function watchMouse runs throughout the lifetime of the tornado. It simply calculates speed directly based on the distance the mouse is from the center of the tornado. Each attached TextTornadoRoto references speed and spins accordingly. Having a centralized speed allows for efficiency of the calculation.

12. As a final step, you need to define an array of words to place into the tornado. You do this at the root of the movie. In the first frame of any layer in the root movie, type the following:

```
       // register root as environment
       Object.environment = this;
```

```
// create array of words to be used by text tornado
this.words = "friends of ed code poetry tornado left climbed
emily stormy weather particle cow time gonna need a bigger boat
data lost swept dead things mikey nothing leaving home today";
this.wordlist = this.words.split(" ");
```

This creates a globally accessible `environment` object containing an array of words visible to the `TextTornadoWord` movie clips. When each `TextTornadoWord` initializes, it chooses, by random, one of the words in this list. This method of sharing variables in a global fashion is repeated for all three systems discussed in this chapter.

13. Drag an instance (or two) of the `TextTornado` onto the stage of your movie and test it (CTRL/CMD+ENTER). You should see spinning words slowly emerging from the background. Move your mouse from one side to the other and watch the tornado switch rotational directions. Watch this new construct for a while and you should begin to see the random levitation, variable gravity, and rotational acceleration that you just programmed into it:

In the following subsections we'll take a look at a couple of modifications to the tornado text movie.

Center-facing words

Thus far, the tornado's text is most readable around the outside edges of the tornado. Words that approach the center gradually become thinner until reaching dead center, at which point they appear paper thin. Suppose you want a movie that makes words most visible in the center—how would you achieve that? In fact, you need only change the code in a few places to create such a system. The file `textTornado_center.fla` contains the following modifications (again, all the examples are available for download from www.friendsofed.com).

1. The `setup` function of the `TextTornadoRoto` has an additional line of code:

```
this.radius=50+random(200);
```

You need a random radius to make things appear chaotic. This radius will place the panel of words 50 to 250 pixels from the center of the tornado.

2. New code also exists in the `TextTornadoRoto` definition layer, where the `_xscale` of the movie clip is calculated. The following line:

```
    this._xscale = xbit * 100;
```

is changed to this:

```
    // make word readable when in center
    this._xscale = ybit * 100;
    this._x = xbit * this.radius;
```

This way, the `TextTornadoRoto` is translated about the axis and scaled normally at the center, keeping it more readable.

Line to origin

As another modification, it might be nice to connect each word to the origin of rotation by a single line. This is a theme that will occur again later in this chapter, and with the drawing API features of Flash MX, this kind of thing is both fun and easy to do. These changes have been implemented in the `textTornado_line.fla` (for more discussion of the drawing API in the context of 3D effects, be sure to check out Chapter 9).

1. First, remove all rotation manipulation from the `TextTornadoWord` definition. You don't want the words to rotate, because it makes it more difficult to track the origin. The modified `tumble` function with no rotation appears as such, with new code shown in bold:

    ```
    TextTornadoWord.prototype.tumble = function() {
    // random levitation
    if (!random(500)) {
    ```

```
    this.vy = this.vy-random(5)-1;
  }

  // variable gravity
  this.vy -= this._y/(1000+random(500));

  // add vertical
  this._y += this.vy;

  // stop word from falling through ground
  if (this._y>50) {
    this._y = 50;
  }

  // fade in if not at 100% opacity
  if (this._alpha<100) {
    this._alpha+=1;
  }

  // draw a line to the origin
  this.drawLineToOrigin();
};
```

2. Notice that the very last line in the preceding code calls a function named drawLineToOrigin. This is a new function that you will write yourself. Type the following in the first frame of the definition layer of the TextTornadoWord movie clip. It should be somewhere toward the end, but not after the class registration.

```
TextTornadoWord.prototype.drawLineToOrigin = function() {
  this.clear();
  this.lineStyle(0, 0x000000, 25);
  this.lineTo(-this._x, -this._y);
};
```

3. This function literally draws a translucent line to the origin of the TextTornadoWord within the TextTornadoRoto. The combined effects of this function clearly show what is actually going on inside the text tornado.

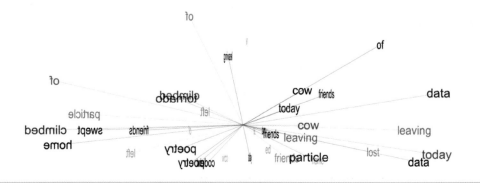

177

An interesting challenge would be to horizontally flip any word on the left side of the tornado so that all words could be easily readable at all times.

Spherical text magnification

Spherical text magnification refers to a displacement technique that moves letter objects around the surface of a three-dimensional sphere:

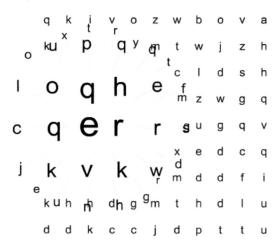

In `sphericalMag.fla`, the characters continually watch the position of the mouse and determine their own positions based on its proximity. If the mouse is outside a certain "sphere of effect," the character remains unchanged, sitting in its original position. Once the mouse enters the sphere of effect, the character is at first pushed away, then drawn in after the mouse reaches the halfway mark. This process of expansion and contraction is smoothed using a sinusoidal function.

Building the spherical text magnifier

To create this system, you will prototype a reactive letter and instantiate a grid of them. As with the previous project, the motivation to build the movie in this way should be easy to understand: the `prototype` gives you the fastest performance possible in Flash MX while providing an easy-to-use modular framework.

1. First, open a new Flash movie and set the frame rate at a comfortable 30 fps. On frame 1 of the main timeline, add the following environmental constants. Your reactive letter objects will be referencing these variables later.

    ```
    // register root as environment
    Object.environment = this;
    // spherical lens radius
    this.frad = 100;
    // spherical magnification amount
    this.mag = 2;
    ```

2. Next, create a new movie clip and name it `TextNode`. Export it with the linkage identifier `textNode`. The `TextNode` is going to become your reactive letter object. Name the first layer definition and create a new layer named body.

3. On the body layer, create a new dynamic text field and assign it the variable `txtWord`. Set the style and size of the type as you desire. Now select the text field and convert it into a movie clip. Name the movie clip `TextNodeBody`; it's not necessary to export it (the reason you are not exporting this movie clip is because you will not be attaching it dynamically and it contains no prototyped functions). Now highlight the instance of `TextNodeBody` that already exists on the body layer of `TextNode`. Give it an instance name of body. You can do this by typing the word body into the <instance name> field of the Property Inspector. The reason you are subclassing the text field is so that you can scale it while keeping the `TextNode` movie clip unaffected.

4. On the layer definition of the `TextNode` movie clip, prototype the movie clip in the usual fashion by typing the following on frame 1 (you can also see this code in `sphericalMag.fla`):

```
#initclip
// build the TextNode object
function TextNode() {
 this.setup();
}
// inherit movie clip object properties
TextNode.prototype = new MovieClip();

// instance functions...
TextNode.prototype.setup = function() {
 // set random character
 this.body.ch = String.fromCharCode(random(26)+97);
 // set size of body
 this.body._xscale=this.bodysize;
 this.body._yscale=this.bodysize;
 // watch mouse for lifetime
 this.onEnterFrame = this.render;
};

TextNode.prototype.render = function() {
 // watch the mouse - move and scale accordingly
 var dx = Object.environment._xmouse-this.x;
 var dy = Object.environment._ymouse-this.y;
 // calculate distance to mouse
 var d = Math.sqrt(dx*dx+dy*dy);
 // if distance is within 'sphere of effect'
 if (d>=Object.environment.frad) {
   // beyond edge of sphere, text remains where it should
   this._x = this.x;
   this._y = this.y;
 } else {
   // within the sphere, conjure from the depths of number
```

continues overleaf

```
        var lensDisp = Math.sin(Math.PI*Math.abs(d/this._parent.frad));
        // position the text
        this._x = this.x-dx*lensDisp;
        this._y = this.y-dy*lensDisp;

        var lensMag = Object.environment.mag*(1-Math.sin(Math.PI *
    ➥Math.abs(d/Object.environment.frad)/2));
        }
    this.body._xscale = this.bodySize*(lensMag+1);
    this.body._yscale = this.bodySize*(lensMag+1);
    };

        // register class
        Object.registerClass("textNode", TextNode);
        #endinitclip
```

5. The construction and initialization of this movie clip is probably familiar by now. In the prototyping style, you begin the definition of the movie clip with a constructing function that calls the setup function. Let's take a look at the essential parts of the setup function:

    ```
        // set random character
        this.body.ch = String.fromCharCode(random(26)+97);
    ```

    This code sets the text field in the body movie clip to some random character, from a to z.

    ```
        // set size of body
        this.body._xscale=this.bodysize;
        this.body._yscale=this.bodysize;
    ```

    Here you are setting the visual size of the movie clip by resizing the small body contained within it. This will be important later, when you add elements to the TextNode that you do not want to be scaled.

    ```
        // watch mouse for lifetime
        this.onEnterFrame = this.render;
    ```

    This final line sets the behavior of the TextNode for the rest of its existence, as defined in the render function.

6. Next up, the render function keeps an eye on the proximity of the mouse and does all the serious mathematical work of the three-dimensional transformations. When the mouse enters a given range set by the environmental constant frad, the TextNode displaces and scales itself so as to appear on the edge of a moving sphere.

    The following diagram shows the behavior of render as a function of the mouse's position. The outer circle represents the active radius set by frad. The inner circle represents the extent to which the letter will travel as the mouse nears. The middle circle represents the halfway mark of frad. Although it is true the letter is displaced from its actual coordinates, notice that in both the first and last positions the letter is precisely where it should be. This can happen because the letter recedes from the mouse until the halfway mark. Once more than halfway there, the letter approaches the mouse. The letter increases in size spherically proportional to the approach. At full size the letter is `bodysize` (the original scale) multiplied by `mag`.

Let's look at the individual elements of the `render` function to learn how it works:

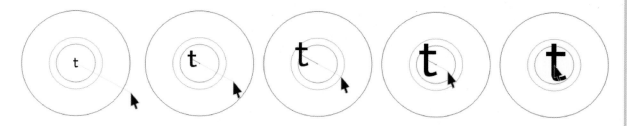

```
// watch the mouse - move and scale accordingly
var dx = Object.environment._xmouse-this.x;
var dy = Object.environment._ymouse-this.y;
// calculate distance to mouse
var d = Math.sqrt(dx*dx+dy*dy);
```

This is a simple calculation of distance (in pixels) between the mouse and the object itself.

```
// if distance is within 'sphere of effect'
if (d>=Object.environment.frad) {
  // beyond edge of sphere, text remains where it should
  this._x = this.x;
  this._y = this.y;
} else {
```

Here you compare the distance to the mouse. If it is greater than the environmental constant `frad`, the position and scale calculations are easy because the letter is outside the sphere of effect. Otherwise, the letter's position and scale need to be modified.

Calculation of the position and scale of the letter involves two sinusoidal curves, two environmental constants, the fractional position of the mouse within the sphere of effect, and some faith.

```
// within the sphere, conjure from the depths of number
var lensDisp = Math.sin(Math.PI*Math.abs(d/this._parent.frad));
```

First, you calculate the displacement intensity as a factor of how close the mouse is to the letter's center. This intensity curves along a sinusoidal arc so the letter appears to move across a sphere, rather than a pyramid. You store this value as `lensDisp`.

```
// position the text
this._x = this.x - dx * lensDisp;
this._y = this.y - dy * lensDisp;
```

Next, you use the displacement intensity as a factor in the positioning of the letter. Starting from where the letter should be, the new position is the difference computed by multiplying the mouse distance by the displacement intensity. As you will see later in this section, these two lines offer great potential for interesting modification.

```
    var lensMag = Object.environment.mag*(1-Math.sin(Math.PI *
➡Math.abs(d/Object.environment.frad)/2));
    }
```

As a final step for letters within the sphere of effect, you compute a value that will be used in the sizing of the letter. This is essentially the same equation used in `lensDisp`, except you want letters to continue to grow larger the entire time the mouse approaches. This requires an extra divisor of 2.

```
    this.body._xscale = this.bodySize*(lensMag+1);
    this.body._yscale = this.bodySize*(lensMag+1);
    };
```

Here you set the scale of the body movie clip to the size it should be, multiplied by the value of `lensMag` plus 1.

Earlier, you created two global constants called `frad` and `mag`. These constants control the size and intensity of the spherical magnification effect. The first, `frad`, sets the radius of the magnification in pixels. Thus, a `frad` value of `100` would produce a spherical magnification 200 pixels wide. The other constant, `mag`, sets the magnification level as a multiplying factor. Thus, a `mag` value of 4.2 would create a spherical magnification of 4.2x, and characters directly under the mouse will appear 420% as large as normal (it's worth noting that negative mag values produce weird results).

7. Now you'll write a nested loop that creates a grid of `TextNode` objects. A nested `for` loop running across the rows and columns of the grid should do the trick. Place the following code in the first frame of the main timeline, just underneath the environmental constants that you defined in step 1 of this tutorial:

```
// creation and positioning of 100 characters
for (gy=0; gy<10; gy++) {
 for (gx=0; gx<10; gx++) {
    // make a letter centered at this grid spot
    // name the new text node
    nombre = "tn"+String(depth++);
    // initialize the text node with the parameters passed
    posy = 200+gy*20;
    posx = 200+gx*20;
    init = {_x:posx, _y:posy, x:posx, y:posy, bodysize:25};
    // attach the text node
    this.attachMovie("textNode", nombre, depth, init);
 }
}
```

```
stop();
```

Notice how each letter is created and initialized immediately after being attached. A `stop()` action at the end of the loop indicates that you are done working. The movie is now ready to test (CTRL/CMD+ENTER).

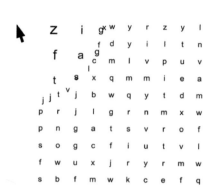

The effect is a seemingly static field of characters, arranged in a grid. Upon closer inspection with your mouse cursor, the letters jump out of their positions, accelerating around the edge of an invisible sphere until they arrive, magnified, under the position of the mouse. When seen in motion, the behavior is very intuitive, and the process of scanning and reading the information can be quickly mastered.

Again, we'll look at a few different ways of extending this project in the subsections that follow.

Line to origin

Adding a simple function that draws a line to the origin of the movie clip further demonstrates the three-dimensional processes used to move it around (extending the line in the other direction is interesting to look at, but not so useful).

1. Somewhere inside the `render` function on the definition layer of the `TextNode` movie clip, add the following function call (see `sphericalMag_line.fla` for further details):

   ```
   this.drawLineToOrigin();
   ```

2. Prototype this new function by adding the following to the `TextNode` movie clip definition:

   ```
   TextNode.prototype.drawLineToOrigin = function() {
    this.clear();
    this.lineStyle(0, 0x000000, 15);
    this.lineTo(this.x-this._x, this.y-this._y);
   };
   ```

3. And that's it! Go ahead and test your new, improved version of this movie. You really get an enhanced sense of depth with this iteration of the effect.

Weird lens

As mentioned earlier, there are two lines in the calculation of the `TextNode` displacement that you can have a lot of fun with. Keep in mind the calculations used to move the letter around the edge of a sphere, and take a look at `sphericalMag_weird.fla`. In this file, we have doubled the effect of the lens displacement by including an extra constant of 2:

```
. . .
// within the sphere, conjure from the depths of number
var lensDisp = Math.sin(Math.PI*Math.abs(d/this._parent.frad));
// position the text
this._x = this.x - dx * lensDisp * 2;
```

```
this._y = this.y - dy * lensDisp * 2;
...
```

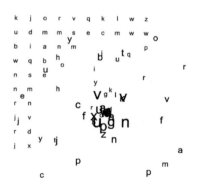

Additionally, including multiples to the calculating of the displacement intensity creates wavy effects. These changes are available in sphericalMag_weird2.fla. To create this file on your own, begin with the original spherical magnification framework, and then change the calculation of lensDisp within the TextNode movie clip to the following:

```
// within the sphere, conjure from the depths of number
var lensDisp = Math.sin(Math.PI*Math.abs(d/this._parent.frad)*4);
```

In essence, this creates a field of text letters where each letter approaches and recedes from the mouse four times after entering the sphere of influence. Moving the mouse about the stage causes quite a stir of computational frenzy. The resulting animation looks like a swarm of letter insects attacking the cursor:

Lost in text space

In this final technique, you'll approach the closest approximation of true three-dimensional perspective rendering yet. However, you are still very far from burdening either your processor or your user with the intricacies of full three-dimensional representation.

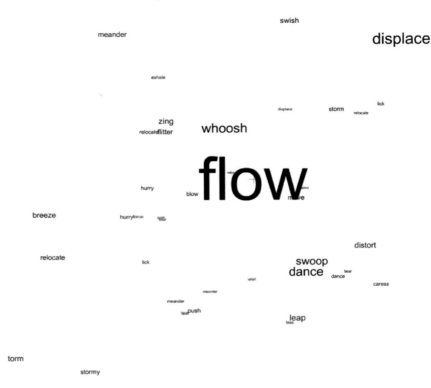

In this system of three-dimensional text, words are fixed in a large spatial area (see `textInSpace.fla`). Clicking on a word zooms the user through the space to focus on the selection. Words that move beyond the camera are replaced in the distance to create the illusion of infinite depth.

You can trick most users into believing your type exists within a third dimension using only scale and screen positioning. The closer a word is to the user, the larger it becomes. The opposite is true for words far away; they are very small. Words also appear to move faster when they are closer.

Building the text space

Lost in text space is a modification of a parallax system (refer to Chapter 6 for more details). It takes only a few simple equations to set the word object up—the rest of the algorithmic work will be devoted to ways in which you can move around in this word space. The completed version of this example can be found in this chapter's source files as `textInSpace.fla`.

1. Let's get busy creating the first crucial object of the system, the SpaceWord. Create a new movie clip and name it SpaceWord. Export the movie clip with the linkage ID spaceWord. Name the first layer definition, and create two new layers called word and button (by now, this setting-up stage is probably a piece of cake for you).

2. On the layer named word, create a dynamic text field and assign it the variable txtWord. Change the style and size of the word as you see fit. Be sure to center the text field and embed font outlines (by clicking the Character... button) for the cleanest possible presentation.

3. On the button layer, create a rectangular button that covers an average-sized word. This button will be used to select the word and focus the camera on its position in three-dimensional space. Give this button an instance name of btnSquare. The instance name will be important later when you assign code and actions to the button.

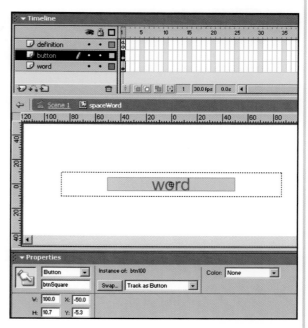

4. On the first frame of the definition layer, type the following to set up the foundation for your prototyped SpaceWord:

```
#initclip
// constructor
function SpaceWord() {
  // set up button functionality
  this.btnSquare.onPress = function() {
    // push the camera towards the word
    Object.environment.cam.dx = this._parent.x;
    Object.environment.cam.dy = this._parent.y;
    Object.environment.cam.dz = this._parent.z+Object.environment.fl*.9;
    // disable and hide button
    this.enabled = false;
    this._visible = false;
  };
  // set continual function to render word
```

continues overleaf

```
    this.onEnterFrame = this.render;
}

// allow SpaceWord to inherit MovieClip properties
SpaceWord.prototype = new MovieClip();

// instance methods go here…

// Connect the class with the linkage ID for this movie clip
Object.registerClass("spaceWord", SpaceWord);
#endinitclip
```

5. In the preceding code, you see right away that there is some initialization that occurs with each instance of the SpaceWord. Primarily, this sets what happens when the button of the SpaceWord is clicked. Also, you are using the onEnterFrame event to drive the behavior of the word. This includes the scaling and positioning of the text to emulate a three-dimensional environment. You'll next write the render function, as you have done before, with some slight modifications (this slots in above the class registration, as usual—see textInSpace.fla):

```
// instance methods go here…
SpaceWord.prototype.render = function() {
 var zActual = Object.environment.fl+this.z-Object.environment.cam.z;
  // has the object moved behind the camera?
 if (zActual>0) {
    // object is still visible
    // calculate scale
    var scale = Object.environment.fl/zActual;
    // set position using camera as an offset
    this._x = (this.x-Object.environment.cam.x)*scale;
    this._y = (this.y-Object.environment.cam.y)*scale;
    // set size
    this._xscale = scale*100;
    this._yscale = scale*100;
 } else {
    // object has moved behind camera
    // reposition further down the line
    this.z += Object.environment.fl*2;

    // enable button
    this.btnSquare.enabled = true;
    this.btnSquare._visible = true;
 }
};
```

Here, each word calculates the fractional influence of its z position based on the location of the camera and the focal length of the environment. This value is calculated on the first line of the function and stored as zActual. If the result is greater than zero, the object is in view of the camera. The screen position and size is calculated by the word's relative location to the camera.

If the value is less than or equal to zero, the object has actually moved behind the camera. In this case, you want to reposition the object in the distance by twice the value of the focal length. Notice also that you are reenabling the button when you reposition it, so you can select the object again.

6. Now you'll write two setter functions to allow you to set the attributes of the word. This includes the actual word displayed and the position of the word. The following needs to be placed just after the `render` function in the `SpaceWord` definition:

```
SpaceWord.prototype.setWord = function(s) {
  this.txtWord = s;
};

SpaceWord.prototype.setPosition = function(x, y, z) {
  this.x = x;
  this.y = y;
  this.z = z;
};
```

The `SpaceWord` object is now complete. However, you are not ready to test your movie because you have not defined the environment in which the words exist, nor have you developed an algorithm that creates instances of the `SpaceWord`. You'll do that next.

7. First, define the `environment` as the root of the movie. On the first frame of the main timeline, in any layer, type the following:

```
// register root as environment
Object.environment = this;

// create camera object
this.cam = {x:0, y:0, z:500, dx:0, dy:0, dz:-500};

// set environmental constants
this.fl = 1000;

// a string of words related to the wind
this.somewords = " wind breeze storm stormy blow gush whoosh
thrash whirl push roar rush caress flow swoop ";

// convert the string of words into an array of words
this.wordList = new Array();
this.wordList = this.somewords.split(" ");
```

The `cam` object holds the location (x, y, and z) and destination (dx, dy, and dz) of the camera object. Initially, the camera is center focused, deep in the space. Its destination is back 500 pixels, the effect being that immediately when the movie runs, the camera is already moving through space, pulling backward. The variable `fl` represents the focal length of the three-dimensional perspective.

8.   You'll also create an empty movie clip called `space` in which you can place all of your `SpaceWord` objects. The advantage to doing it this way is that you now have a nice, tangible handle on the text space's vanishing point (0,0). In effect, the vanishing point of the text space system is set by the screen position of the `space` object. Here is the code that creates the `space` movie clip and positions it in the center of the movie's stage:

```
// create 'space' to which all words will be attached
this.createEmptyMovieClip("space",1);
// center 'space' on the stage
space._x=400;
space._y=300;
```

9.   Now you can program the loop that actually creates instances of your `SpaceWord`. The following should be typed on the first frame of the main timeline, immediately after creating the `space` object:

```
// create one instance for each word in the list
for (n=0;n<this.wordList.length;n++) {
// pick a word from the list
 var word = Object.environment.wordList[n];
 var x = random(800)-400;
 var y = random(800)-400;
 var z = random(Object.environment.fl*2)-Object.environment.fl;

// create an instance of the SpaceWord object
 nombre = "word"+String(depth++);
 initialization = {txtword: word, x: x, y: y, z: z};
 space.attachMovie("spaceWord", nombre, depth, initialization);
}
```

10. As one final step, you need a function at the environmental level that moves your camera. The function will execute continuously because it is assigned to the `onEnterFrame` event of the main timeline. This code immediately follows the preceding, on frame 1 of the main timeline:

```
this.onEnterFrame = function() {
// move the camera to its destination
this.cam.x+=(this.cam.dx-this.cam.x)/10;
this.cam.y+=(this.cam.dy-this.cam.y)/10;
this.cam.z+=(this.cam.dz-this.cam.z)/30;
};
```

The camera moves by a speed defined within each of the preceding equations. Whenever the destination of the camera changes, the camera automatically moves toward it. For the x and y positions, the translation per frame is divided into tenths; for the z position, the translation is divided into thirtieths. Essentially, the larger the divider, the slower the camera will move into position.

Your *lost in text space* system is now complete. Test your movie (`textInSpace.fla`) and you should immediately see words streaming into the background. Select a word and you should be drawn through the space, focusing slowly on your selection:

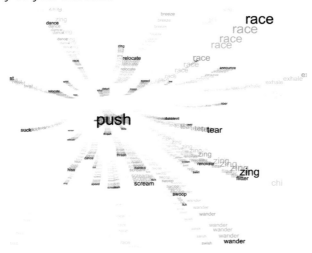

If everything is coming together, you are now flying through space. If you can pull yourself away from clicking around these new planetary text objects, you can continue to develop this system and make it even more interesting.

Free-floating words

As a potentially interesting exercise, you might allow your words to move themselves. These modifications exist in a file called `textInSpace_floating.fla`. For the sake of simplicity, you will allow words to move only along their x- and y-axes. You need only extend the current functionality of the `SpaceWord` prototype to include a function called `float` (positioned just after the `render` function's definition):

```
SpaceWord.prototype.float = function() {
  // float about the space randomly
  // apply random forces to velocities
  this.vx += (random(101) - 50) / 500;
  this.vy += (random(101) - 50) / 500;
  // add velocities to position
  this.x += this.vx;
  this.y += this.vy;
  // bound check
  if (this.x<-400) {
    this.x=-400;
    this.vx*=-.85;
```

continues overleaf

```
      } else if (this.x>400) {
        this.x=400;
        this.vx*=-.85;
      }
      if (this.y<-400) {
        this.y=-400;
        this.vy*=-.5;
      } else if (this.y>400) {
        this.y=400;
        this.vy*=-.5;
      }
    };
```

Now you must also be sure to call this function. The best way to do this would be a simple function call embedded in the `render` function, as such:

```
SpaceWord.prototype.render = function() {
  var zActual = Object.environment.fl+this.z-Object.environment.cam.z;
  // has the object moved behind the camera?
  if (zActual>0) {
    // object is still visible
    // calculate scale
    var scale = Object.environment.fl/zActual;
    // set position using camera as an offset
    this._x = (this.x-Object.environment.cam.x)*scale;
    this._y = (this.y-Object.environment.cam.y)*scale;
    // set size
    this._xscale = scale*100;
    this._yscale = scale*100;
  } else {
    // object has moved behind camera
    // reposition further down the line
    this.z += Object.environment.fl*2;

    // enable button
    this.btnSquare.enabled = true;
    this.btnSquare._visible = true;
  }

  // let the word move about!
  this.float();
};
```

The position of the `SpaceWord` is modified by two velocity variables: `vx` and `vy`. In turn, very small random forces modify the velocity variables. The `SpaceWord` is kept within a reasonable range by checking to see if it has exceeded the boundaries. When the object does exceed the boundary, the word is placed back within the limits and its velocity is reversed and dampened.

Camera autofocus

One potential problem of the free-floating words feature is that the camera is now unable to focus on a moving word. You can fix this problem by writing a small function allowing the camera to track a target. The best place to put this new function is within the loop the camera is already using to move to its destination. As you may recall, this loop is on frame 1 of the main timeline. You simply need a few additional lines of code to reassign the destination if the word has moved (these changes have also been made in `textInSpace_floating.fla`):

```
this.onEnterFrame = function() {
  // does the camera have a moving target
  if (this.cam.targetWord!=null) {
    // yes - reassign the destination to the target's current position
    this.cam.dx = this.cam.targetWord.x;
    this.cam.dy = this.cam.targetWord.y;
  }

  // move the camera to its destination
  this.cam.x += (this.cam.dx-this.cam.x)/10;
  this.cam.y += (this.cam.dy-this.cam.y)/10;
  this.cam.z += (this.cam.dz-this.cam.z)/30;
};
```

You also need to append some code in the selection event of the `SpaceWord` so that the camera knows which word it is focused on. You do this by adding a single line to the constructor function in frame 1 of the `SpaceWord` definition layer:

```
// constructor
function SpaceWord() {
  // set up button functionality
  this.btnSquare.onPress = function() {
    // push the camera towards the word by setting destination just a
➥bit in front
    Object.environment.cam.dx = this._parent.x;
    Object.environment.cam.dy = this._parent.y;
    Object.environment.cam.dz =
this._parent.z+Object.environment.fl*.9;

    // disable and hide button
    this.enabled = false;
    this._visible = false;

    // inform the camera of its new target
    Object.environment.cam.targetWord = this._parent;

  };
  // set continual function to render word
  this.onEnterFrame = this.render;
}
```

The new text system is a bit more irregular as the camera may or may not always be able to keep up with the SpaceWord, but this is how you might expect things to happen in the real world.

Atmospheric fog

One final enhancement you can make to this system involves another trick of the faux-3D trade: *fog*. In real-world scenarios, fog, or atmospheric perspective, can be a natural indication of distance. The further away an object is, the more the particulate matter in the atmosphere will obscure its visibility. You can simulate this effect with attractive results using the _alpha movie clip property. Introducing fog also eliminates the distracting side effect caused by repositioning words in the distance. Instead of simply popping into existence, each word gradually fades in from the bright white background. This final modification exists in a file called textInSpace_fog.fla.

To add fog, you simply compute some value for _alpha within your SpaceWord's render function. The most logical place to place the code is just after the setting of the size:

```
// set size
this._xscale = scale*100;
this._yscale = scale*100;

// set fog
this._alpha = 100 - 100 * zActual/(Object.environment.fl*1.1);
```

Though the fog effect does require a significant amount of additional computation, the results, we believe, are worth it:

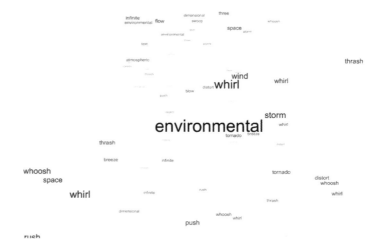

Summary

Three-dimensional space is an absolutely wonderful place to exist. Indeed, we are very well suited for it! The closer you get to displaying typographic data in this space, the more successful your design with text will become. At the same time, you must keep your distance from the heavy computational requirements typically involved in this type of display. In this chapter, we've discussed only three possible solutions that work well in the Flash MX environment. There are still many other elegant solutions waiting to be invented.

Drawing API and Math for 3D

Graphical content used in Flash movies is typically generated before the movie is published. Designers may import graphics from external sources or they may create artwork using the drawing tools in Flash MX. These graphics are then packaged into a SWF when the movie is published and their representation becomes fixed or static.

Alternatively, when graphic content is generated while a Flash movie is being played, we say that the graphics are generated at *runtime* or that they are *dynamically* generated. The Flash MX drawing API makes this type of content possible. We can use the drawing API to draw graphics that are interactive: as a user interacts with the movie, he or she can make complex changes to the content that would simply not be possible using static graphics. One such application of the drawing API is generating dynamic 2D representations of 3D geometries or building what many people refer to as 3D engines.

In this chapter, we begin by describing the Flash drawing API. We then introduce a 3D engine based on the drawing API and, using this 3D engine, we explore some of the math behind 3D and use this knowledge to create some interesting examples.

The Flash MX drawing API

In this section, we will introduce the core methods of the Flash drawing API. These methods enable you to dynamically add shapes made up of basic lines and curves to a movie clip. It also allows you to control basic properties of these shapes such as fill type, fill color, line color, and line weight. Let's get started by learning how to draw some simple shapes.

Drawing shapes

Like many drawing engines, the Flash drawing engine is essentially a *state* machine. What this means is that any operation you perform affects the current state of the underlying drawing engine. For example, when you draw a line with the drawing API, you only specify the end point of the line. The beginning point of the line is taken from the current state of the drawing engine. Usually, this will be the point you specified in a previous draw or move operation. Because the drawing engine relies on state information, the order in which you perform operations is very important.

Consider the four points that make up a square. One specific sequence of the points will form a square, but the same points written in a different order may form a bow tie. It's the ordering of the points that determines which shape is drawn:

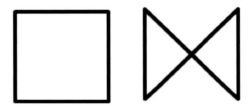

There are three important methods in the Flash drawing API that let us specify how shapes should be drawn from lines, curves, and points, and another that allows us to delete our dynamic creations.

Drawing Method	Description
moveTo(x, y)	Sets the current drawing position to (x, y).
lineTo(x, y)	Draws a line from the previous drawing position to (x, y). It then sets the new drawing position to (x, y).
curveTo(control_x, control_y, x, y)	Draws a curve from the previous drawing position to (x, y) using the control point (control_x, control_y). It then sets the new drawing position to (x, y).
clear()	Clears all of the drawing paths that have been created in the movie clip.

Before you tackle some pseudo-3D drawings, you'll do a few simple warm-up exercises to show how these methods work (if you're already up to speed with the drawing API in Flash MX, feel free to skip ahead to the section *Moving from 2D to 3D*):

1. Create a new movie (CTRL/CMD+N) and then select Modify > Document. Set the window dimensions to 150x150.

2. To draw the square in the previous figure, you just need to click on frame 1 of the timeline and add this code in the Actions panel, which you open by pressing F9 (refer to drawing1.fla):

```
createEmptyMovieClip("square", 1);
with (square) {
 lineStyle(4);
 moveTo(25, 25);
 lineTo(125, 25);
 lineTo(125, 125);
 lineTo(25, 125);
 lineTo(25, 25);
 }
```

3. Test the movie (CTRL/CMD+ENTER) and you should indeed see a square.

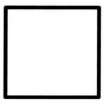

4. Next, to draw the bow tie that you saw earlier, you can just change the order of the `lineTo` methods ever so slightly (`drawing2.fla`):

```
createEmptyMovieClip("bowtie", 1);
with (bowtie) {
 lineStyle(4);
 moveTo(25, 25);
 lineTo(125, 125);
 lineTo(125, 25);
 lineTo(25, 125);
 lineTo(25, 25);
 }
```

5. Additionally, you can make a rounded shape by using the `curveTo` method instead of the `lineTo` method (`drawing3.fla`):

```
createEmptyMovieClip("rounded", 1);
with (rounded) {
 lineStyle(4);
 moveTo(25, 25);
 curveTo(75, 0, 125, 25);
 curveTo(150, 75, 125, 125);
 curveTo(75, 150, 25, 125);
 curveTo(0, 75, 25, 25);
 }
```

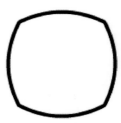

6. Try tweaking the values of the control point parameters in the `moveTo` methods to gain an understanding of the significance of these controls:

```
createEmptyMovieClip("rounded", 1);
with (rounded) {
 lineStyle(4);
 moveTo(25, 25);
```

```
    curveTo(125, 50, 125, 25);
    curveTo(200, 125, 125, 125);
    curveTo(125, 200, 25, 125);
    curveTo(50, 125, 25, 25);
    }
```

Using fills

Flash provides three methods that are used to control the fill of shapes that you define.

Fill Method	Description
beginFill(rgb, alpha)	Begins a filled shape with the specified rgb value provided in hexadecimal format and an integer alpha value that ranges between 0 and 100
beginGradientFill(fillType, colors, alphas, ratios, matrix)	Begins a filled shape with either a linear or radial fillType, an array of colors provided in hex format, an array of alphas that corresponds to the colors array, an array of integer color distributions named ratios that range between 0 and 255, and a transformation matrix represented as a nine-element array
endFill()	Ends a fill that was begun either with beginFill or beginGradientFill

The beginGradientFill method is obviously much more powerful and more complex than the beginFill function. Let's look at some examples.

1. Adding a red fill to your square shape is easy (see also drawing4.fla):

```
createEmptyMovieClip("square", 1);
with (square) {
 lineStyle(4);
 beginFill("0xFF0000", 100);
 moveTo(25, 25);
 lineTo(125, 25);
 lineTo(125, 125);
 lineTo(25, 125);
 lineTo(25, 25);
 endFill();
}
```

2. However, adding a red-to-white gradient is slightly more complex (refer to drawing5.fla):

```
createEmptyMovieClip("square", 1);
with (square) {
 lineStyle(4);
 colors = [0xFFFFFF, 0xFF0000];
```

```
    alphas = [100, 100];
    ratios = [0, 0xFF];
    matrix = {a:150, b:0, c:0, d:0, e:150, f:0,
➥g:75, h:75, i:1 };
    beginGradientFill("radial", colors, alphas,
➥ratios, matrix);
    moveTo(25, 25);
    lineTo(125, 25);
    lineTo(125, 125);
    lineTo(25, 125);
    lineTo(25, 25);
    endFill();
}
```

Although the 3D drawing engine that we will introduce later in this chapter will employ the relatively straightforward `beginFill` method, it's obvious that `beginGradientFill` has great potential for creating the shaded surfaces of 3D objects.

Line styles

You have already been using the last method in the Flash drawing API.

Line Style Method	Description
`lineStyle(thickness, rgb, alpha)`	Sets the current line weight to `thickness`, the current line color to the hexadecimal value provided by `rgb`, and the current opacity to `alpha`

So you can change your box's border to a thick blue line by changing a single line in the original script (see `drawing6.fla`):

```
createEmptyMovieClip("square", 1);
with (square) {
  lineStyle(12, "0x0000FF", 100);
  moveTo(25, 25);
  lineTo(125, 25);
  lineTo(125, 125);
  lineTo(25, 125);
  lineTo(25, 25);
}
```

Moving from 2D to 3D

As you can see, Flash has a fairly complete 2D drawing API. If we can somehow *project* 3D geometry into a 2D representation that Flash can draw, we can bridge this 3D-to-2D gap. That said, the problem of transforming 3D geometries to 2D isn't specific to Flash—all applications that render 3D graphics on a 2D format (like the computer screen) must make this transformation. Unfortunately, this can be a computationally expensive transformation. This is why modern graphic adaptors support hardware acceleration for many of these expensive 3D transformation operations.

Since Flash wasn't designed with 3D in mind, as we've been emphasizing throughout this book, we won't have the advantage of 3D hardware acceleration. This means that there will be a serious trade-off with regard to complexity versus speed when producing faux-3D in Flash. In order to keep things fast, we also need to keep them simple!

We will begin our journey from 2D to 3D by considering a simple cube:

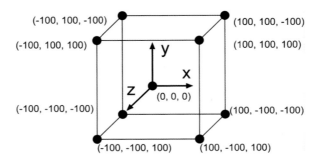

A cube is made up of eight vertices (otherwise known as points) and six faces. We will use multidimensional arrays in ActionScript to store each vertex value and then use the Flash drawing API to draw the faces. You can work through this tutorial in detail or just take a look at `drawing7.fla` while you read along.

1. Create a new movie and set the window dimensions to 400x400. Select frame 1 on the timeline and add the following ActionScript. The code begins by creating an array of points with the coordinates of the cube:

    ```
    points = new Array(8);
    points[0] = new Array (100, 100, -100);
    points[1] = new Array (100, -100, -100);
    points[2] = new Array (-100, -100, -100);
    points[3] = new Array (-100, 100, -100);
    points[4] = new Array (100, 100, 100);
    points[5] = new Array (100, -100, 100);
    points[6] = new Array (-100, -100, 100);
    points[7] = new Array (-100, 100, 100);
    ```

2. At each frame in the animation, you will need to know the transformed coordinates, which you will store in another array:

```
xpoints = new Array();
for (i=0; i<8; i++) xpoints[i] = new Array();
```

3. You'll also rotate or spin the points about the y-axis. We'll cover rotation and other transformations in more depth a little later in the chapter.

```
theta = 0;
createEmptyMovieClip ("cube", 1);

this.onEnterFrame = function () {
 theta += 0.01;
 if (theta > 6.28) theta -= 6.28;

 // transform the points
 for (i=0; i<8; i++) {
   xpoints[i][0] = points[i][2]*Math.sin(theta) +
➡points[i][0]*Math.cos(theta);
   xpoints[i][1] = points[i][1];
   xpoints[i][2] = points[i][2]*Math.cos(theta) -
➡points[i][0]*Math.sin(theta);
   p = 500 / (xpoints[i][2] + 500);
   xpoints[i][0] *= p;
   xpoints[i][1] *= p;
   xpoints[i][0] += 200;
   xpoints[i][1] += 200;
 }
```

4. Once the original cube vertices have been transformed, use the Flash drawing API to render the faces:

```
with (cube) {
  clear();
  lineStyle (4);

  // draw face 1
  moveTo (xpoints[0][0], xpoints[0][1]);
  lineTo (xpoints[1][0], xpoints[1][1]);
  lineTo (xpoints[2][0], xpoints[2][1]);
  lineTo (xpoints[3][0], xpoints[3][1]);
  lineTo (xpoints[0][0], xpoints[0][1]);

  // draw face 2
  moveTo (xpoints[4][0], xpoints[4][1]);
  lineTo (xpoints[7][0], xpoints[7][1]);
  lineTo (xpoints[6][0], xpoints[6][1]);
  lineTo (xpoints[5][0], xpoints[5][1]);
  lineTo (xpoints[4][0], xpoints[4][1]);
```

continues overleaf

```
                    // draw face 3
                    moveTo (xpoints[0][0], xpoints[0][1]);
                    lineTo (xpoints[4][0], xpoints[4][1]);
                    lineTo (xpoints[5][0], xpoints[5][1]);
                    lineTo (xpoints[1][0], xpoints[1][1]);
                    lineTo (xpoints[0][0], xpoints[0][1]);

                    // draw face 4
                    moveTo (xpoints[1][0], xpoints[1][1]);
                    lineTo (xpoints[5][0], xpoints[5][1]);
                    lineTo (xpoints[6][0], xpoints[6][1]);
                    lineTo (xpoints[2][0], xpoints[2][1]);
                    lineTo (xpoints[1][0], xpoints[1][1]);

                    // draw face 5
                    moveTo (xpoints[2][0], xpoints[2][1]);
                    lineTo (xpoints[6][0], xpoints[6][1]);
                    lineTo (xpoints[7][0], xpoints[7][1]);
                    lineTo (xpoints[3][0], xpoints[3][1]);
                    lineTo (xpoints[2][0], xpoints[2][1]);

                    // draw face 6
                    moveTo (xpoints[4][0],
            ➥xpoints[4][1]);
                    lineTo (xpoints[0][0],
            ➥xpoints[0][1]);
                    lineTo (xpoints[3][0],
            ➥xpoints[3][1]);
                    lineTo (xpoints[7][0],
            ➥xpoints[7][1]);
                    lineTo (xpoints[4][0],
            ➥xpoints[4][1]);
                }
            };
```

5. Test your movie by pressing CTRL/CMD+ENTER.

These first steps into the world of 3D were fairly successful, but there are a few things we haven't addressed. First, this example was a simple wire frame. If we had filled the faces of the cube, this example wouldn't have worked, because as the cube turns the same faces would always be rendered on top. Second, although the transformation we chose here worked nicely, it's a little difficult to follow—we've got a few sine and cosine functions, and it's not immediately clear what they mean or how they are affecting the cube. And third, we haven't yet considered how lighting might affect the color of the cube.

What we need is a higher-level interface that abstracts such functionality so that we do not have to concern ourselves with the scene-rendering implementation details.

A basic 3D drawing engine

In this section we'll introduce some of the core methods of a basic 3D drawing engine. The file for this 3D engine is `draw3d.as`, available for download from www.friendsofed.com along with the other example files in this chapter. You can open this file in your favorite text editor to analyze the implementation in more depth. In this section, we will describe the API and take another stab at the spinning cube from the last section.

Our engine uses a single class called `Draw3D` to store polygonal geometry. It defines several methods to represent the points and lines that make up an object and provides several methods to transform that geometry.

Draw3D	Method Description
`Draw3D(pointCount, faceCount)`	Constructor; creates a new `Draw3D` object with the specified number of points and faces allocated
`Draw3D.setPoint(i, x, y, z)`	Sets the point at index `i` to the coordinates (`x`, `y`, `z`)
`Draw3D.setFace(i, a)`	Defines a face at index `i` with an array of point indices given in `a`
`Draw3D.clearTransform()`	Clears any transformations that have been applied thus far
`Draw3D.scale(sx, sy, sz)`	Scales (or multiplies) the points in the mesh along the x-, y-, and z-axes by the values `sx`, `sy`, and `sz`, respectively
`Draw3D.translate(dx, dy, dz)`	Translates the points in the mesh along the x-, y-, and z-axes by the distances `dx`, `dy`, and `dz`, respectively
`Draw3D.rotateX(theta)`	Rotates the points in the mesh about the x-axis by an angle of `theta` radians
`Draw3D.rotateY(theta)`	Rotates the points in the mesh about the y-axis by an angle of `theta` radians
`Draw3D.rotateZ(theta)`	Rotates the points in the mesh about the z-axis by an angle of `theta` radians
`Draw3D.applyPerspective(p)`	Applies a simple perspective function using `p` as the basis for the amount of perspective to apply
`Draw3D.setFillColor(r, g, b)`	Sets the fill color to use when rendering polygons
`Draw3D.setFillAlpha(alpha)`	Sets the fill alpha to use when rendering polygons
`Draw3D.setLineColor(r, g, b)`	Sets the line color to use when rendering polygons
`Draw3D.setLineWeight(w)`	Sets the line thickness to `w`
`Draw3D.setShadeOn()`	Turns on a very simple lighting and shading model
`Draw3D.setShadeOff()`	Turns off the simple lighting and shading model
`Draw3D.render()`	Renders the scene

The `render` method is really the heart of the engine. Once the geometry and its transformations have been set up, `render` translates that information into drawing functions that Flash understands. This rendering function is slightly more intelligent than the loop you used to draw the wire frame cube in the last example. It sorts the faces so those that are supposed to be in front are on top of faces that should be in back. It also uses information about the face to compute its relationship to a fixed light source, which in turn can be used to alter the shading of the faces.

With these new features, you should really be able to improve the last example. For this example, refer to the file `drawing8.fla`.

1. Create a new movie and set the window dimensions to 400x400. Using the infrastructure developed in `draw3d.as` (incorporated via the `#include` command) you can re-create your cube.

   Select frame 1 on the timeline and add the following code. The script begins by creating an array of points with the coordinates of the cube:

   ```
   #include "draw3d.as"

   // Initialize the 3d drawing object with 8 points and 6 faces
   m = new Draw3D (8, 6);

   // Define the point list
   m.setPoint (0,   100,   100, -100); // Point 0
   m.setPoint (1,   100,  -100, -100); // Point 1
   m.setPoint (2,  -100,  -100, -100); // Point 2
   m.setPoint (3,  -100,   100, -100); // Point 3
   m.setPoint (4,   100,   100,  100); // Point 4
   m.setPoint (5,   100,  -100,  100); // Point 5
   m.setPoint (6,  -100,  -100,  100); // Point 6
   m.setPoint (7,  -100,   100,  100); // Point 7

   // Set the fill and line properties
   m.setShadeOn ();
   m.setLineWeight (2);
   m.setLineColor (0, 0, 0);
   m.setFillColor (.4, .4, .8);

   // Define the faces
   m.setFace (0, new Array (0, 1, 2, 3));
   m.setFace (1, new Array (4, 7, 6, 5));
   m.setFace (2, new Array (0, 4, 5, 1));
   m.setFace (3, new Array (1, 5, 6, 2));
   m.setFace (4, new Array (2, 6, 7, 3));
   m.setFace (5, new Array (4, 0, 3, 7));
   ```

2. You may be wondering why we have one list of vertices and then each face has a list of indices into that list of vertices. Wouldn't it be easier to have a point list for each face rather than a combined point list? A cube has eight points that need to be transformed, but if each face has its own point list, then there are 24 points we will need to transform (6 faces multiplied by 4 points per face equates to 24 points). That's quite a few redundant calculations! In addition to being more computationally efficient, this scheme makes it easier to update point values.

To finish the program, add on this `onEnterFrame` function that effectively renders your cube:

```
theta = 0;

m.scene.onEnterFrame = function () {
 with (_root) {
   m.clearTransform();
   m.rotateY (theta);
   m.applyPerspective (500);
   theta += .02;
   if (theta > 6.282) theta -=
➥6.282;
   m.render ();
 }
};
```

3.   Finally, test your movie (CTRL/CMD+ENTER).

3D transformations

We mentioned transformations earlier, and we just used the `clearTransform` method, but we haven't really described them in detail. Three of the most common 3D transformations are translation, scaling, and rotation. These operations allow us to change the position, size, and orientation of objects in a scene.

In many advanced 3D systems, all transformations are represented as 4x4 matrices. This is useful because one transformation matrix can be multiplied by another transformation matrix to create an aggregate transformation matrix. Multiplying the transformation matrix by a position vector results in a transformed position vector.

In complex systems, this can be an efficient way of applying a complex transformation to a large number of points. This is useful in 3D games, medical imaging applications, and scientific visualization applications that often must deal with thousands or even millions of points, and numerous transformations. The 3D transformations we will introduce are slightly less complex. These operations will be applied directly to the points that we are transforming instead of to an intermediate transformation matrix.

If you're starting to get a little worried about how freely we're using mathematical terms such as *vector* and *matrix*, just relax. We're going to explain how and why the math does what it does, but if you don't completely get it, that's OK—it's more important that you understand the high-level concepts and *why* they work, if not *how*.

Our 3D drawing engine defines four transformations: **translation**, **scaling**, **rotation**, and **perspective**. We will now examine each operation a little closer.

Translation

Translation boils down to simple addition. In ActionScript, you could translate a point `p` by values `tx`, `ty`, and `tz` like this:

```
p[0] += tx;
p[1] += ty;
p[2] += tz;
```

After this transformation, `p` will be offset along the x-, y-, and z-axes by distances `tx`, `ty`, and `tz`, respectively.

Scaling

Scaling is equivalent to multiplication. In ActionScript, you could scale a point `p` by values `sx`, `sy`, and `sz` like this:

```
p[0] *= sx;
p[1] *= sy;
p[2] *= sz;
```

Rotation

Rotation is measured as an angle about an axis. Our 3D drawing engine defines rotation transformations about the x-, y-, and z-axes. With these three functions it is then possible to represent any arbitrary rotation as being made up of x, y, and z rotational components.

A point `p` can be rotated about the x-axis with the following ActionScript:

```
y = p[1]*Math.cos(theta) - p[2]*Math.sin(theta);
z = p[1]*Math.sin(theta) + p[2]*Math.cos(theta);
p[1] = y;
p[2] = z;
```

The point `p` can be rotated about the y-axis with the next code snippet:

```
z = p[2]*Math.cos(theta) - p[0]*Math.sin(theta);
x = p[2]*Math.sin(theta) + p[0]*Math.cos(theta);
p[2] = z;
p[0] = x;
```

And finally, point `p` can be rotated about the z-axis using this code:

```
x = p[0]*Math.cos(theta) - p[1]*Math.sin(theta);
y = p[0]*Math.sin(theta) + p[1]*Math.cos(theta);
p[0] = x;
p[1] = y;
```

Notice that when we rotate a point about a particular axis, the value associated with that axis does not change.

View transformation and perspective

When you look at the two-dimensional floor plan of a house, you are viewing what is called a **parallel projection**. In a parallel projection, the x- and y-axes of the screen or viewing surface correspond to the x- and y-axes of the scene. The imaginary lines, or rays, that we use to project points from 3D space onto the 2D projection plane are parallel. In parallel projections, objects do not change size when they move in a direction perpendicular to the plane of projection.

What we would like to develop is a transformation that imparts a sense of perspective. We will use a very simple equation to find a value *perspective* that we will multiply by the point's x and y values:

$$Perspective = \frac{c}{c+z}$$

The value c can be tweaked to adjust the amount of perspective. As c gets larger the perspective effect lessens.

The corresponding ActionScript code to transform a point p with the constant c is thus:

```
if (c-p[2] == 0) perspective = 1;
else p = perspective / p[2] + perspective;
if (c <= 0) perspective = 1;
p[0] *= perspective;
p[1] *= perspective;
```

Using the 3D drawing engine

We have provided quite a bit of background on how the 3D drawing engine works, and it's now time to delve into some deeper examples.

Interactive rotating cube

By now you should have a pretty good grasp on how transformations work, so you will revisit the cube example one last time and add a degree of interactivity. The FLA file that accompanies this example is `drawing9.fla`.

1. Create a new movie and set the window dimensions to 400x400. Select frame 1 on the timeline and add the following ActionScript code:

```
#include "draw3d.as"

// Initialize the 3d drawing object with 8 points and 6 faces
m = new Draw3D (8, 6);

// Define the point list
m.setPoint (0,  100,  100, -100); // Point 0
m.setPoint (1,  100, -100, -100); // Point 1
m.setPoint (2, -100, -100, -100); // Point 2
```

```
m.setPoint (3, -100,  100, -100); // Point 3
m.setPoint (4,  100,  100,  100); // Point 4
m.setPoint (5,  100, -100,  100); // Point 5
m.setPoint (6, -100, -100,  100); // Point 6
m.setPoint (7, -100,  100,  100); // Point 7

// Set the fill and line properties
m.setShadeOn ();
m.setLineWeight (2);
m.setLineColor (0, 0, 0);
m.setFillColor (.4, .4, .8);

// Define the faces
m.setFace (0, new Array (0, 1, 2, 3));
m.setFace (1, new Array (4, 7, 6, 5));
m.setFace (2, new Array (0, 4, 5, 1));
m.setFace (3, new Array (1, 5, 6, 2));
m.setFace (4, new Array (2, 6, 7, 3));
m.setFace (5, new Array (4, 0, 3, 7));

theta = 0;

m.scene.onEnterFrame = function () {
 with (_root) {
   mx = ((m.scene._xmouse) / 200);
   my = ((m.scene._ymouse) / 200);
   m.clearTransform();
   m.rotateZ (theta);
   m.rotateY ((-mx*45)*.0174);
   m.rotateX (my*90*.0174);
   m.applyPerspective (500);
   theta += .02;
   if (theta > 6.282) theta -= 6.282;
   m.render ();
 }
};
```

2. Finally, add a background image to taste, and test your movie (CTRL/CMD+ENTER).

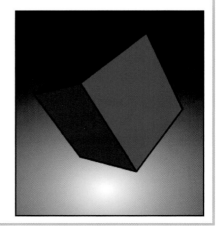

3D star

The cube is one of the classic 3D shapes, but it's only one of an infinite number of possible shapes that we can represent. In this example, you'll create a 3D star block (see `drawing10.fla`).

1. A star is made up of ten points. If you were to plot a star on a piece of graph paper, you might come up with the following point assignments:

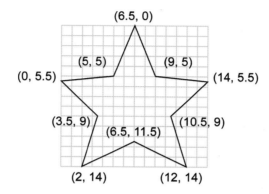

2. Create a new movie with window dimensions 400x400, and then select frame 1 on the timeline and add the following ActionScript:

```
#include "draw3d.as"

m = new Draw3D (20, 12);

// Create the points we extracted from our graph paper drawing

// Top Star
m.setPoint (0, 6.5, 0, 4);
m.setPoint (1, 9, 5, 4);
m.setPoint (2, 14, 5.5, 4);
m.setPoint (3, 10.5, 9, 4);
m.setPoint (4, 12, 14, 4);
m.setPoint (5, 6.5, 11.5, 4);
m.setPoint (6, 2, 14, 4);
m.setPoint (7, 3.5, 9, 4);
m.setPoint (8, 0, 5.5, 4);
m.setPoint (9, 5, 5, 4);

// Bottom Star
m.setPoint (10, 6.5, 0, -4);
m.setPoint (11, 9, 5, -4);
m.setPoint (12, 14, 5.5, -4);
m.setPoint (13, 10.5, 9, -4);
```

continues overleaf   **209**

```
m.setPoint (14, 12, 14, -4);
m.setPoint (15, 6.5, 11.5, -4);
m.setPoint (16, 2, 14, -4);
m.setPoint (17, 3.5, 9, -4);
m.setPoint (18, 0, 5.5, -4);
m.setPoint (19, 5, 5, -4);

// Set shading and color characteristics of the star
m.setShadeOn ();
m.setLineWeight (0);
m.setLineColor (1, .4, 0);
m.setFillColor (.1, .4, 1);
m.setFillAlpha (100);

// sides
for (i=0; i<9; i++) {
 m.setFace (i, [i, i+1, 11+i, 10+i]);
}
m.setFace (9, [0, 9, 19, 10]);

theta = 0;

m.scene.onEnterFrame = function () {
 with (_root) {
   mx = ((m.scene._xmouse) / 200);
   my = ((m.scene._ymouse) / 200);
   m.clearTransform();
   m.translate (-7, -7, 0);
   m.scale (10, 10, 10);
   m.rotateZ (theta);
   m.rotateY ((-mx*45)*.0174);
   m.rotateX (my*90*.0174);
   m.applyPerspective (140);
   theta += .04;
   if (theta > 6.282) theta -= 6.282;
   m.render ();
 }
};
```

3.   Test your movie (CTRL/CMD+ENTER) and you should be seeing stars! Well, one star anyway.

Origami swan

In the next example, you will render an origami swan. Origami is the Japanese art of folding paper, and origami artists have created some amazingly complex and beautiful works with only a single sheet of paper to work with. One popular figure that beginning origami students learn to make is the swan (remember to check out the swan in our example file `drawing11.fla`).

1. You will begin by drawing the folded paper pieces that make up the swan on a sheet of graph paper. You can then use the grid to get the x- and y-coordinates of the polygonal pieces:

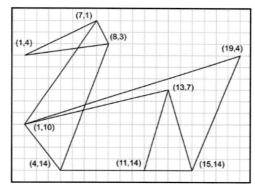

We could then use a second piece of graph paper to plot a front view of the swan and then extract the z-coordinates of each piece. This particular model is fairly simple and we can probably guess approximately how far the points should extend from the x-y plane.

2. Open up a new movie and give it window dimensions of 500x300. Select frame 1 on the timeline and add the following script:

```
#include "draw3d.as"

m = new Draw3D (14, 10);

// Create the points we extracted from our graph paper drawing:
m.setPoint (0, 1, 4, 0);
m.setPoint (1, 7, 1, 0);
m.setPoint (2, 8, 3, 1);
m.setPoint (3, 8, 3, -1);
m.setPoint (4, 1, 10, 0);
m.setPoint (5, 4, 14, 2);
m.setPoint (6, 4, 14, -2);
m.setPoint (7, 13, 7, 5);
m.setPoint (8, 13, 7, -5);
m.setPoint (9, 11, 14, 8);
m.setPoint (10, 11, 14, -8);
m.setPoint (11, 15, 14, 6);
m.setPoint (12, 15, 14, -6);
m.setPoint (13, 19, 4, 0);
```

continues overleaf

```
    // Make the swan a translucent yellow with thin red lines
    m.setShadeOn ();
    m.setLineWeight (1);
    m.setLineColor (1, .4, 0);
    m.setFillColor (1, 1, 0);
    m.setFillAlpha (70);

    // Define the surfaces that make up the swan

    // head
    m.setFace (0, new Array(0, 1, 2));
    m.setFace (1, new Array(0, 1, 3));

    // neck
    m.setFace (2, [4, 1, 2, 5]);
    m.setFace (3, [4, 1, 3, 6]);

    // outside wings
    m.setFace (4, [5, 4, 7, 9]);
    m.setFace (5, [6, 4, 8, 10]);

    // inside wings
    m.setFace (6, [5, 4, 7, 11]);
    m.setFace (7, [6, 4, 8, 12]);

    // body
    m.setFace (8, [5, 4, 13, 11]);
    m.setFace (9, [6, 4, 13, 12]);

    theta = 0;

    // Provide a 'show room floor' style rotation:
    m.scene.onEnterFrame = function () {
     with (_root) {
       m.clearTransform();
       m.scale (10, 10, 10);
       m.rotateY (theta);
       m.applyPerspective (500);
       m.translate (50, -150, 0);
       theta += .03;
       if (theta > 6.282) theta -= 6.282;
       m.render ();
     }
    };
```

3.   As usual, press CTRL/CMD+ENTER to test the movie.

There are actually a few subtle problems with this example. Many of the points that make up faces on the swan are not coplanar so, as the swan turns, if you examine the individual polygons that make up the swan you'll notice that some of them are not flat. When the 3D drawing engine renders them, it renders a polygonal shape that crosses itself (like the bow tie example at the beginning of the chapter). For the most part, this isn't a big problem itself. The technique we have chosen to draw nonplanar polygons is at least consistent. Shading them correctly is a bigger problem. Because the polygon isn't planar, there is no single angle between the surface and the light source that we can use for shading. There are also multiple interpretations of how such a surface should be shaded, if at all. The engine ignores this issue and uses the first three points in a polygon to form a flat surface to compute shading information.

Flying rocket

In the previous examples, you created point and face information either from your head or with the help of some graph paper. More complex shapes are often harder to describe with these techniques. In this example we will show you a 3D modeling application that can be used to produce data you can render with your rendering engine. For this example, refer to the file `drawing12.fla`.

1. We began this exercise by creating a simple model of a spaceship in Blender, a free 3D modeling application. You can download the latest version of Blender from www.blender3d.org.

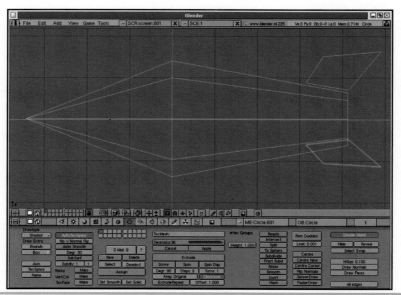

213

2. Next up, we exported the model into Virtual Reality Modeling Language (VRML) format. The resulting file has the following structure:

```
#VRML V1.0 ascii
# Blender V2.0

Separator {
Switch {
 DEF Body
 Separator {
   Coordinate3 {
     point [
           -2.213190 3.029455 0.314176,
           -2.051762 0.365852 0.152740,
                 .
                 .
                 .
           -0.386417 -0.200915 0.604752,
           -0.722432 1.243950 0.940768,
     ]
   }
   IndexedFaceSet {
     coordIndex [
           0, 1, 2, 3, -1,
           4, 7, 6, 5, -1,
                 .
                 .
                 .
           27, 31, 35, 39, -1,
           28, 32, 35, 31, -1,
     ]
   }
  }
 }
}
```

This file is basically a list of points and a list of faces given in terms of the point indexes. Translating this file into something the drawing engine can use is a simple matter of cutting, pasting, and some minor editing. The first list of numbers in this example (abridged) represents points. Each point is space-separated and ends with a comma. The second list represents faces, and each face is represented with the indices into the point list that make up the face (the face ends with a -1 since this is not a valid index).

When designing characters, remember that Flash wasn't designed with 3D in mind. It's not optimized for 3D in the way that OpenGL or DirectX are, and it certainly can't compete with C, C++, or even Java in terms of computational speed. So keep everything simple!

3. Now we bring Flash into the procedure. Create a new movie and set the background color to black in the Property Inspector.

4. Click on frame 1 and then open the Actions panel. You will reuse all the classes you have created thus far. These are already available in the file named `3D.as`, so you only need to include these classes using the `#include` action:

   ```
   #include "draw3d.as"
   ```

5. There's a little bit of "hand waving" in this step—you've taken a VRML file that was exported from the 3D modeler (Blender) and extracted the point and face lists. Each point entry in the VRML file corresponds to a `Draw3D.setPoint()` command and each face entry in the VRML file corresponds to `Draw3D.setFace()`. While you add the faces you also add some color and shading information:

   ```
   m = new Draw3D (29, 22);

   // First enter the point list. The index is implicit
   // in the VRML file; they are given in order.
   m.setPoint (0, 2.532231, -2.585503, -14.208573);
   m.setPoint (1, 1.097652, -1.116318, -12.507711);
   m.setPoint (2, 1.366280, -1.391427, -10.272746);
   m.setPoint (3, 2.361356, -2.410507, -11.191585);
   m.setPoint (4, -2.536146, -2.538829, -14.208573);
   m.setPoint (5, -1.090759, -1.080277, -12.507711);
   m.setPoint (6, -1.361411, -1.353395, -10.272746);
   m.setPoint (7, -2.363985, -2.365099, -11.191585);
   m.setPoint (8, -0.000001, 3.614895, -14.208574);
   m.setPoint (9, -0.000001, 1.561478, -12.507711);
   m.setPoint (10, -0.000001, 1.945987, -10.272747);
   m.setPoint (11, -0.000001, 3.370310, -11.191586);
   m.setPoint (12, 2.195727, 2.195726, -3.261939);
   m.setPoint (13, 3.105227, -0.000000, -3.261939);
   m.setPoint (14, 2.195727, -2.195727, -3.261939);
   m.setPoint (15, -0.000000, -3.105227, -3.261939);
   m.setPoint (16, -2.195727, -2.195727, -3.261939);
   m.setPoint (17, -3.105227, -0.000000, -3.261939);
   m.setPoint (18, -2.195727, 2.195726, -3.261939);
   m.setPoint (19, -0.000001, 3.105227, -3.261940);
   m.setPoint (20, -0.000001, 1.414213, -12.454270);
   m.setPoint (21, -1.000000, 0.999999, -12.454270);
   m.setPoint (22, -1.414214, -0.000001, -12.454270);
   m.setPoint (23, -1.000000, -1.000001, -12.454270);
   m.setPoint (24, -0.000000, -1.414214, -12.454270);
   m.setPoint (25, 1.000000, -1.000001, -12.454270);
   m.setPoint (26, 1.414213, -0.000001, -12.454270);
   m.setPoint (27, 1.000000, 0.999999, -12.454270);
   m.setPoint (28, -0.032325, 0.007158, 4.384903);
   ```

continues overleaf

```
// Set some properties for the base of the rocket.
m.setShadeOn ();
m.setLineWeight (0);
m.setFillColor (1, .2, .2);

// Begin entering faces that make up the rocket.
m.setFace (0, new Array (0, 3, 2, 1));
m.setFace (1, new Array (4, 7, 6, 5));
m.setFace (2, new Array (8, 11, 10, 9));
m.setFace (3, new Array (19, 12, 27, 20));
m.setFace (4, new Array (19, 20, 21, 18));
m.setFace (5, new Array (18, 21, 22, 17));
m.setFace (6, new Array (17, 22, 23, 16));
m.setFace (7, new Array (16, 23, 24, 15));
m.setFace (8, new Array (15, 24, 25, 14));
m.setFace (9, new Array (14, 25, 26, 13));
m.setFace (10, new Array (27, 12, 13, 26));
m.setFace (11, new Array (18, 28, 19));
m.setFace (12, new Array (12, 19, 28));
m.setFace (13, new Array (12, 28, 13));
m.setFace (14, new Array (17, 28, 18));
m.setFace (15, new Array (16, 28, 17));
m.setFace (16, new Array (13, 28, 14));
m.setFace (17, new Array (14, 28, 15));
m.setFace (18, new Array (15, 28, 16));

// The next three faces correspond to the back
// of the rocket. We will make them yellow.
m.setFillColor (1, 1, .2);
m.setFace (19, new Array (22, 25, 24, 23));
m.setFace (20, new Array (21, 26, 25, 22));
m.setFace (21, new Array (20, 27, 26, 21));
```

6. The final block of code defines the behavior of your rocket. We want this example to be a bit more attention-grabbing than our previous examples and have some interesting motion interactions. You will base the rocket's position and angle on the mouse position, but you will also add a gentle back-and-forth thrusting motion and a slight rotation to the rocket to make it seem like it's moving:

```
thrust = 0;
rocket_rotation = 0;

m.scene.onEnterFrame = function () {
 with (_root) {
    // Mouse coordinates scaled to be between -1 and 1
    mx = ((m.scene._xmouse) / 200);
    my = ((m.scene._ymouse) / 200);
```

```
            // Reset all transformations
            m.clearTransform();

            // Scale the rocket a bit bigger
            m.scale (15, 15, 15);

            // Appy a subtle rotation to the rocket so it's always
            // spinning
            m.rotateZ (rocket_rotation*.0174);

            // Orient the rocket in the right direction
            m.rotateX (180*.0174);

            // Use the mouse position to angle the rocket
            m.rotateY ((180-mx*20)*.0174);
            m.rotateX (my*45*.0174);

            // In addition to a translation based on the
            // mouse we add a little back and forth thrusting
            m.translate (100*mx, 100*my, Math.abs(thrust-100));

            // Set a moderate level of perspective
            m.applyPerspective (500);

            // Render the scene
            m.render ();

            // Update a few variables for the next iteration
            thrust += 5;
            if (thrust == 200) thrust = 0;
            rocket_rotation += 5;
            if (rocket_rotation == 360) rocket_rotation -= 360;
        }
    };
```

7. That's the end of the code. Now you just need to put the rocket into context. On a new layer, draw about 20 stars or so. Select all of the stars and then convert them to a movie clip by selecting Insert > Convert to Symbol…. Name this movie clip stars.

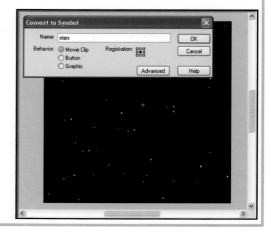

8. Select the stars symbol and select Insert > Convert to Symbol… again. Name this symbol star_field.

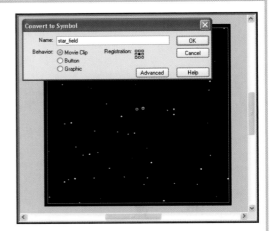

9. Double-click the `star_field` symbol to begin editing it. Create a new layer and copy the frame in the first layer to the second layer. Add keyframes to frame 30 on both layers.

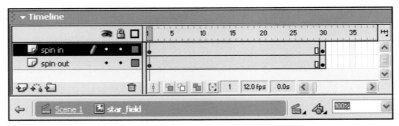

10. Now go to frame 1 and select the movie clip on the *top* layer. Open the Property Inspector and set the alpha to 4%. In the Transform window (CTRL/CMD+T), set the rotation to 45 degrees and the x and y scaling to 60%.

11. Next, go to frame 30. Select the symbol on the *bottom* layer. Open the Property Inspector and set the alpha here to 4%. In the Transform window, set the rotation to -45 degrees and the x and y scaling to 160%.

12. Finally, click on frame 1 of each layer and then select Insert > Create Motion Tween (or use the Property Inspector).

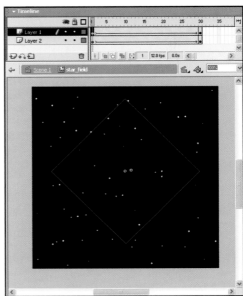

13. If you test the movie now, the rocket should seem to be spinning into space while the mouse steers it.

  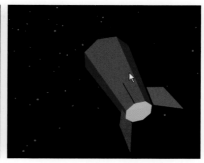

Summary

In this chapter, we've shown how ActionScript can be used to draw dynamic content with the Flash MX drawing API. We introduced a 3D drawing engine, the `Draw3D` class framework, based on the drawing API, and we talked a little about 3D transformations and operators. We then used the 3D drawing engine to render several examples.

This drawing engine and the examples that you've studied are hardly the end of the road—there are many more features you can add to the drawing engine code and, of course, an infinite number of applications for it. What we have done in this chapter is given you a taste of the potential for Flash as a mechanism for 3D content delivery. This is an exciting area of Flash development and one that will likely be full of new developments and exciting new applications.

3D Slice Engine

The initial inspiration for this project came while examining a topographical map that showed contours dividing a landmass into portions of equal altitude. By examining the contour lines defining areas of a similar altitude, we were able to imagine how the landmass would look if we were actually there. These contours gave us insight into the shape and dimensionality of the landmass as perceived from the ground, from the air, or from any other arbitrary point around it. It was from this insight that the Flash 3D *slice engine* was born.

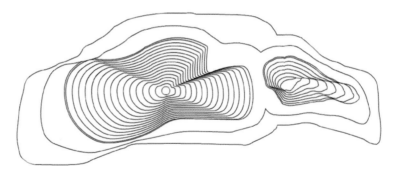

In this chapter, we'll go through the development stages of the 3D slice engine, before presenting some examples of the slice engine in action.

Core engine development

Before we get to grips with the construction of the slice engine, it's a good idea to see what the engine can do. As a teaser of what's to come in this chapter, open the files `3D_slice_engine.swf` and `3D_perspectives.swf`, and take note of the contours and the way in which they react to mouse movement relative to each other. Also note that the combination of contours form the context of an object, in this case a landmass.

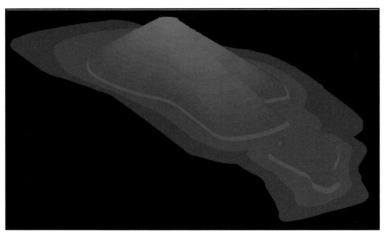

Basic principles

It's important to understand how the engine works in a general sense before you familiarize yourself with the ActionScript that makes it possible. What we are attempting to do is represent a three-dimensional object in two-dimensional space. The topographic map analogy used earlier is an appropriate starting point, so we'll discuss the process of building a multilayered and interactive landmass.

The fundamental principle is to create a series of layers representing the contours of a landmass object. You then place them relative to one another and use the mouse as a way of rotating the object and defining the angle of the view. An understanding of how the objects and layers are structured will be extremely useful when you get into the scripting side of things.

In order to simulate a 3D object made up of slices, the individual slices have to be skewed. You should be familiar with skewing shapes and symbols using the Free Transform Tool with the Rotate and Skew modifier in the authoring environment. Unfortunately, Flash MX does not have any native support for skewing *at runtime* (hopefully it will in later versions), so you need to simulate a skewing effect through the nesting of movie clips.

The principle of mimicking runtime skewing in Flash can be a little tricky to understand at first, so it is important that you read and understand the following outline. In this demonstration, we'll be manually replicating the procedure in Flash to help you understand the skewing effect. However, ultimately we'll implement the slice engine functionality through ActionScript to achieve the same result.

1. The shape to be skewed (represented here as a black box) is turned into a movie clip.

2. The movie clip is then placed inside another movie clip (represented by the blue box). This movie clip will be referred to as the `container` movie clip. The shape we wish to skew is contained or nested within this movie clip.

3. The nested movie clip (our shape movie clip) is rotated *within* the `container` movie clip.

4. The `container` movie clip is then scaled along a single axis (in this case the y-axis).

5. Next, the `container` movie clip is rotated in the opposite direction to which we rotated the shape movie clip earlier.

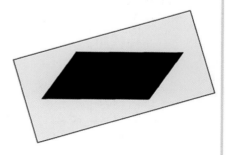

6. Finally, the `container` is scaled the along the y-axis again. If you are trying to manually reproduce this effect, you will have to break apart the `container` movie clip in order to scale along the y-axis of the stage rather than the movie clip's own y-axis. The diagram shows your final result (left) with the original shape movie clip nested inside your container movie clip (right).

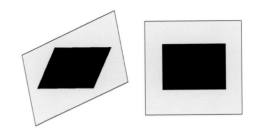

It's difficult to see without context, but this simple skewing technique, coupled with some basic trigonometry, forms the core principle behind the slice engine. The engine uses this skewing method in that it builds a stack of movie clips, each containing a nested clip. The nested (or inner) clips are rotated while the clips themselves (the *slices*) are scaled. By stacking these slices on top of each other and controlling their skewing in relation to each other, we are able to simulate a topographical map or a series of contours and dynamic angles. By placing a number of these slices close enough to each other, we can simulate three-dimensional objects.

Open `3D_perspectives.swf` and you'll see a series of contours representing a landmass. The contours have been progressively manipulated to demonstrate change in angle and rotation.

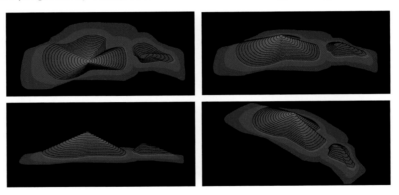

Creating the object clip

Now that you've looked at some of the theory behind the Flash 3D slice engine, you're ready to study how it is created. For the first step, you need to create a movie clip with a series of frames containing the contours of your object. As you are producing a landmass, the initial movie clip contours can be created by hand in Flash and do not require any external tools, files, or knowledge.

1. The object clip creation step can be followed by opening the file `step1_final.fla`, though we recommend that you attempt to create the object from scratch. On the stage, use the Pencil Tool (Y) with the Smooth option selected to create the outline of a landmass approximately 200 pixels wide and 100 pixels high. Fill it with a linear gradient or solid color of your choosing (keeping in mind that as this example is a landmass, you may wish to choose earthy tones).

2.   Convert it to a movie clip (F8) and name it `slice container`. This will be the movie clip that contains your object's layers.

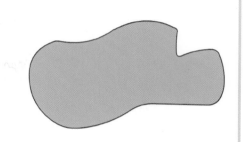

3.   Next, choose to edit the `slice container` movie clip by double-clicking on its icon in the Library, and create a keyframe (F6) at frame 15. On this frame, select the shape, reduce it in size, and fill it with a gradient or solid color (make it noticeably different from the color or gradient used in the shape on frame 1).

4.   Imagine this shape to be the uppermost point of your landmass, and position and modify it accordingly. Make a shape tween between frame 1 and 15. With the Onion Skin Outlines button switched on, you should be able to recognize the contours of your landmass like so:

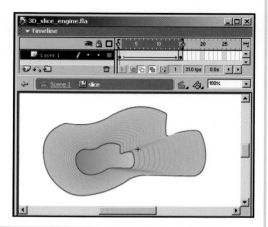

Setting up assets and global variables

In this step, you need to set up the assets and variables required by the slice engine. You need to link your `slice container` movie clip so that you can use it remotely with ActionScript, and you need to declare some environmental variables that will be used by the slice engine code.

1.   Again, this step can be followed by opening the file `step2_final.fla`. To display the object, the engine needs to attach multiple instances of the `slice container` movie clip from the Library. To facilitate this, go the Library panel (F11), select `slice container`, and choose Linkage… from the panel options menu (or right-click/CMD-click for the context-sensitive menu). Check Export for ActionScript (Export in first frame should also become checked automatically), and then name the identifier `inner`. Note that this is what you will be referring to the movie clip as when constructing your objects with ActionScript:

225

2. Next, on frame 1 of your main timeline place the following ActionScript:

```
_quality = "low";

sliceNum = 15;
step = 4;
angle = 20;
scaleFactor = 0.5;
rotSpeed = 0.05;
offsetX = 200;
offsetY = 200;

createEmptyMovieClip("base", 0);
base._x = offsetX;
base._y = offsetY;
```

Before moving on to the next developmental stage, let's break down and analyze the preceding code line by line:

```
_quality = "low";
```

This engine has the capacity to be rather CPU intensive, so in this first line you turn the movie playback quality to low in order to facilitate a greater number of layers and more responsive interactivity (note that setting _quality to low will stop all antialiasing and bitmap smoothing).

```
sliceNum = 15;
```

With this line you define the number of slices that will be used to represent the "landmass."

```
step = 4;
```

The step is the distance, in pixels, between each slice.

```
angle = 20;
```

The angle variable refers to the default angle at which your landmass will be viewed.

```
scaleFactor = 0.5;
```

The scaleFactor controls the amount that you scale the slices relative to the amount of mouse movement on the y-axis. Depending on the type of object and its environment, this variable could also be perceived as the amount that the object rotates or the elevation of the view of the object (both with respect to the y-axis).

```
rotSpeed = 0.05;
```

The rotSpeed variable affects the rotational speed of your landmass. In the first instance, you will make the rotation of the landmass reactive to the mouse, so this value will represent rotational speed relative to the distance of the mouse from the center of the landmass. In simple terms, the higher the value of `rotSpeed`, the faster the rotation.

```
offsetX = 200;
offsetY = 200;
```

These offsets define the x and y position of the center of the base of the landmass. You then create an empty movie clip named `base` to attach all of the slices to:

```
createEmptyMovieClip("base", 0);
```

Finally, you position the `base` movie clip on the stage. Both `offsetX` and `offsetY` are used as the center point from which all your mouse positions will be relative to:

```
base._x = offsetX;
base._y = offsetY;
```

Adding slices to the base movie clip

Now that you've set some global variables, you can go about the creation of the landmass, based upon the `slice container` movie clip (remember that you gave it the linkage name `inner`). Refer to `step3_final.fla` to follow along with this stage. First, you need to create a loop that will attach multiple instances of `inner` and will modify their properties. This code will follow on directly from the previous script:

```
_quality = "low";

sliceNum = 15;
step = 4;
angle = 20;
scaleFactor = 0.5;
rotSpeed = 0.05;
offsetX = 200;
offsetY = 200;

createEmptyMovieClip("base", 0);
base._x = offsetX;
base._y = offsetY;

for (i=0;i<sliceNum;i++) {
 base.createEmptyMovieClip("slice"+i,i);
 base["slice"+i].attachMovie("inner","inner"+i,i);
 base["slice"+i]._y = - i*step*Math.cos(angle*Math.PI/180);
 base["slice"+i]._yscale = Math.sin(angle*Math.PI/180)*100;
 base["slice"+i]["inner"+i].gotoAndStop(i+1);
 base["slice"+i].myNum = i;
 }
```

Here you're using a `for` loop to build up your slice stack by creating empty movie clips (`"slice" + i`) and attaching the `inner` clip to them:

```
for (i=0;i<sliceNum;i++) {
  base.createEmptyMovieClip("slice"+i,i);
  base["slice"+i].attachMovie("inner","inner"+i,i);
```

As you build the slices on top of each other, you need to space them along the y-axis. As the object is to be built upward from `0`, you need to use a negative value (remember that the y-axis runs from top to bottom in Flash) of the slice number, `-i`, multiplied by the distance between each slice, `step` (described in the previous section). Given that `step` is a distance measured on the y-axis and you are projecting the y-axis from a 3D space to a 2D space, you need to consider the rotation of the object:

```
base["slice"+i]._y = - i*step*Math.cos(angle*Math.PI/180);
```

Some basic trigonometry is required to do this, and this is best understood if you imagine how the object would appear if viewed along the x-axis:

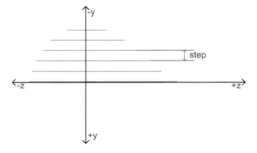

As you are measuring each slice from its center, it helps to imagine each slice as the center point of the 3D object. The following diagram indicates the center points of each slice and the separation distance, represented by the variable `step`:

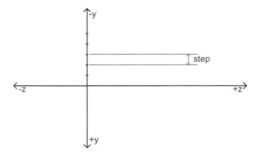

As the angle increases when you rotate the object, the projected y aspect of `step` decreases:

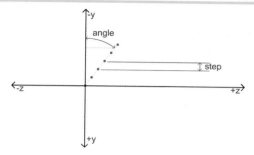

The final vertical (y) distance for a certain `angle` can be calculated using a basic rule of trigonometry with this simple equation:

```
y = step * Cosine(angle*Pi/180)
```

Note that your angle in degrees is multiplied by a factor of `Pi/180` to give the angle in radians that Flash requires. Hence, your final line of code, factoring in the y aspect projection of the `step` variable, looks like this:

```
base["slice"+i]._y = - i*step*Math.cos(angle*Math.PI/180);
```

The next line of ActionScript follows the same principles as outlined previously:

```
base["slice"+i]._yscale = Math.sin(angle*Math.PI/180)*100;
```

In this case, you are calculating the projection of the height of the slice, rather than the projection of `step`, so you use the sine function instead of cosine.

Now, in order to represent the landmass as a series of layers, you need to tell each instance of `inner` to go to their respective frames:

```
base["slice"+i]["inner"+i].gotoAndStop(i+1);
```

You then assign each slice with a variable `myNum` equal to its order in the slice stack (which is also `i`):

```
base["slice"+i].myNum = i;
```

Although it's not necessary to include this variable in the core engine, it becomes invaluable in later samples as it allows you to identify each slice by an integer value as opposed to a string value (determined by _name). You can shortcut this step by naming each inner slice `i` instead of `"inner" + i` and then referring to _name instead of `myNum`.

To recap what we've covered so far, at this point your code looks like this:

```
_quality = "low";

sliceNum = 15;
step = 4;
angle = 20;
scaleFactor = 0.5;
```

continues overleaf

```
rotSpeed = 0.05;
offsetX = 200;
offsetY = 200;

createEmptyMovieClip("base", 0);
base._x = offsetX;
base._y = offsetY;

for (i=0;i<sliceNum;i++) {
 base.createEmptyMovieClip("slice"+i,i);
 base["slice"+i].attachMovie("inner","inner"+i,i);
 base["slice"+i]._y = - i*step*Math.cos (angle*Math.PI/180);
 base["slice"+i]._yscale = Math.sin (angle*Math.PI/180)*100;
 base["slice"+i]["inner"+i].gotoAndStop(i+1);
 base["slice"+i].myNum = i;
 }
```

Test the movie so far (CTRL/CMD+ENTER), and the end result should look something like this (refer to `step3_final.fla` if you're having any trouble):

You can now start to experiment with the slice engine by changing some of the variables. With the `step`, `angle`, and `offsetX` and `offsetY` variables, you can control the overall height, viewing angle, and position of the object. For instance, try the following new values:

```
sliceNum = 15;
step = 50;
angle = 75;
scaleFactor = 0.5;
rotSpeed = 0.05;
offsetX = 300;
offsetY = 300;
```

These changes result in some specific differences in the look of your slice object:

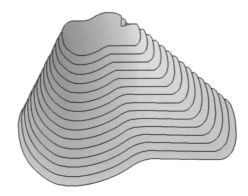

You can also experiment with the shape of the object by changing the shapes used on keyframes and the length of the tween used in the `slice container` movie clip. Make sure that the variable `sliceNum` always reflects the length of the tweens used in `slice container`.

Adding interactivity

There are two basic types of interactive features that you can now add to the functionality of your 3D slice engine: rotational and angular.

Rotational interactivity

Before you add any interactivity, it is important to note that for the sake of an efficient engine you need to create further global variables. In this case, you need to create a function that is triggered by the `onEnterFrame` event handler on the main timeline.

1. Open the file `step4_final.fla` and refer to the new ActionScript on the first frame of the main timeline:

    ```
    onEnterFrame = function () {
     rot = (this._xmouse-offsetX)*rotSpeed;
    };
    ```

    This script is executed every frame and updates variable `rot`, which is a measure of the x distance between the center of the landmass (`offsetX`) and the current mouse position (`this._xmouse`), multiplied by the rotation speed (`rotSpeed`).

2. After creating variable `rot`, which is constantly updated, you can add a simple function that defines your object's rotation:

    ```
    function rotateMe() {
     this._rotation +=_root.rot;
    }
    ```

3. As discussed earlier, this engine is based on skewing, so in order to effect a skew on each slice, you need to add this function to the `onEnterFrame` of each instance of `inner`. You do so within the `for` loop, as follows:

    ```
    for (i=0;i<sliceNum;i++) {
     base.createEmptyMovieClip("slice"+i,i);
     base["slice"+i].attachMovie("inner","inner"+i,i);
     base["slice"+i]._y = - i*step*Math.cos (angle*Math.PI/180);
     base["slice"+i]._yscale = Math.sin (angle*Math.PI/180)*100;
     base["slice"+i]["inner"+i].gotoAndStop(i+1);
    ```

continues overleaf

```
         base["slice"+i]["inner"+i].onEnterFrame = rotateMe;
         base["slice"+i].myNum = i;
      }
```

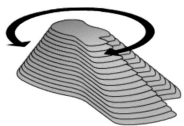

4. If you test the movie with these updates, you'll see that the landmass can now be viewed at the any angle. It rotates around the y-axis in relation to the position of the mouse cursor.

Angular interactivity

To take things a little further, you can also add angular interactivity.

1. First, you'll add some script that updates your `angle` value. This works in a similar way to your rotation script but uses the `_ymouse` coordinates rather than `_xmouse`. Open the file `step5_final.fla` and refer to the additional ActionScript on the first frame of the main timeline:

```
onEnterFrame = function() {
 rot = (this._xmouse - offsetX)*rotSpeed;
 angle = (this._ymouse)*scaleFactor;
}
```

2. Before you add instructions to each instance of `slice`, note that you no longer require the following lines of code:

```
angle = 20;

base["slice"+i]._y = - i*step*Math.cos(angle*Math.PI/180);
base["slice"+i]._yscale = Math.sin(angle*Math.PI/180)*100;
```

You're going to dynamically modify the `_y` position and the `_yscale`, so these lines are now redundant. Go ahead and delete them (or comment them out).

3. You can now create the function that defines the way in which the dynamic angle is translated into the `_yscale` of each instance of `slice`:

```
function scaleMe() {
 this._y = - this.myNum*_root.step*Math.cos (_root.angle*Math.PI/180);
 this._yscale = Math.sin (_root.angle*Math.PI/180)*100;
}
```

Note that we have created a custom function that will be used by each instance of base["slice"+i]. We used the `this` scope to ensure that each instance using this function uses it in reference to its own timeline, thus the term `this`. The function `scaleMe` calculates and displays the scale and position of each slice relative to the changing value of variable `angle` (this relies on the same trigonometry techniques that we explained earlier).

4. Once again, you follow a similar process undertaken when adding rotational interactivity, only in this case you'll be adding an `onEnterFrame` function for each instance of `slice` movie clip (remember earlier that you scaled the container and rotated the nested movie clip to simulate skewing):

```
for (i=0;i<sliceNum;i++) {
  base.createEmptyMovieClip("slice"+i,i);
  base["slice"+i].attachMovie("inner","inner"+i,i);
  base["slice"+i]["inner"+i].gotoAndStop(i+1);
  base["slice"+i]["inner"+i].onEnterFrame = rotateMe;
  base["slice"+i].myNum = i;
  base["slice"+i].onEnterFrame = scaleMe;
}
```

5. On testing this code, you'll see that you've now got an extra degree of angular interactivity.

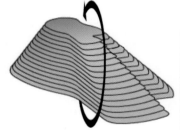

That's essentially all that makes up the core components to the slice engine. For completeness, your resulting code should look like this:

```
_quality = "low";

sliceNum = 15;
step = 5;
scaleFactor = 0.5;
rotSpeed = 0.05;
offsetX = 200;
offsetY = 200;

createEmptyMovieClip("base", 0);
base._x = offsetX;
base._y = offsetY;

onEnterFrame = function() {
 rot = (this._xmouse - offsetX)*rotSpeed;
 angle = (this._ymouse) *scaleFactor;
};
```

continues overleaf

```
for (i=0;i<sliceNum;i++) {
 base.createEmptyMovieClip("slice"+i,i);
 base["slice"+i].attachMovie("inner","inner"+i,i);
 base["slice"+i]["inner"+i].gotoAndStop(i+1);
 base["slice"+i]["inner"+i].onEnterFrame = rotateMe;
 base["slice"+i].myNum = i;
 base["slice"+i].onEnterFrame = scaleMe;
}

function rotateMe() {
 this._rotation +=_root.rot;
}

function scaleMe() {
 this._y = - this.myNum*_root.step*Math.cos (_root.angle*Math.PI/180);
 this._yscale = Math.sin (_root.angle*Math.PI/180)*100;
}
```

Notes and considerations for using the slice engine

As you progressed through the development of the core engine, you might have noticed that there are some limitations. Accordingly, in the following subsections we'll present an outline of these main limitations. This can act as a guide to the "do's and don'ts" when using your Flash 3D slice engine.

Processor intensity

Although the code has been optimized to do the smallest number of calculations possible, there is still the overhead of Flash having to handle multiple objects and their constantly changing position, scale, and rotation. It is a good idea to limit the number of slices to the minimum required to achieve the desired effect. It is also suggested that when using bitmaps, the player quality is turned to low in order to reduce the processor requirements normally used for bitmap smoothing and antialiasing.

In addition, it is important to make sure that there are no unnecessary calculations and that all global variables are calculated on the main timeline rather than every individual instance of slice or inner. The importance of this point will become obvious as you progress through the various implementations of the slice engine in the next section.

In the event that you want to maximize the processing power of the end user machine, it is possible to approximate the processor speed of the machine playing the piece. We have seen many methods of testing processor speed, most of which are based on combining the getTimer() method and some processor-intensive calculations or animation. The time in which it takes the machine to complete a certain process can be used to place it in a range. This classification can then be used to define the number of slices to be used in a given object. If, for example, a machine takes a relatively long time to complete the process, then you could use one-third of the number of slices and use every third frame of the slice container movie clip. If the machine completes the process in ample time, then you know you can use the maximum number of slices and every frame of the movie clip.

Angle limitations

You may also have noted that as the angle of the view approaches 0, the layers cease rendering. This is because `Math.cos(angle*Math.PI/180) = 0`; therefore, so does the `_yscale` of each object. It *is* possible to use angular offsets to render slices at different angles to each other to prevent this, but in most cases, the desired effect is best achieved through a modular 3D box engine as opposed to this slice engine. Feel free to experiment in any case.

Z-order

So far, we have discussed the making of objects so that they can be viewed within an angle variance of 0 to 180 degrees. This has been mostly due to the angle limitations outlined in the previous sections. Taking this into consideration, it is still possible to create an object that can rotate 360 degrees on all axes. To allow this to happen, you need to make sure that your old friend the z-order (or *depth*) of your slices is managed appropriately.

When you first built the slice object, you made the uppermost slice have the highest z-order—that is, it was always on top. You may have experimented with the engine already and discovered that rotating the object less than 0 or greater than 180 degrees gives a strange, reversed mirrored object. To avoid this, you need to reverse the z-order of the slices whenever the angle is less than 0 or greater than 180. To be more accurate, the variable `angle` is accumulative, and as alternate lots of 180 degrees are passed you need to alternate the z-order.

A simple way of determining alternate lengths of 180 degrees is by dividing the angle by 180, rounding down, and then determining if the result is an odd or even number. For example:

- If the angle is 90 degrees: Divide 90 by 180 to get 0.5, round down to 0, which is *even*.
- If the angle is 270 degrees: Divide 270 by 180 to get 1.5, round down to 1, and the result is *odd*. Therefore, you need to swap the z-order.

Now let's look at implementing this into the core engine script. Open the file `z-order_fix.fla` to take a peek at what you are about to achieve. You need to determine the order of the slices every frame, so you'll add some ActionScript to the `onEnterFrame` function of the root timeline:

```
onEnterFrame = function() {
 rot = (this._xmouse - offsetX)*rotSpeed;
 angle = (this._ymouse) *scaleFactor;
 temp = Math.floor(angle/180);
 if (Math.floor(temp/2) == temp/2){
   order = 1;
 }else{
   order = -1;
 }
};
```

In the first new line, you are using variable `temp` to divide the angle by 180 and round down to determine a whole integer. You then determine if `temp` is odd or even by dividing `temp` by 2, rounding it down, and then comparing the result to `temp` divided by 2 (not rounded). All even numbers will return a `true` result, while all odd numbers will return a `false` result. From here you can set the variable `order`, which contains the required order of the slices (either positive or negative).

Now that you know if the order is positive or negative, you can leave it up to each slice to determine its order in the stack. Though there are a number of ways of changing the z-order of the slice stack, we prefer to have each slice determine its own position in the stack. You can do this by adding some script to the `scaleMe` function, which occurs in `onEnterFrame` for each slice:

```
function scaleMe() {
    this._y = - this.myNum*_root.step*Math.cos (_root.angle*Math.PI/180);
    this._yscale = Math.sin (_root.angle*Math.PI/180)*100;
    this.swapDepths(this.myNum*_root.order)
}
```

Here you are using each slice's unique identifier `myNum` and multiplying it by `_root.order`. In the case of the core engine outline thus far, the resulting z-order is 1 through to 15 if the order is positive, or –15 to –1 if the order is negative. Don't worry about the fact that you are using negative depth values, because Flash will make them positive values while retaining the order of each slice relative to one another.

Test `z-order_fix.fla` to see the effect of your z-order fix.

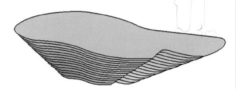

3D slice engine in action

In the remaining half of this chapter you'll study several implementations of your slice engine. Though the engine has an expansive scope with the potential to produce pseudo-3D effects in many different areas, we have attempted to isolate several main possibilities. The key to achieving optimum results from this 3D engine is first to understand how it works and realize what it is doing, and second to experiment with both layer and tween techniques, as well as the core engine functions.

Sample 1: Building primitive and organic objects

Although we've discussed building a 3D landmass, the engine is not confined to just these object types. As the engine represents objects by slices, you need to manipulate the slices to take advantage of that fact. For instance, if you replace your original landmass tween with a simple square and run the engine, you will notice that there is nothing defining the separate faces of the resulting 3D box. In order to do this, you need to shade the square so that each edge is a slightly different color.

The resulting object looks like this:

You can now see that each face of the object is beginning to show its own definition. Only the top face of the object still shows the shading of the layers beneath. In order to remove this visible shading, you need to cap the top of your object. To do this, you simply place a keyframe on the final frame of the movie clip, where the last frame is equal to the total number of slices as determined by the `sliceNum` variable. In this frame, just fill the shape with a solid color. Now that all the slices have shaded edges and the last slice (or top slice) has a solid color, the final object renders as a box.

Experiment with different shapes and shading to get different results. For example, take a look at the file `sample1_primitives.fla`. This file illustrates the way in which motion and shape tweens combined with multiple layers allow you to achieve all sorts of primitive objects. Open the `slice container` movie clip from the Library (F11) and spend some time examining the structure of its timeline.

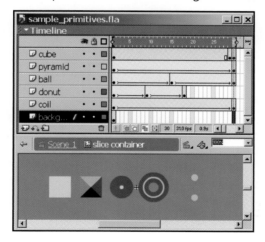

It is important to experiment with shapes, tweens, and slices to get a feel for how they all work with each other. You may also find that you can achieve certain effects by making simple changes to the `slice container` movie clip instead of adjusting the engine code. Make sure to experiment with lines, text, and transparency, but pay attention to how they affect the overall performance.

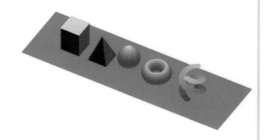

Note, however, that using shaded shapes and shape tweens can result in undesirable frames. You may have to use shape hints in order to gain better control of the tweened shapes. To execute more organic shapes, it is best to use a combination of shapes, graphics, movie clips, and multiple layers.

In the more advanced example shown below (`sample1_vase.fla`), you will see that we've used the same core engine to represent a still life of a vase, plate, fruit, and glasses. Using this engine allows you to create pretty much any real-world object you could imagine.

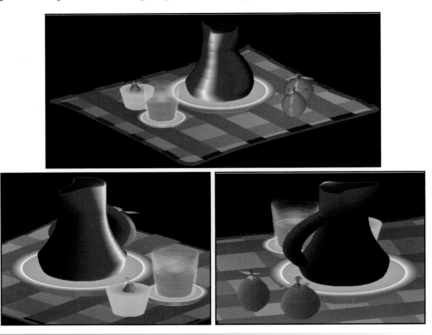

Sample 2: Layer interactivity

One of the easiest ways of introducing layer interactivity into your objects is to define event handlers that would normally be used for buttons. `sample2_layer_interactivity.fla` is a good example of how layers can be made interactive. To demonstrate this, let's take the core engine code and add some functions that change the `_alpha` (opacity) of each slice:

```
function hideMe() {
 this._alpha = 0;
}

function showMe() {
 this._alpha = 100;
}
```

You then add these event handlers to each instance of `slice`:

```
for (i=0;i<sliceNum;i++) {
  base.createEmptyMovieClip("slice"+i,i);
  base["slice"+i].attachMovie("inner","inner"+i,i);
  base["slice"+i]["inner"+i].gotoAndStop(i+1);
  base["slice"+i]["inner"+i].onEnterFrame = rotateMe;
  base["slice"+i].myNum = i;
  base["slice"+i].onEnterFrame = scaleMe;
  base["slice"+i].onRollOver = hideMe;
  base["slice"+i].onDragOver = hideMe;
  base["slice"+i].onRollOut = showMe;
  base["slice"+i].onDragOut = showMe;
}
```

Whenever the mouse is moved over a slice, whether the mouse is down or not, the event handlers `onRollOver` and `onDragOver` trigger the `hideMe` function. Whenever the mouse is moved out of the slice, the event handlers `onRollOut` and `onDragOut` trigger the `showMe` function. These small additions to the core engine allow for a high level of layer interactivity. As you roll in and out of each slice, the `_alpha` switches from `0` to `100`, respectively.

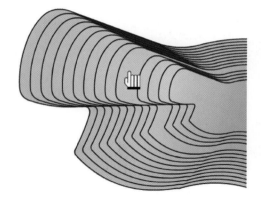

Event handlers can be added to the individual slices to facilitate layer and section interactivity and animation. Refer to the file `interactive_combo.swf` in the `SWF_samples` directory as an example of how layer interactivity could be integrated into a menu system.

Sample 3: Organic masks

The true power of this 3D engine is best illustrated through the use of textures. Most Flash 3D techniques that use bitmaps for textures are based around the use of squares and/or triangles as masks for bitmaps. In the following example, you will discover how organic 3D-looking objects can be built through the use of progressive organically shaped masks.

Open `sample3_organic_masks.fla` and take a look at the `slice container` movie clip in the Library. Here you'll see that instead of using a series of shapes to define our final object, we are using a series of masks and a single bitmap image. Much like the topographical map metaphor, we are taking elevation contours and, instead of filling them with a color, we are filling them with the raster image that would be visible at each specific elevation.

The following image illustrates the series of contours that are being used as masks and the image that is to be masked by these contours:

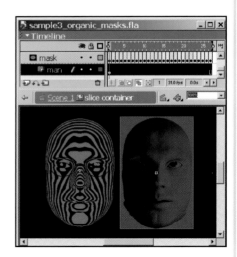

These contours were created by building a model in 3D Studio Max and then animating a plane passing through the object. By making the model solid black in color and the plane self-illuminating white, it is easy to render a series of images that represent the masks. These images were then imported into Flash MX, bitmap traced (Modify > Trace Bitmap...), and then cleaned up for use. As ever, it's best to experiment with what tools you have knowledge of and access to, as well as ways of processing the image series once imported into Flash.

An effective way of converting bitmaps to shapes without creating excessive shapes is to use a large color threshold. Bitmap tracing often results in small extraneous shapes around the edges of your main shape. To remove these, simply select and copy the main shape, then select and delete all the shapes and paste the main shape back in place. The main shape can then be optimized, though you must be careful not to alter it too much.

When you view the main engine script in frame 1 of the root timeline sample3_organic_masks.fla, you'll notice that there are some minor changes to the original core code (note that these changes have been made to suit this particular example and are not always required when building organic models):

```
_quality = "low";

sliceNum = 27;
step = 3;
scaleFactor = 0.5;
rotSpeed = 0.5;
offsetX = 200;
offsetY = 200;

createEmptyMovieClip("base", 0);
base._x = offsetX;
base._y = offsetY;

for (i=0;i<sliceNum;i++) {
 base.createEmptyMovieClip("slice"+i,i);
 base["slice"+i].attachMovie("inner","inner"+i,i);
 base["slice"+i]["inner"+i].onEnterFrame = function() {
   this._rotation =_root.rot;
```

```
      }
      base["slice"+i].myNum = i;
      base["slice"+i].onEnterFrame = function() {
         this._y = - this.myNum*_root.step*Math.cos
➥(_root.angle*Math.PI/180);
         this._yscale = Math.sin (_root.angle*Math.PI/180)*100;
      }
   }

   onEnterFrame = function() {
    rot = (this._xmouse - offsetX)*rotSpeed;
    angle = (this._ymouse) *scaleFactor;
    base._rotation = -rot;
   };
```

The variables `sliceNum` and `step` are changed to reflect the length of the `slice container` movie clip and the desired distance between the individual slices. This line from the original code:

```
   this._rotation +=_root.rot;
```

has now been changed to the following:

```
   this._rotation =_root.rot;
```

and this line has been added to the `onEnterFrame` function:

```
   base._rotation = -rot;
```

These subtle code changes affect the way in which the object rotates. Previously, mouse movement on the x-axis would change the speed in which the object rotated. In this case, it is not the *speed* of rotation that changes with `_xmouse` but simply the *amount* of rotation. The additional line of code rotates the base object to counteract the rotation of the base object's content, making the final object remain in a vertical position. Getting a smooth result is dependent on the alignment of your slices relative to the center of the `slice container` movie clip.

For a bit of fun, try replacing the image used in slice container with a photo of a friend or yourself. Try and make the facial features (eyes, nose, lips, and outline) line up with those of the original image to get a cleaner effect.

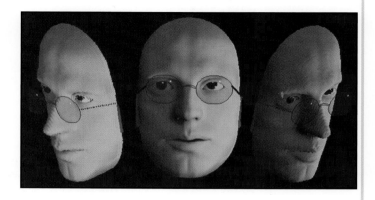

Sample 4: Global to local object space

Previously, we discussed building and manipulating objects in global space—that is, the object sits in a set position and changes according to mouse movement relative to the object and the stage. In this example, we'll discuss how to use the `base` object and its properties to define the way in which we render its layers.

The sample we will be using to illustrate this is a pseudo-3D representation of a car (refer to `sample4_car.fla`). This image is practical in the sense that it is fairly small, and therefore relatively CPU-efficient—it does not require the use of the full 3D space. It could easily be adapted to game engines, and it also facilitates 3D collision detection as well as component animation (tires, indicators, lights, and so on).

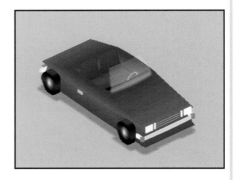

Earlier in this chapter, when you created the original landmass, you first created the `base` object and attached the slices to it. Previously, you used global mouse positions to control the angle and rotation of the object. In this example, you are going to use the object's position to define its angle and rotation. Though this example allows you to drag the object around the screen and watch it change angle and rotation, the engine is not confined to using just a mouse drag. You can experiment with adding key controls to make the vehicle turn and move forward and backward.

The changes to the original engine code for this example (`sample4_car.fla`) are as follows:

```
_quality = "low";

sliceNum = 49;
step = 1;
scaleFactor = 0.2;
rotSpeed = 0.5;
offsetX = 200;
offsetY = 200;

createEmptyMovieClip("base", 0);
base._x = offsetX;
base._y = offsetY;
base.onPress = function() {
 startDrag(this);
}
base.onRelease = function() {
 stopDrag();
}

onEnterFrame = function() {
```

```
    rot = (base._x)*rotSpeed;
    angle = (base._y)*scaleFactor;
};

for (i=0;i<sliceNum;i++) {
  base.createEmptyMovieClip("slice"+i,i);
  base["slice"+i].attachMovie("inner","inner"+i,i);
  base["slice"+i].onEnterFrame = scaleMe;
}

function rotateMe() {
  this._rotation =_root.rot;
}

function scaleMe() {
  this._y = - this.myNum*_root.step*Math.cos (_root.angle*Math.PI/180);
  this._yscale = Math.sin (_root.angle*Math.PI/180)*100;
}
```

The first few changes are pretty self-explanatory and are specific to each different object you build:

```
sliceNum = 49;
step = 1;
rotSpeed = 0.5;
```

More important, the changes to the onEnterFrame function greatly affect the way in which your object reacts to its position on the stage:

```
onEnterFrame = function() {
  rot = (base._x)*rotSpeed;
  angle = (base._y)*scaleFactor;
};
```

Previously, you were using mouse positions to control your angle and rotation. By changing the control mechanism from mouse positions on the stage (*global*) to your object's position (*local*), you can see how the object's rotation and angle relate to its screen position. As the object approaches the bottom of the stage (base._y), the viewing angle increases, and as the object approaches the right of the stage (base._x), the rotation increases.

Though this is, of course, a simplified example, it outlines the foundation of a car-related game engine. Although it is possible to use the car as a local object and have the race track (or environment) as a global object, it would require an entire chapter to explain the processes required to complete it.

As an exercise, examine the slice container movie clip in sample4_car.fla and pay attention to the way in which movie clips, layers, and tweens are used to build up the object. Try adding features to the vehicle and try taking away features, layers, and slices to optimize the processor requirements.

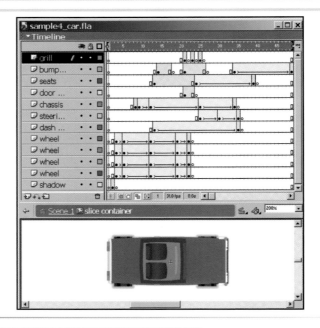

Sample 5: Dynamic shading and blurring

Following on from the global to local example, you are going to look at using local object properties to create dynamic shading. Accordingly, open `sample5_meteor.fla`. In this example, the object has each slice layer shaded respective to its position on the screen and its order in the stack of layers. The `_alpha` property is used to shade and blur each layer:

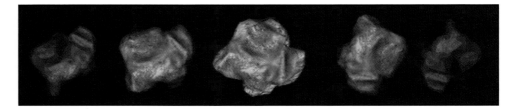

The code is basically the same as the previous vehicle sample, with the addition of some distance calculations and the setting of `_alpha` for each slice:

```
_quality = "low";

sliceNum = 19;
step = 5;
scaleFactor = 0.25;
rotSpeed = 0.5;
offsetX = 200;
offsetY = 200;
```

```
createEmptyMovieClip("base", 0);
base._x = offsetX;
base._y = offsetY;

base.onPress = function() {
 startDrag(this);
}
base.onRelease = function() {
 stopDrag();
}

onEnterFrame = function() {
 rot = (base._x-offsetX)*rotSpeed;
 angle = (base._y-offsetY)*scaleFactor + 90;
 dist = Math.sqrt((base._x - offsetX) * (base._x - offsetX) + (base._y
➥- offsetY) * (base._y - offsetY));
};

for (i=0;i<sliceNum;i++) {
 base.createEmptyMovieClip("slice"+i,i);
 base["slice"+i].attachMovie("inner","inner"+i,i);
 base["slice"+i]["inner"+i].gotoAndStop(i+1);
 base["slice"+i]["inner"+i].onEnterFrame = rotateMe;
 base["slice"+i].myNum = i;
 base["slice"+i].onEnterFrame = scaleMe;
}

function rotateMe() {
 this._rotation =_root.rot;
}

function scaleMe() {
 this._y = - this.myNum*_root.step*Math.cos X(_root.angle*Math.PI/180);
 this._yscale = Math.sin (_root.angle*Math.PI/180)*100;
 this._alpha = 200 - _root.dist - this.myNum * 10;
}
```

Open the file sample5_meteor.fla and test the movie (CTRL/CMD+ENTER). As with the vehicle example, you are able to move the object about the stage with the mouse. The fundamental difference in this case is that the object progressively fades and blurs as it approaches the edges of the stage. To do this, you must first calculate the distance that the object is from its original positions. At the start of the chapter, you defined the variables offsetX and offsetY as the initial starting coordinates for your object. It is these coordinates that you will use to measure the distance that the object has moved (though you could use any arbitrary point):

```
dist = Math.sqrt((base._x - offsetX) * (base._x - offsetX) + (base._y
➥- offsetY) * (base._y - offsetY));
```

This is the standard measure of distance (using a little bit of trigonometry again) between the two points (`base._x`, `base._y`) and (`offsetX`, `offsetY`).

You then change the `_alpha` of each layer. It is initially set to `100`, from which you subtract the distance that the object is from its initial coordinate:

```
this._alpha = 100 - _root.dist * (this.myNum+10)/20;
```

Note that you want the layers to fade out individually, so you need to make the `_alpha` of each slice a factor of its unique identifier. The use of the `+10` simply increases the range of slices from 1–19 to 11–29 to give a more even distribution of the fade effect. You divide by `20` to reduce the effect of `dist` combined with the unique identifier. Increasing the number that you divide by will increase the distance at which the object fades.

In this example, you have used `_alpha` to achieve a fade and slight blur effect. It's also possible to create a fade-only effect by using the color object or to create just a blur effect by using `_alpha` and placing a solid noneffected layer at the bottom of the slice stack.

Sample 6: Including nonlayer elements

Now that you understand some of the more advanced iterations of the engine, you're ready to examine a way in which you can include additional elements to your object. Nonlayer elements are objects that render as part of the model but do not act like the slices that are used to make the model.

The fact is, we're still exploring the use of nonlayer elements and the different ways to introduce them into the 3D object, so there are currently some restrictions and complications to keep in mind. One of the biggest issues is that your element is best restricted to a point-style object—that is, the element joins to the 3D object at a single point. Another consideration is that z-order and rotational scale have to be factored into the element and, in doing so, can fundamentally affect the code structure of the core engine.

To alleviate some of these complications and to ease your use of nonlayer elements, we are going to discuss the addition of a tree into a landmass object environment. As the landmass is a very organic shape, z-ordering issues (as discussed earlier in this chapter) can be prohibitively complex. So for this example, you are going to add the tree to the top layer of the landmass. (If you choose to explore z-ordering further, we suggest you begin by implementing a z-order fix similar to that required for the rotational z-order mentioned earlier in this chapter.)

Open the file `sample6_final.swf` and notice the way the tree acts in relation to the landmass and mouse movement:

Now that you've seen what we're talking about, you'll learn how to do it:

1. Open the file `sample6_start.fla` and go to the Library to edit the `slice container` movie clip.

2. Create a new layer above the current one and an empty keyframe at frame 30 (to correspond to your uppermost object slice).

3. Into this keyframe, place an instance of the `node` movie clip (just drag it from the Library) and align it to the desired point above the landmass slice. The `node` clip is used purely as a point of reference and does not require a name or contents (though in this case it contains a small circle so that you can see it at runtime).

4. With this instance of `node` still selected, open the Actions panel (F9) and add the following ActionScript:

```
onClipEvent(enterFrame) {
 point = new object();
 point.x = 0;
 point.y = 0;
 localToGlobal(point);
 _root.myX = point.x;
 _root.myY = point.y;
 updateAfterEvent();
}
```

This code is a good example of using `localToGlobal()`. For those unfamiliar with this useful method, we are creating an object at 0,0 (relative to `node`), and then converting it from `node` coordinates (local) to the stage coordinates (global).

If you test the movie and trace or debug the `point` object, you will see that `node` moves relative to the slice object and that `point.x` and `point.y` show coordinates relative to the top right of the stage.

5. Now that you have globalized your point coordinates, you can concentrate on adding the element. Drag an instance of the `tree` movie clip onto the stage. You need to make this movie clip sit in front of the landmass, so you attach the following code to it to force the clip to a depth of `100` (an arbitrary number that is higher than the number of slices in your slice object):

```
onClipEvent(load) {
 this.swapDepths(100);
}
```

6. Next, you need to make the object conform to the (global) coordinates of `node`. Extend the code as follows:

```
onClipEvent(load) {
 this.swapDepths(100);
}
onClipEvent(enterFrame) {
 this._x = _root.myX;
 this._y = _root.myY;
}
```

7. At this point, test the movie with (CTRL/CMD+ENTER) and you'll see that the tree does not rotate in relation to the rotation of the landmass slices. In some cases this may be desirable, but in this case it is not. You can solve this problem with a little bit of trigonometry again, but before you do so, you need to work out the rotation of the landmass. In the core engine code, you calculate the rotation increment for each frame as the variable `rot`. Thus, you need to use `rot` to calculate the accumulative rotation like so:

```
onClipEvent(load) {
 this.swapDepths(100);
}
onClipEvent(enterFrame) {
 this._x = _root.myX;
 this._y = _root.myY;
 tempRot +=_root.rot;
}
```

8. Additionally, you need to add a little bit of trig to scale the `tree` clip depending on the landmass rotation:

```
onClipEvent(load) {
 this.swapDepths(100);
}
onClipEvent(enterFrame) {
 this._x = _root.myX;
 this._y = _root.myY;
 tempRot +=_root.rot;
 this._xscale = Math.sin(tempRot*Math.PI/180)*100;
}
```

This calculation is fundamentally the same as the trig required for the landmass slice scaling, as discussed in the start of the chapter, only in this case it is applied to the _xscale of the object.

9. So you have successfully created an object that follows a point and scales relative to the landmass rotation. The only problem now is that the object gets thin when it reaches the x-coordinate extremities of the landmass.

A simple yet effective solution is to place another movie clip at the same location as the original object one, but to make it appear perpendicular to the original object. Drag a copy of the tree2 movie clip onto the stage and place it next to the instance of tree. Copy the code from tree, place it on tree2, and make the following changes:

```
onClipEvent(load) {
 this.swapDepths(101);
}
onClipEvent(enterFrame) {
 this._x = _root.myX;
 this._y = _root.myY;
 tempRot +=_root.rot;
 this._xscale = Math.cos(tempRot*Math.PI/180)*100;
}
```

All you have done here is change the z-order to 101 so as to not conflict with the z-order of tree, and you've changed the trig equation from sin to cos in order for the two movie clips to appear at right angles to each other. Play around with the finished movie (sample6_final.swf) to see your 3D tree in all its glory!

Summary

There is a wide scope for the use and extension of the core slice engine and samples outlined in this chapter. We discussed some pretty fundamental implementations of the core engine all based around a single object. There are many ways in which this engine can be extended—for instance, for use in 3D logos, navigation systems, instructional and education applications, game engines, and even good old creative Flash experiments. It's possible to create multiple base objects, each with its own unique functionality that can work independently or with other objects. Try replicating some of the samples in the `SWF_samples` folder, available with this chapter's downloaded example files, or try creating your own effects. The key to success is plenty of experimentation, while keeping things simple and tidy.

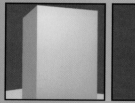

Departure Lounge

In this final chapter we're going to take a quick look at the next natural step on our journey through Flash 3D: moving beyond 3D cheats and looking toward the use of specific 3D graphics software with Flash. In the past couple of years, companies such as Electric Rain and Discreet have come out with some pretty amazing software, and they're slowly bridging the gap between 3D and Flash.

For instance, Swift 3D from Electric Rain (see www.swift3d.com and www.erain.com) includes a couple of vital 3D tools: an extrusion editor to create basic custom-shaped planes and a lathe editor to create lathed objects. With the most recent release, version 3, you can create very complex extrusions, and it also includes a new bitmap texturing tool, so you can export some pretty amazing graphics for such a simple and inexpensive piece of software. It can export bitmap (JPEG) as well as vector graphics (SWF).

Last year, Discreet released Plasma (www.discreet.com/products/plasma/) based on the same technology as 3D Studio Max (www.discreet.com/products/3dsmax/). The export capability of Plasma is a little more advanced than that of Swift 3D, and you can also do a lot of mathematical equations and neat random things. The compromise is that the learning curve on this software is rather higher compared to Swift 3D, but if you're serious, it's worth the effort.

For the purpose of demonstration, we'll focus our attention on Swift 3D in this chapter. If you're inspired to start playing around with Swift 3D after reading this chapter, you should find that it is quite attuned to the beginning-to-intermediate Flash user.

Working with external 3D applications

As this chapter mainly deals with the graphics once they are inside of Flash, we are not going to discuss how these files were made. For that, you should pick up a good book on Swift 3D. Instead, we'll concentrate on importing 3D files into Flash and manipulating them there.

> *For a solid introduction to Swift 3D, it's worth taking a look at* Foundation Swift 3D *(friends of ED, ISBN: 1-904344-19-4). This book even has a couple of chapters specifically devoted to using Swift 3D with Flash MX.*

Creating a 3D navigation movie

In this example, you'll see just how easy it is to import Swift 3D files into Flash. In fact, even the Swift files that you'll use are pretty straightforward to construct in Swift 3D. All you need is version 2 or higher, and, of course, Flash MX.

As we mentioned earlier, we'll avoid the finer details of how this was created, as it's a little beyond the scope of this book. That said, something worth keeping in mind when creating your animation in Swift 3D is to always go back to the same point you zoomed into. This is critical so that you can get a fluid animation throughout. That probably doesn't make much sense right now, but hopefully it will very soon. In this case, you'll click on a 3D building graphic to zoom in and then click the main screen again to zoom back out to the exact same spot, no matter what building you are on (you'll see this in action very shortly).

So, assuming your Swift 3D files have already been created (and you can find ready-made sample Swift files in this chapter's example files, available for download from www.friendsofed.com, as ever), let's get started. Note that the finished version of the example is `swift3D_FlashExample.fla`.

1. First things first, if you don't already have it, you'll need to download the Smart Layer Importer (for PC or Mac—whichever you are using) to import the external Swift 3D file. It couldn't be easier to do—just go to www.erain.com/technology/smartlayer.asp, follow the short and snappy instructions from the good folks at Electric Rain, and you'll be up and running with the Smart Layer Importer in no time at all.

2. Now, open a new Flash MX document and import the file `swift3DExample_export.swft` from this chapter's examples (File > Import... and then browse for the file through the Import window). After import, it will create a new layer in your Flash file called Colors.

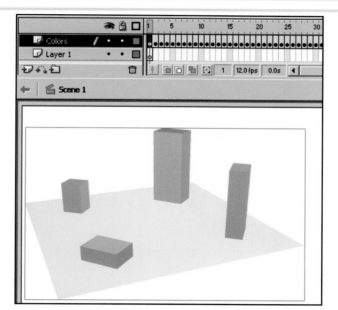

3. At this point, you'll notice that Flash has imported this file as a series of keyframes, each being a different view/zoom. Press ENTER and Flash will take you on a quick tour of the animation. Every frame is different except for frames 1, 20, 40, 60, and 80. This is because these will be the zoomed-out starting points. What you will need to do next is create three more layers (from top to bottom): Actions, Buttons, and Text (Colors is already created, and we've renamed this layer 3d).

4. In your Actions layer, create blank keyframes (F7) at frames 1, 10, 20, 30, 40, 50, 60, 70, and 80, and write `stop();` actions on each one of these frames.

5. Next, on the Buttons layer, draw a rectangle with no stroke. Select it and press F8 to convert it to a button with the name `Blank Button`. Now double-click this button and move the Up frame (first frame) to the Hit frame (fourth frame). Your button is now invisible, and it will function the same as a normal button without showing itself.

6. Place this button over the back left "building" and scale it to be a little larger than the entire building itself. Duplicate the button and do the same thing with the rest of the buildings. When you've finished, you should have four buttons overall, and the stage will look something like this:

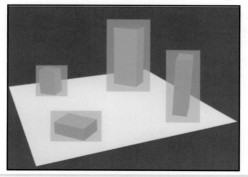

253

7. Select the back-left building button and put the following actions in the Actions panel (F9) (note that we're using the attached scripting technique in this example for ease of understanding—you could, of course, give each button an instance name and control all the actions remotely from a single script):

    ```
    on (release) {
       gotoAndPlay(2);
    }
    ```

8. Attach the following actions to the back-right building button:

    ```
    on (release) {
       gotoAndPlay(21);
    }
    ```

9. Put the following actions on the front-right building button:

    ```
    on (release) {
       gotoAndPlay(41);
    }
    ```

10. Finally, place this script on the front-left building button:

    ```
    on (release) {
       gotoAndPlay(61);
    }
    ```

11. Next, you will need to insert a blank keyframe (F7) on frame 2 of the Buttons layer. Select both frames 1 and 2, and while holding the ALT (OPTION) key, drag the frames to frame 20, 40, 60, and 80. Delete frame 81, as it will never be used. When you've finished, your timeline should look like this:

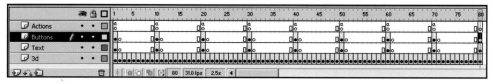

12. Next, select frames 1 and 2 again, and while holding the ALT (OPTION) key, drag it to frame 10. Select frame 10 and delete all buttons on the stage except one (it doesn't matter which one, as long as you have one). Take this button and scale it to be the size of the stage. Select the button and put the following actions in the Actions panel:

    ```
    on (release) {
       gotoAndPlay(11);
    }
    ```

13. Next, select frames 10, and 11, and while holding the ALT (OPTION) key, drag these frames to frames 30, 50, and 70. Now select frame 30, edit the ActionScript on the button to **gotoAndPlay(31)**,

do the same for frames 50, and 70, but make them go to 51 and 71 (see also `swift3D_FlashExample.fla`).

14. To finish, add some simple textual navigational instructions to each frame. Select frame 1 of the Text layer, and create a dynamic text box. Type "Click on each building to zoom in" in the text box. Position it in the lower-right corner of the stage.

15. Insert a blank keyframe in frame 2 of the Text layer. Select frames 1 and 2, and while holding the ALT (OPTION) key, drag these frames to frames 20, 40, 60, and 80. Next, create a keyframe on frame 10 of the Text layer and add another dynamic text box. Type "Click on the screen to zoom out" and then position this text box on the stage somewhere. Insert a blank keyframe on frame 11. Select frames 10 and 11, and drag them to frames 30, 50, and 70. You now have text on each frame instructing the user how to navigate through the buildings.

16. If you now test your movie (CTRL/CMD+ENTER), you can click on each building and the camera will zoom into it. When you click anywhere on the screen, the camera zooms back out ready to zoom into another building. By creating the blank keyframes after each button, you disable the user from clicking that button again before it is zoomed in/out:

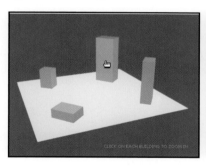 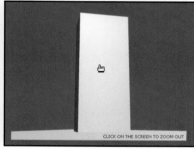

Your finished Flash design is pretty flexible and could be used in many different ways: a navigation interface for a website, an attention-grabbing presentation, or whatever else you can dream up!

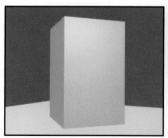 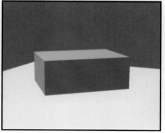 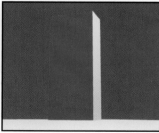

You've seen how easy it is to import graphics from an external 3D program, but it's important to remember that once the objects have been imported into Flash, changing or editing the 3D images becomes very complicated. The crucial point is that when you change one frame, you must change the rest. This might not be that bad on a 10-frame animation, but in our example we were working with an 80 frame animation.

However, a couple of properties that are fairly easy to edit are alpha and color values and the scaling. Changing the opacity or color is particularly easy for mouseovers, as they are not included in the animation. Take a look at the bonus example in this chapter's source file. Open `swift3D_FlashExample_mouse.fla` and notice the subtle yet effective mouseover animation that we've added:

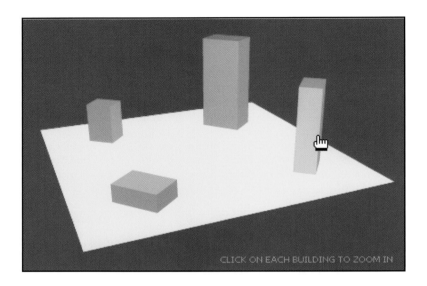

Summary

In this book, you've learned how to fool people into thinking you've got the time, money, and brainpower to create real 3D. And this chapter's rounded off your deceitful ways rather nicely by introducing the basics of using external 3D applications with Flash.

At the very least, we hope you've learned a few cool techniques to pep up your web pages. You should now have some good, practical techniques under your belt, and hopefully you'll also have gotten to grips with the more advanced and impressive 3D engines that we covered in the latter few chapters. Looking at the bigger picture, you've checked out the capabilities of Flash 3D—everything you need to know if you really do want to branch out into 3D. Take these tricks and use them well!

Index

The index is arranged hierarchically, in alphabetical order, with symbols preceding the letter A. Many second-level entries also occur as first-level entries. This is to ensure that you will find the information you require however you choose to search for it.

Z

z-order 69. See also 3D slice engine (tutorial); interactive landscape (tutorial)

URLs

http://iias.leidenuniv.nl 65
http://sourceforge.net 63
www.blender3d.org 213
www.compuphase.co 66
www.discreet.co 251
www.erain.com 251
www.gamedev.net 71
www.indie-rpg.net 91
www.iuav.it 66
www.macromedia.com 44
www.onrelease.org 85
www.swift3d.com 251